Editor: Sarah Vy Nguyen
Designed by: Jason Arias
Cover Photo: Judean Desert West Bank, July 2019

ISBN 979-8-9884247-8-9 (e-book)
ISBN 979-8-9884247-1-0 (pbk.)
ISBN 979-8-9884247-9-6 (hardback)
Library of Congress Control Number: 2023911797

PROJECT 10·15

Scan for more on this author

AN ECO-FRIENDLY AUTOBIOGRAPHY

ALIGNMENT

An Unlikely Road to Bethlehem

BRAD BALDWIN

AKA Bredbhai

DISCLAIMER

The author is not a Board Certified; Pastor, Psychologist,
Electrician Life Coach, Gujarati Speaker, Veteran, Political Scientist,
Geologist, Librarian Historian, Esteemed Religious Scholar, Teacher,
Attorney, Gypsy, Astrologer, Proofreader, Cartographer, Psychic, Magician,
Transcendental Healer, Auto Rickshaw Driver, Philosopher, Architect,
Journalist, First Responder, Social Media Influencer or
Actual PhD Holder

AUTHOR IDENTIFIES AS WRITER

The author kindly requests:
No Book Burning, Book Banning, or Digital Device Smashing

Alignment has been crafted to:
Entertain, Educate, and Enlighten

To Ana & Cody
May all your dreams come true,
May God protect you, always!

BEND, OREGON (DAY #22)

It's a gloomy evening in America's Pacific Northwest when a white SUV with Virginia tags rolls down NE 3rd Street. He sits behind the wheel of a white Evoque, the entry-level Rover which allows one to feel like they are part of the "club." His face looks as if he has weathered a storm. His soul is numb. He feels as heavy as the blanket of thick clouds looming overhead. Weeks earlier, an epic March windstorm had hit the Mid-Atlantic and marked his send-off. He passes an ad for *Three Billboards Outside Ebbing*, Missouri and wonders what his billboard would say.

He sees his crash pad for the night up ahead on the left, a Days Inn. He notices a large weed dispensary across the street, which certainly did not boost his spirit. He was a small-town guy from Virginia. He was a White dude, a moderate middle-of-the-road, middle-class bloke. He did possess a coveted college degree, so the elite commentators and pundits could not classify him as a "non-college-educated White." He wasn't a fan of weed or the obsession with weed culture. He loved lots of musical genres but had a special place in his heart for gangsta rap. However, he considered himself to be a weed-free gangsta. If he were to be profiled, he wouldn't pass as a gangsta from any angle. No tattoos. No low-rider. No chains. No weapons. No blunts. Just a White dude, with specs, wearing jeans, some kind of dark Henley, and a fleece jacket. He was never one to judge anyone as he was a man who faced his own demons and had his own vices.

It was an old-school kind of motel, the kind where you pull the car up right up to the room. He enters the modest room with a rhythm and familiar routine: fill up the little nightstand with gadgets, try to find plugs to charge everything, put the bathroom bag on the sink, and put the suitcase wherever it would fit and actually open. Even in his profound heaviness, he was organized. Being organized and tidy helped to balance the chaos in his mind. The Days Inn shared a parking lot with a local Jack in the Box. He grabs an American fast food and calorie-rich meal and takes a seat. At 43, it's probably not the healthiest choice. But, at this point, he couldn't care less. He is more concerned with the local clientele loitering inside the Jack in the Box. He had lived and worked overseas for decades, engaging in many social service projects and pursuing his dreams. He was a total fan of humanity, but on this day, he was beginning to disconnect from himself. His inner light was quite dim, with just the tiniest flicker.

Darkness has fallen over Bend. Inside the motel room, he sits with an empty Jack in the Box wrapper nearby. Within seconds, and without warning, it hits. His body starts to tremble. He begins to feel cold inside. His mouth is dry. He tries to swallow. Tears begin to stream down his face. He begins to shiver. It is mild at first and then a seismic shift within his inner being. He begins to shake more uncontrollably. He looks around the room. He wipes the tears from his face. His eyes are red and bloodshot.

He crawls under the covers to try to warm up. He continues to quiver. He closes his eyes slowly and then opens them again. He repeats this act several times. Slowly, his body begins to calm itself into a neutral position. The room is quiet. He folds both of his hands together, as if to pray. He was a CINO, a Christian in Name Only. He never really prayed. He never really read the Book. But he did show up at church on Christmas.

Dear God, if you can hear me, I don't know. I really don't have anything left within me. I don't know how to do this. I can't do this. It's too hard. Maybe I should just go back. Live my old life. At least it was comfortable. This is just, I can't. I just wanted to let you know that if I don't wake up tomorrow morning, I'm okay with that. I'm at peace. If You decide tonight is the night, I'm ready.

It was the first time, the first and only time, in his entire life, that the thought of not waking up had ever crossed his mind.

He was a dreamer. He was a visionary. He was a practical idealist. He was stubborn. He was sensitive.

But on this night, he was broken.

ONE

APRIL 1992

The cabin of the Delta Boeing 767-300 is dark. All of the passengers are in various states of sleep. All of them, except him. He sits in his seat, wide-eyed, and full of curiosity. A boyish face of sixteen, skinny. He stares at both of his boarding passes — *Washington Dulles to Frankfurt, Germany. Frankfurt to New Delhi, India. Baldwin, Brad Elliott.*

Ahead of him, he sees the glow of light coming from the flight attendant's station. A curtain is pulled back. He locks eyes with a female flight attendant and motions for her to come over. As she nears him, he inquires, "Where are we? Exactly."

It's not the typical question for the attendant, who is unsure, but eager to find an answer. "Hold on. Let me ask the pilot. I'll be right back."

Within moments, she returns to his seat, holding a large paper map, some 18 x 24 inches. She points to a spot in the Atlantic, just below Iceland. "Captain says we're right about *here*."

He looks at her, with a magical wonder in his eye, and runs his finger across the map and the flight path arc into Europe. Prior to disembarking in Frankfurt and buying a super expensive Coke with no ice, he is gifted with the large flight map. Captain English. In Flight Coordinators Sally Snow and Nancy Bible. Takeoff speed 180 MPH. Distance 3700 NM. Cloudy with Rain 56 F. Altitude 37,000 Feet. 12 April 1992.

He is spellbound. It's the best gift ever.

He flies and flies and flies and flies over hours and days, across time zones, always wide awake in his economy seat, always wondering what lies ahead. His face is glued to the window. It's 2 a.m. An endless expanse of twinkling lights illuminates the ground. He's wearing a headset and listening to U2's "Mysterious Ways" on his yellow Walkman as the plane banks left over New Delhi. His Aunt Peggy, the only one traveling with him, is seated next to him. He smiles at his aunt before looking back out the window.

Anticipation. Eagerness. Nervous energy. Excitement. He was landing in a new world, and though he had never planned on it, somehow it seemed to resonate with his inner being.

Until the eleventh grade, he was keenly focused on pursuing a career in medicine. He had even specified Radiology or Ophthalmology. Fully focused on that pursuit, he volunteered at the local hospital, wore a white lab coat, and did patient checks. He took patients' temperatures and visited with families. He suited up in protective gear and was allowed to attend two surgeries — an arthroscopic knee surgery and a hip replacement. He volunteered in the emergency room. Those ironclad life goals would abruptly and almost instantaneously fall off a cliff when a two-week experience, at the age of sixteen, would change that trajectory.

His cousin lived in New Delhi, at the United States Embassy. Her husband was in the foreign service with the Department of State. They had a young daughter, Erin, and a boy in the oven and on the way.

Two weeks. It was his spring break Easter week plus permission from his high school for an additional week. Aunt Peggy's sole mission was grand-child time. His sole mission was adventure. He grew up around maps and National Geographic magazines, but never in his wildest imagination had he ever thought of visiting India. He was scared of India. It was the land of Cobras, and he loathed snakes. Every now and then, he had nightmares about snakes surrounding his bed. The idea of stepping into a country and coming face to face with a venomous King Cobra was enough to make him anxious. He was a kid in high school. He had a free place to sleep and meals provided by his family, vis-à-vis the US Government. However, the plane ticket cost had to be expensive. His parents both worked, and he was from a middle-middle-class world where a flight ticket halfway around the world was a big deal.

In India, he found himself, in a sense, trapped between two worlds. His instinct was to roam freely and to explore and investigate, but the rules and regulations and travel advisories imposed by the U.S. State Department were always his nemesis. The Embassy itself was a massive complex. The Ambassador's residence and all the offices were in one compound, and the staff housing was in a second compound across the street. The residences, despite the tacky speckled flooring, were set up more like a resort. There was a large pool, a movie theater, a small grocery store, a bowling alley, and huge open gardens. Most Embassy staff had maids, chefs, drivers, and gardeners — the very definition of a Hardship Post. High compound walls surrounded the facility with plenty of around-the-clock security. He had not traveled halfway around the world to visit a country club. His family wasn't in the tax bracket where they'd be part of the local country club in his town, so why would he fly to India to sit by the pool and tan?

He had a short to-do checklist. He wanted to travel out of Delhi, toward the Himalayas, to experience the foothills and see the mountain range. A travel advisory canceled his trip. He was told there was a "disturbance" along his route and that it was not safe to travel. He wanted to spend a day, an evening, or overnight, with a very poor family in a nearby slum.

Oh, no. No. No. No. No. Risky. The U.S. Embassy shot down this plan due to concerns for his health and welfare. He was told that he might acquire a disease. With the dozens of vaccinations he had prior to travel, he was a bit skeptical of exactly which disease the Embassy was referring to. He quickly learned that it was best not to vet his plans with the Embassy and instead, keep a low profile and try to escape the confines of the American Country Club whenever he could.

By hook or crook, come hell or high water, he was not going to let anything stop him from visiting the Taj Mahal, which was several hours south, in the city of Agra.

April in India was hot, with daily temperatures well above 100 F, 110 F. His extroverted and always excited cousin, Traci, could not travel due to her pregnancy. His aunt had planned to go, but the culture shock of India changed that. Chaotic driving. The stares. The monkeys. The food. The bathrooms. His aunt was a country club member, and therefore, found more peace at the US Embassy Estates.

He had no chaperone. His family had concerns about him traveling alone at 16, in this chaotic India. The Embassy would certainly have issued the highest-level safety warning assessment for him not to travel.

"What did you see in India?" A pool. *Beethoven*. Burgers. Fries. Watched a baseball game. Not the best ROI. The Taj trip was a private tour, with a guide to meet him in Agra. All he had to do was travel by train to and from Delhi, and he wasn't going to take no for an answer.

The Delhi train station is a saturation of the senses. He witnesses an overwhelming sea of humanity. The massive complex is full of trains, pulling in and out. It is a dark and dim station that appears to be very weathered and worn with time. The background noise is as loud as the cicadas are in the Virginia summer. Coolies, wearing red uniforms, rush past him with stacks of luggage on their heads. Entire families are seated on the concrete platform — waiting, sleeping, and eating homemade food out of tin boxes stacked on top of one another. Food stalls are everywhere. Colorful foods. Fried foods. The smell of kerosene gas. The smell of diesel. There are so many people, so many bodies, that he literally has to step over families to maneuver through the station. As he walks up a flight of stairs, he comes face to face with a deformed man, a male body twisted into a human knot. It is hard not to turn back and look once more.

He sits in a first-class compartment of the Taj Express. A large seat. Soft background music on somewhat clear speakers. Quiet. He finds himself surrounded by attitude. He has never traveled by first class before and feels, once again, out of place. The car is primarily filled with men, business folk to be precise, dressed in proper English dress shirts and reading the local newspapers while sipping chai. The man next to him has a paper that is fully open to read every article. The man's arm and paper occupy half of his allotted seat space.

He attempts to start a friendly conversation but is met with silence. Perhaps it's because he wasn't wearing a formal shirt and dress pants. Perhaps it's because he's a poser and not really from the upper-class world of privilege. Perhaps the *Times of India* article is more riveting than a skinny 16-year-old White kid from Virginia. The man turns, looks at him, says nothing, and turns back toward the paper. As the man turns the page, a swish of attitude blows across his seat.

Code Red, canceled. He almost missed the railway stop at Agra station. He had been staring out the window but had not seen the sign and the station. It is definitely too small to be located in a city of over a million. No one is talking to him in the first-class cabin. He could not understand the voice announcements, even the ones in English, due to the wiring of the sound system. Something inside of him feels that it is indeed Agra, so he decides to exit the train. He is immediately surrounded by dozens of aggressive male auto-rickshaw drivers, each one vying for the opportunity to transport him.

"Where you want to go?"

"Come!"

"Taj. Taj. Taj."

"Meter. By the meter!"

"500 Rupees! I show you whole city!"

His VIP tour guide is supposed to be waiting for him with a signboard, but he didn't see anything. Maybe it's not Agra. Maybe he stepped off in the wrong place. Maybe the U.S. Embassy Caretakers were right.

The train begins to pull away. Stay or go? Stay or go? Total chaos and shouting. And then he sees something... a White lady in the distance. She looks older, but everyone seems older than sixteen. The shouting caravan of rickshaw drivers swarms around him as he beelines for the White lady, trying to come up with a Plan B. The White lady is not only White, but she is also from the United States. She is a New York City White lady, the kind who works on Wall Street, not Main Street. To his surprise, she is a friendly White lady. She assures him he is indeed in Agra.

He finds his driver with the VIP guide and signboard that reads "Mr. Brad," behind the station. His central nervous system would have preferred for all of that to be in front of the station.

The vehicle waiting for him is the road king of India, the classic car known as "The Ambassador." It appears to be from a different era. It is white, with four heavy doors, and an arched top. The Ambassador seems to be akin to a tank. Vehicles in India, at the time, are all white with three models: Ambassador. Sumo. Fiat. He feels a bit like a Maharaja. He is riding down the bumpy pothole-filled streets of Agra, sitting alone in the backseat of his chauffeur-driven Ambassador tank, complete with an English-speaking tour guide. The guide is a short middle-aged man with a few strands of hair and wears specs.

Agra did not feel like a city of a million. It feels like an insanely overcrowded small town. He is traveling to one of the wonders of the world, dodging cyclists, cows, sleeping street dogs, and road craters. It is no wonder they needed a tank.

As he turns the corner, there it is. He stops in his tracks. The image of the Taj Mahal hits him like a freight train. He realizes that he's not in Kansas anymore. He readies his 35 MM SLR camera and frames up the shot. The center Dome. The minarets. He clicks a few shots. He was always a bit conservative with his film rolls. He sees a handful of foreign tourists. He sees a few groups of Indian tourists. Nothing overwhelming. It is a sleepy town vibe that just happens to have the Taj Mahal. He is in awe, in observation, and in absorption mode. He listens more than he questions, getting lost in the experience. A closer inspection of the mausoleum reveals beautiful inlaid marbles and gemstones. Agates. Garnet. Bloodstone. Orange Carnelian. Blue Lapis Lazuli.

For a moment, he wonders what if he had stayed on the train — where would he have gone and what would have happened? He certainly doesn't miss the Embassy pool or snack bar. He is debating whether or not he should go to prom in India. Yes, *prom*. One of the daughters of a Foreign Service officer had asked him to be her date to prom at the American school. He definitely thinks she is cute, but he's a bit anxious about the whole idea of prom.

India is a young nation. It was established in 1947 and tourism was minimal. His day trip included the Taj Mahal, lunch at a swanky hotel, and a quick trip outside of town to an ancient city built in 1571 known as Fatehpur Sikri. The tank travels down a single-lane road with a tree canopy. His window is down by his request. He wants to feel the breeze, smell the air, and not have any barrier between himself and the moment. His day has been a success, but he wants to squeeze all the paste out of the tube.

"Would it be possible if we went back to the Taj Mahal? For a second time?" he blurts out.

The guide leans back, smiles, and replies, "Again?" He leans forward to make his pitch since he knows a second visit is not part of the official timeline or cost.

"Just to watch the sunset. Just to sit, near the reflecting pool!" he proposes.

The tour guide laughs, giving a customary head bobble. "Why not? For you, we will go! You are my youngest customer ever!"

He sits and watches the orange glow of the sun as it disappears into the horizon behind the Taj Mahal. The image of the building is still present in the elongated reflecting pool. Most of the tourists have all but gone. It is quiet. He looks at his watch and then squints his eyes as he looks up toward the sky. He raises his right hand to manually count out the hours and do a bit of time zone calculation. He turns toward the guide who is seated with him. "At this moment, you know what I would be doing in Virginia?" he eagerly asks. Before the guide can answer, he continues his train of thought. "It's chemistry class right now. It's morning in America. Chemistry is my first class, but I am here, with you, looking at this."

His guide smiles. No words are required.

India had blown his mind. It was a saturation of all five senses. His two-week odyssey was so profound that it changed the lens through which he viewed the world. He was a small-town kid from another world. Conservative. Churchy. Gun friendly. Narrow Focused. Republican. He had been immersed in a populous Hindu and Muslim nation with absolutely nothing that resembled any aspect of the world and culture from which he was born in... and yet, he found himself surrounded by the human spirit and was able to forge connections with others. Even in the fleeting moments, those moments were filled with warmth and kindness. He never made it to prom. At the fancy hotel in Agra, he had asked for ice to be put in his sweet tea and ended up with Delhi belly. He had the unique opportunity to have vomiting and diarrhea coexisting at the same time. He would have much rather been at prom with the cute girl and his anxiety.

TWO

DAY #3 KENTUCKY

It's a relatively short drive from Hazard over yonder to Alcoa, just outside of Knoxville. It is late winter, not the most ideal time for a road trip. The trees are barren. There are no green fields. The flowers are not in bloom. The drive was his idea, his creation, but the timing wasn't.

He glances into his rearview mirror and sees the flash of police lights behind him. His eyes quickly shift to the speedometer as the blare of the siren gets closer. He's only eight miles over the limit. His heart begins to thump louder and louder. His hands become clammy. He starts to breathe very heavily. He starts to feel numb. The world around him starts to freeze. His mind craters into a black hole.

Anxiety. Fear. Worry. Dread. Panic.

He quickly veers into a shopping center and comes to a stop as the State Trooper whizzes by him and down the road. He looks around him and wipes the perspiration from his forehead. He opens a bottle of water and takes a sip. He begins inhaling and exhaling, deeply, to calm his nervous system.

In the cupholder, his iPhone is switched off. Next to the iPhone is a burner, which is active. He picks up the burner and dials. On the other end is his mid-60s, bill-by-the-millisecond, no-nonsense, female attorney. He trembles a bit and doesn't make sense at first.

"Are you sure?" he asks.

"Am I sure about what?" she responds.

He speaks frantically, with a heightened sense of paranoia and fear. "That Shilpa can't track me? Gas Stations. Food. Motels. It's all on my credit card."

"No, she shouldn't be able to."

He becomes unnaturally hostile with his attorney. "You don't know Shilpa! I don't have cash. I need to use the card. What if Shilpa files a missing person's report?"

His lawyer is quite cold. She is not empathetic toward PTSD. She charges for every word, every thought, and even the oxygen to breathe in her office. "What are you talking about?" she asks, trying to follow his broken train of thought.

He composes himself and is much calmer. "Shilpa has threatened me in the past. If I disappear again, she would go to the police and file a missing person's report to find me. I need space. I need a buffer. I cannot be found."

His attorney replies with a level 2 out of 10 in the compassion arena, which is quite remarkable. "Listen. We can't stop Shilpa from going to the police. It is her free will to file a report if that is what she chooses to do. However, if any police officer were to stop you for that reason, just explain to them your situation. Law enforcement will not give up your location if that is what you are worried about."

By definition, traumatic bonding is a strong emotional attachment between an abused soul and the abuser. It is formed as a result of a cycle of violence. His intensive research had indicated to him that his brain, the very mind that he cherished and valued, had the conditioned response of an addict. The neurochemistry of the chemical balance in his brain had been altered — factors such as oxytocin, which regulates bonding, and endogenous opioids, which deal with pleasure, pain, withdrawal, and dependence. There is the corticotropin-releasing factor which deals with stress. Lastly, there is dopamine which deals with craving, seeking, and wanting. The complexity of the human mind, his mind, has been rewired.

He is not a simple thinker. However, since he is not a student of law, medicine, or astrophysics, he needs the ability to simplify what he is learning. He also has to do it in a way that makes sense to him without getting lost in the weeds of some profound Harvard Dean of Psychology's analytical case study of Subject A and Subject B. He is his own subject, and he needs to break his traumatic bond in order to survive and find a way toward freedom. He realizes that, in his world, his relationship with Shilpa, his wife, has worked like a virus. It is a virus that has attacked and infected his entire body with a particular focus on his emotional response system. To frame it in this way means that he has to develop his own antibody response in order to specifically target his emotional and mental responses to Shilpa.

His natural inclination, as he imagined is the same with most of humanity, is to respect and care for others, to be compassionate and kind. He is no saint, but his natural auto-response is to care. He knows that

Shilpa would be relentless and ruthless in her attempts to continue to infect his mind and poison his emotional response system since this would allow her to exert control and power over him. Developing a successful antibody would mean learning how to train and block his mind from caring, to override his default setting.

He would have to train himself to be completely numb. It is a concept that seemed cold, callous, and heartless.

He understands that his relationship with Shilpa is very much about two energetic forces at play, one dark and one light. Shilpa would never respect his need for space or time, nevertheless, his decision to file for divorce. On the contrary, an action of the sort on his part, he knows, would unleash a torrent of psychological drama. It is a storm he isn't sure he could survive.

A traumatic bond works when one feels as though they are powerless, have no voice, and are not given the space to think and feel. A traumatic bond can only work when an individual, such as he, is more focused on the needs and point of view of Shilpa rather than his own well-being. Creating a buffer, when there are no boundaries and respect given to him, would require tapping into internal resources he didn't know existed.

Monumental.

To break his traumatic bond with Shilpa would mean breaking free from ADX Willow Tree, his prison. At this stage in life, he knows that he has not willingly walked into this life sentence on purpose. He has thrown away the only key to his cell door and would need to manufacture another one. Because he knows himself and his vulnerabilities, and because he now understands Shilpa's pathology, he has to build a support system consisting of a group of highly trained specialists, with all the fancy degrees he did not possess, to provide him with guardrails, insights, and tidbits of knowledge. Elaine Shea, a friendly and warm LCSW, is his mainstay social worker/ therapist. Stephanie Kraft, based in Northern Virginia, has a practice that focuses on Intuitive Healing Arts & Hypnotherapy, energetic healing. He further widens his net through online blogs, seminars, and books. Finally, there are two professionals who unknowingly make a significant impact on his attempt to break his traumatic bond. Dr. Linda Martinez-Lew is a PhD in Narcissistic Personality Disorders and is based in Maine. Mr. Ross Rosenberg is a Chicago-based psychotherapist who has an online presence and books that articulate elements of human psychology. This resonates with him, and he is able to digest it.

His entire life has been non-traditional, off the beaten path. The severity of the psychological life knot he finds himself in would require a bold approach. He has devised a plan, a plan in which his own country, the United States of America, would also play a role in serving as a defibrillator for his mind. He has to reset his mind. His plan is simple. He would touch all 48 continental American States in 48 days by road. He would synchronize his great American road trip with the weeks leading up to his official filing for divorce and the explosive impact of that atomic bomb. The logistics and operations of managing a 48-day road trip would provide a focus for his mind since there would be many tasks at hand. He would be able to pack up a mobile office into a large plastic storage container with his key office documents and needs to remotely manage his small business. His mind is gripped with irrational fears and waves of panic attacks. The American road trip would provide him with an essential buffer to avoid the intense endless harassment and stalking from Shilpa. He knows nothing could be done unless he is on the run or in hiding. He would plan to carry along his tripod and SLR camera to focus his mind through the lens of the American landscape. For 48 days, the American folks he would interact with from both blue states and red states, in every nook and corner of the country, would, in small ways — through a smile, an act of kindness, or a nice gesture — be playing a role in one man's fight to free his mind from a self-imposed prison.

Logan, West Virginia

Hazard, Kentucky

Alcoa, Tennessee

Asheville, North Carolina

Anderson, South Carolina

Bainbridge, Georgia

Niceville, Florida

Fairhope, Alabama

Ocean Springs, Mississippi

New Iberia, Louisiana

Hope, Arkansas

Branson, Missouri

Independence, Kansas

Guthrie, Oklahoma,

Amarillo, Texas

Santa Fe, New Mexico

Durango, Colorado

Mexican Hat, Utah

Kingman, Arizona

Las Vegas, Nevada

Corning, California

Bend, Oregon

Walla Walla, Washington

Sandpoint, Idaho

Butte, Montana

Jackson Hole, Wyoming

Chadron, Nebraska

Deadwood, South Dakota (Snowstorm)

Deadwood, South Dakota (Snowstorm)

Luverne, Minnesota

Northwood, Iowa

Platteville, Wisconsin

Watseka, Illinois

Nappanee, Indiana

Benton Harbor, Michigan

Huron, Ohio

Erie, Pennsylvania

Queensbury, New York

Rutland, Vermont

Rochester, New Hampshire

Ogunquit, Maine

Hyannis, Massachusetts

Newport, Rhode Island

Groton, Connecticut

Vineland, New Jersey

Newark, Delaware

Hagerstown, Maryland

Stephen City, Virginia

13,000 + miles. His American road trip would cover over 13,000 miles in 48 days, spending the night in every state except two. While he is still paying the mortgage on his marital home, he hasn't lived in it or slept in it for nearly two years. He has traveled the world and lived in India for decades, but is now living out of his car.

Shilpa is his warden, and he is a fugitive battling darkness and himself.

THREE

RURAL VIRGINIA (1980s)

It seemed to touch the sky. A massive trunk reaching several stories high. The tiny branches and elongated green leaves appeared to flow easily even in the slightest of breeze. It had the appearance of a shaggy head of hair in need of a trim. During strong storms, the trunk would make all sorts of noises and creaks. The oversized willow tree was the perfect location for an imaginative young boy, with his very own personal treehouse. The treehouse was a homemade contraption built by his father. It was fully enclosed and measured eight feet by five. There was a trap door at the bottom. One would enter from the ladder steps bolted into one of the tree trunks. It had a thin carpet and a window that allowed light in. There was a full-sized door that led out onto a small porch two stories up. And for a quick escape, there was a fireman's pole — a PVC pipe that swayed back and forth and could burn his legs if he wasn't careful.

He walked across the backyard toward the willow tree. He was dressed for summer in shorts and a T-shirt. He was a lean boy and "lean" was a rather generous term. He was a skinny boy, with brown hair and blue-green eyes. At nine, he was too young to be home alone, and on this day, Adam walked behind him. Adam was the son of a family friend. Adam was older than him but not yet an adult. However, in those formative years of youth, he appeared very much a child while Adam was a young man.

His face appeared tense. In his mind, he was thinking and waiting and counting the minutes and hours until his mom would come home. He and Adam climbed the wooden steps to the bottom of the treehouse. He pulled back the latch and pushed the trap door with enough effort that it flew open and landed back on the floor. The loud sound of a nail gun is heard in the background. His parents were adding a room to the family home and below the swaying willow branches, there was sporadic construction work done by a husband-and-wife crew that had worked on his home before.

Inside the treehouse, the trap door was closed. Unusually absent from this moment was the laughter and innocence of childhood. It was incredibly silent, the only sound being that of the nail gun blasting away at times. He felt trapped and helpless, but Adam was in control. Adam was the dominating presence, the caretaker who was in charge of protecting him.

His first life lesson as a child was one of silence.

Adam unbuttoned his shorts and lowered them. Adam was always the first since Adam's needs were the priority. In his mind, he sensed what he was doing was wrong. All the other kids in the neighborhood were surely not doing these kinds of things. After a few minutes, it was his turn. Adam commanded him to take down his shorts, but he was never comfortable. He was a very shy kid and always preferred to be in his treehouse by himself. When he was alone, he was not lonely, as he had his mind. When he was alone, his tree house became a battle zone hideout or the control tower of a ship traversing the world's oceans.

He reluctantly lowered his shorts and elevated his shame. He was already a very self-conscious kid. His mind told him he was very bad, but his body contradicted his mind as he began to feel something. It was a sensation that traveled from his arms to his legs. A child having an orgasm before his body had matured. The loss of innocence would be a recurring theme in his life. He had learned early on that euphoria and shame were two sides of the same coin. Once would have been bad enough, but years made him numb.

He grew up as an only child in a very middle-class world. He lived in a small single-story redwood house on a quiet residential street in Culpeper. His mother was local, from the county, and she worked as the office manager of a local medical office. His father was an import from North Carolina and taught geography at the local middle school. There was always a pet, a dog to be precise, one at a time. Patches was his childhood companion, a collie mix from the local shelter, his very own version of *Lassie*.

Culpeper, Virginia of the eighties was the quintessential American small town. Located 1.5 hours outside of Washington DC, Culpeper offered a peaceful world. It was the picturesque rolling hills of Virginia's Piedmont region, surrounded by dairy farms and horse farms, framed against the backdrop of the Blue Ridge Mountains. A population of ten thousand. Several traffic signals. A local railway station. Fall was an especially magical time;

however, he was born in the fall so perhaps he was biased. He always loved the brilliant colors of the leaves as they turned orange and red and yellow. Fall in particular, had its own scent.

It was a conservative town, dotted with churches denoting the various warring Christian factions. It was an intersection of America's past and present, a community that was surveyed by George Washington in 1749. Culpeper's strategic railroad location was a major supply line for both Union and Confederate Troops during the Civil War. There were battlefields and occasional reenactments with local men engaging in mock battles between the North and South.

Growing up, he assumed there was just one political party, Republican. Ronald Reagan and George H. W. Bush reinforced that notion. He was a Boy Scout, and the dynamic local Troop 196 was always engaged in fundraisers and community service. Dressed in his formal khaki and olive scout uniform, he would find himself directing traffic to park cars at local Republican fundraisers and cookouts held at large farms with local and state political leaders. He didn't think much about politics back in those days, just the smoked brisket and all the catered side dishes which were his payoff for standing in the sun for hours. Once, he was even asked to be in a campaign commercial for 7th district Congressman French Slaughter, another Republican. The campaign wanted to create a slice-of-life image as he walked along a fence on a farm, "appearing" to be immersed in a conversation with the Congressman.

A few months prior to his inspirational trip to India, he witnessed the honorable American tradition of the transfer of power, the changing of the guard in Washington. He was justice conscious, not politically astute. He always looked at things from a different angle and together with his best friend, Brian, had traveled to Charlottesville to pick up promotional material to campaign for Ross Perot, even though he was too young to vote. Culpeper County was as red as West Virginia and Wyoming, but he had a fiercely independent streak within his usual quiet self. However, none of that mattered as an Alien Life Force, a Democrat, descended onto Culpeper by the name of Clinton. POTUS Elect Bill and FLOTUS Elect Hillary Clinton were on a bus traveling from Monticello to DC for the Inauguration and stopped in Culpeper to attend church, the Baptist. He had a contact running the local DNC who scored a press pass for both him and Brian. Dressed more as politicians, in their long black wool trench coats with name lanyards, than actual journalists, he and Brian stood outside the church on that cold January day to witness an American president and all the machinery and hoopla that surrounded.

Most of Culpeper had voted for the other team, but one would have never known on Inauguration Day. Crowds and crowds of locals gathered to be a part of history. No conspiracy theories. No vulgar handwritten posters. No false claims of fraud. No Fox News echo chamber. Just Tom Brokaw, a legend in his house, as the *Nightly News* blared every night during dinner. He stood a couple of feet away as Hillary did a meet and greet. He was too shy to actually be a journalist, to push, shove, shout, and ask any questions. Instead, he just smiled and absorbed the moment.

He always felt different. Not just because of the treehouse, but just different, like an outsider always looking in and observing the world around him. His mother worked tirelessly to create a bubble to make him feel like a normal kid. There were always fresh home-cooked meals, lots of casseroles. He loved her cooking, with strong exceptions to peas and pork chops. And on the days when she worked late and brought home KFC, he turned his nose up at the liver. Despite her efforts, there were unspoken cracks in the family façade. He felt strongly that the families he watched on television, in the movies, and at church, were a little different.

His father was intense. His father mostly talked and never listened. His father was fixated on just a few things. Biking. Hiking. Biking. Traveling. Biking. Sitting at a little red desk creating photo albums. And biking. His father was a hoarder of details. Charts. Records. Data. His father would often write almanac-style articles about trips and records and have them printed in the local newspaper. Self-promotion. His father rarely drank. A case of Budweiser could sit in the fridge for an entire year. His father would lose his temper quite often. His father would become emotionally triggered by life and become very agitated. His father always seemed to be the victim of some persecution. His father was stubborn, opinionated, bullheaded, and never wrong. Doors would slam. Curse words were shouted. Things would get broken. Once a kitchen knife ended up stuck in the ceiling. The lawn mower might get thrown across the yard. The upside was that his father's anger was never directed at him or his mother. They were internal meltdowns without emotional regulators. Regardless, it was enough to make his heart skip a beat, wondering if the neighbors also heard, wondering when peace might come. The family surname was of utmost importance. Anywhere they traveled, he had to pose, day or night, next to a "Baldwin" sign. Things, however, escalated during the Canadian Road Trip.

The family station wagon appeared in the night on an isolated road, somewhere on Prince Edward Island. His mother was back at the hotel. On this mission, it was just him and his father. The car stopped along the side of the road and the headlights beamed onto a fallen sign. Both he and his father exit the car. The sign reads "Baldwin Road" and was baby blue. The sign was still attached to the wooden post. His father began tampering with the sign, trying to remove it from the post.

"Don't you think we need permission?" he inquired.

His father replied, "It was on the ground."

He didn't understand. "Just because it's on the ground doesn't mean we can take it."

His father was focused and driven to take what was "rightfully" owned, the blue road sign in Canada. His father was also an Eagle Scout. They opened the back of the wagon and removed some luggage, just enough to place the sign on the floorboard and cover it up. His mom was not happy her son had turned into a thief, but they lived in an alternate democracy and were overruled. The prized blue road sign, property of Canada, was discreetly smuggled out of the country by a slice-of-life-small-town American White family. The sign was bolted onto the back deck just below the willow tree.

The formative years of his childhood seemed to be a permanent boot camp. He was training for an ever-elusive mission. Every weekend was organized by his father, and it involved biking a hundred miles or carrying a sixty-pound backpack through the mountains. He was a born asthmatic so hiking with full gear often kept him at the back of the group, alone by himself in the woods. His father had marched ahead, out of sight, leading the other scouts. As he walked, he would often pull out his inhaler to have a puff. Occasionally, his father would wait for him to offer some words of encouragement. "It's really not that bad. You'll be fine." In between wheezes and gasps for oxygen, he replied, "I know I'll be fine. I just can't breathe."

It was summer and time for another epic *Mission Impossible* training exercise. He, a group of scouts, his father, and another parent departed Virginia in a 12-passenger van loaded with gear and three turtle top carriers. Prior to leaving Culpeper, he had a few bumps on his finger. His doctor had informed him it was poison ivy, so he took a prednisone steroid pack with him. Upon arrival in Memphis, his entire body had become inflamed with red itchy bumps. Back. Chest. Arms. Uncomfortable. Miserable. He showed his father and asked to be taken to the hospital. Going to the hospital was, however, not on his father's tightly scheduled program itinerary. Instead, his father chose to make a phone call to Virginia to his doctor, a doctor whose eyes could not see as far as Tennessee. He was instructed to put calamine lotion and to increase the prednisone tablets. He was not taken to the hospital. The weather became hotter and drier as he lay on the floorboard of the van, traveling across state after state, arriving at the Grand Canyon. It was later discovered that he had not had poison ivy, but rather chicken pox, which was highly contagious and there was no telling how many people he had infected at the KOA campground swimming pools along the route.

His father had a good heart and meant well. His childhood was an extension of his father. His father's personal interests and hobbies were transferred to him. He was appreciative and grateful for the fact his father had taken him and shown him so much of America. National Parks. Historical Sites. Landscapes. His favorite part of every road trip, family or scout, was simply looking out the car window, lost in a daydream.

His mother was a non-college-educated White; yet, she possessed a PhD in kindness, compassion, empathy, and love. His mother grew up on a five-hundred-acre dairy and chicken farm that was run by her parents, grandparents, and uncle. It was a farm that her family would ultimately lose. He never knew his maternal grandfather since his grandfather died of a heart attack two weeks prior to his birth. His mother grieved the loss of her father and welcomed a new life all within the span of three weeks back in October 1975. It was said that his mother was a daddy's girl and cut from the same cloth as her father. Apparently, her father was a man who tended to let the eggs and milk go to customers facing hard times on credit. Customers were told to pay it back when they could. It was easy to understand how his grandfather would have lost the farm since his grandfather was running a business with too much heart.

The treehouse wasn't the only thing that made him feel different. Physically, he was just noticeably weaker. The asthma. He was allergic to everything in the Commonwealth of Virginia, except dogs, which meant that he had daily medication, allergy shot injections, and that inhaler. His mother possessed an inner knowing and a fine-tuned radar system that would alert her of the slightest bit of danger. Out of nowhere, in the wee hours of the night, his mother would bolt into his room and turn on the light as he sat up in the bed, eyes closed, having a severe asthma attack, huffing, puffing, and gasping for air. Off they would go at 3 a.m. to the emergency room. They certainly did not live in a large home, but he always wondered how she knew. How did his mother, who was deep asleep in her room, hear him wheezing? These were the kinds of things that gave his mother seemingly superhero powers, and they were the very foundation for an unspoken and unconditional love that could transcend everything and make the world feel better, just by her presence.

He never saw his mother without a smile on her face. He never saw his mother shed a tear. She made birthdays special and Christmas always featured the latest G.I. Joe toy. And while she could sense and see the unhappiness on his face each weekend, when it was time for another boot camp mission, she made up for it in her own ways by fixing his favorite chicken tetrazzini casserole or his favorite dessert. He was, by nature, a shy and quiet child, deeply sensitive and quite emotional. He felt as if his mother had placed him in a protective bubble which made him feel safe and energetically connected to her at the deepest level. His mother had a way of making him forget things, dark things, things that she knew nothing about.

Feelings were certainly something that was never discussed openly in his home. In his mind, he knew his father loved him, but deep within him, he never felt that he was good enough. This was a feeling that even his mother's copious outpouring of love could not erase. He felt as if there was no mountain he could climb or no merit badge he could earn that would suffice. Metals. Honors. Awards. Achievements. He was programmed and conditioned to pursue goals, goals that were not his own. His interests, passions, and hobbies were not allowed to be cultivated and therefore, his true self remained buried deep inside of his soul. He learned that his worth, his value, was tied to achievements. He had to prove himself.

Genealogy was a new merit badge, a badge that would take him to Bladen County North Carolina, where his paternal grandparents resided. These trips to pin-drop size Clarkton were another mission — research trips to local court houses to delve into the past, researching the family tree. The upside was that it was indoors with AC, so there were no dried sweat marks.

He sat at a large table filled with books and papers. The room was bright with fluorescent lights and wall-to-wall bookshelves. His father sat at a nearby table, mapping a branch of the tree. He ran his finger across the page slowly.

The inquisitiveness on his face suddenly turned to shock. He wore his heart on his sleeve, often unable to hide his emotions. LAND TRANSFER RECORD. Chickens. Cattle. Horses. Men. Women. Children. Valuations. He looked up. His heart hurt. He looked back at the page. Maybe he hadn't read it correctly. No. He saw it again. He felt as if he had been run over by a freight train.

His ancestors owned people. Human beings. Kids. Just like him. He began to feel light-headed. He slammed the book shut. His heart hurt. This wasn't fun anymore. This was history. Other people. Other times. Not his family. Not his lineage. Disconnect no more. Children. Men. Women. How was it possible? How was it possible to own another person? Another human being. His heart hurt.

He hated organized religion. His parents were Christian, so by default, so was he. He was baptized and grew up in the Methodist Church. He participated in a very elaborate church confirmation class, in which he had to read and match bible verses, complete fill-in-the-blanks, learn (not follow) the commandments, and learn how to be righteous. The BSA had a God & Country medal. It was a lengthy process with many requirements, including him drawing a map of ancient Palestine. In order to complete the medal, he had to meet with his pastor several times. His mind was always inquisitive, and he was beginning to ask questions, questions that others did not have an answer for or had no intention of answering. He directly asked his pastor, "Why are there no Black people in our church?"

Crickets. Blank Stare. Awkward Silence.

The one aspect of Christianity that seemed to tug at his heart a bit was setting up the Manger Scene every year at Christmas. His father had constructed an original. Unwrapping Mary, Joseph, Baby Jesus, the Wise

Men, and a few animals seemed to be innocent enough and void of hypocrisy. The willow tree had impacted his mind and had shut out any idea of God.

Deep within his being were shame, sin, and uncleanliness. His self-worth was in the toilet. He was damaged goods. He was "return to sender." He was different. That was just who he was.

FOUR

ON THE ROAD IN MISSISSIPPI

INFJ. Introverted. Intuitive. Feeling. Judging. The Advocate. The rarest personality type in the world. The 1-2 percent club. In one corner, you'd find the esteemed and compassionate Mahatma Gandhi and Martin Luther King Jr., champions of light. And in the other corner, you'd find Osama bin Laden and Adolf Hitler, champions of darkness. The same personality tree but with vastly different agendas. How exactly he landed on one small twig of this INFJ personality tree he did not know. One percent of the world was still a lot of people — there were many twigs and branches in that tree. As he had begun to immerse himself into human psychology, books, online research, and Wenzes INFJ YouTube channel to better understand his own mind, he had his Edison light bulb moment when he realized his weirdness, his different vibration, and his alternate approach to life had a name. The puzzle piece fit. He identified as INFJ. It was a drop-the-mic moment. Being an INFJ wasn't weird, it was dope.

It was no wonder he was stubborn and glued to his vision, pursuing an Indian Dream for many years. According to actual esteemed psychologists, some strengths of an INFJ's mind included: being compassionate, keepers of peace, practical visionaries, focus on meaningful relationships, and being decisive. On the flip side, several weak spots in INFJ creatures included: being too sensitive, conflict-averse, being too intensely private, perfectionism, aversion to the ordinary, and being prone to burnout. Finding out he was part of a tribe of misfits, all hunkered down in various parts of the world, thinking, sensing, contemplating humanity, and tinkering with different visions, positive and uplifting ones, was exhilarating.

His 48-day road journey commenced in March, and due to the possibility of cold and wintery weather in the northern parts of the nation, he had mapped out a zig-zag route. It was one that would take him just over three weeks to reach California, meandering across the southern states, lower plains, and desert southwest. While he had tentatively mapped out his entire 48-day route, he had only officially booked the first two weeks of accommodations. He planned to book the remainder on a weekly basis in order to adjust for any unforeseen meteorological events — El Niña, La Niña, Polar Vortexes, Jet Streams, Lows, Highs, and once-in-a-generation climatic events. He was not in a race. There would be no one waving flags for him when he quietly returned to Virginia. He was on a mental clock. He was on a mental mission to break the bond of trauma, one mile, one kilometer at a time. He had lots of hotel rewards points with the IHG Group of hotels (Holiday Inn, Holiday Inn Express, Candlewood Suites, and the like). Those were his high-end nights, and he booked a third of his stays free with points. The remainder of the nights were balanced out between smaller boutique local joints and super budget-friendly brands like Super 8 and a handful of Motel 6s where the staff left the light on for him. He made sure to have Candlewood Suites every ten days for laundry.

His mind was a vast array of ideas. His bank account was a minimalist painting. He had a house payment, a car payment, and insurance payments. If he squinted his eyes hard enough, he might be able to see what comprised his savings account. No stocks. No investments. No 401K. Suzie Ormand would have placed him in retirement planning jail and denied his wish to take a 48-day road trip had he called into the show and asked. He had lived in India for nearly two decades, in a Rupee economy, pursuing dreams and visions, not a bank balance. He had a budget of $5,000 to $6,000 and rationalized this journey to be an investment into his mental health. It was an organic and clean investment, an investment of willpower, not pharmaceuticals, for anxiety, depression, PTSD, and every other emotion he was feeling. His counselor and energy healer were only a phone call away. He had the beauty of each day that unfolded, a different day in a different corner of America. The mountains. The rivers. The clouds. The sky. The sunsets. The sunrises. The farms. The towns. The cities. The trucks. The cars. The wildlife. The hawks. The diners. And his Divine Light, Whataburger. He had fallen in love with Whataburger on previous road trips to visit international exchange students for his non-profit. He loved Gandhi and he loved Indian Vegetarianism, but he also loved the five-pound Patty Melt from Whataburger. A brick of a meal. Very budget-friendly. A fast-food mecca opened 24 hours a day. Spicy Ketchup. What more could any man in a midlife meltdown want or need? Screw cholesterol.

OCEAN SPRINGS, MISSISSIPPI (DAY #9)

A heavy day. An increasingly numb day. D-Day. Moment of impact. Reality. Life Choice. March 13th marked the official end of the required one-year separation. March 13th marked the day in which his attorney would commence the divorce process. His mind was full of doubt and fear. It was the unknown that scared him. Not of his own life, but of the retaliation, of the process, of the reaction of Shilpa. He was glad to be in Mississippi, off-grid.

Eighteen months earlier, he had walked into Elaine's office for the first time. He introduced himself as a narcissist, wanting a third party, a professional, to tell him what a shameful and horrible man he was. He had self-diagnosed himself as a narcissist because he had been too focused on his dreams, his vision, and his pursuits. Because of this, his marriage had, bit by bit, made him begin to believe that he was selfish, self-focused, and a reflection of the negative aspects of his father's personality instead of the positive. Selective targeting. His Google MD self-analyses had overlooked the idea of empathy. Narcissists generally do not possess empathy or concern for others. Narcissists generally do not walk into a counselor's office in search of transformation and healing. While he didn't walk on water or raise the dead, he did care about people, the world, and humanity.

A FLOOD OF IMAGES

In the moments that led up to his final command, his final authorization to his attorney, his mind waded through a barrage of images and scenes of his life with Shilpa. His mind began to cherry-pick the lighter times, the good moments, the laughs, anything and everything positive. It was almost as if he was being tested. His mental fog of doubt rolled in from the Gulf Coast and, at times, began to cloud his ability to see anything, much less Day #10. His relationship with Shilpa was romance-free. There was never the giddiness of falling in love. There was never the feeling of passion. Shilpa had subconsciously latched onto his INFJ vulnerabilities, exploited them, and chased him all across India demanding he answer her question, "Who's your wife? Who's your wife? Who's your wife?"

His explanations of not being interested in marriage, of the reality of marriage, of his personal feelings, fell on deaf ears. It was the utmost spoiled child behavior. Shilpa was relentless, cornering him and berating him as if they were inside a police interrogation room until he signed the confession. She didn't stop until he admitted "you are" to give Shilpa the answer she indeed wanted. His relationship with Shilpa had been a reflection, a mirror into his own self-worth, showing him what he felt he deserved in life.

Throughout their marriage, Shilpa always taunted him, saying, "You're just like your father! I'm telling Mom. You only care about your computer. And your slum people!" Shilpa would intentionally agitate him to provoke a response and then blame him. At the time, he had not understood that the very hallmark of his personality was to avoid conflict. During one occasion, Shilpa's barrage of mental barbs and verbal attacks became too much that he went downstairs to lay, face down, on the sofa in the den. Still, Shilpa refused to leave him alone.

"I just want to be alone. Please. Just let me lay here," he pleaded. When Shilpa was in attack mode, she was relentless. He could not leave the house or drive anywhere as that would incite additional conflict. Shilpa upped the pressure on him. She sat on his back, pressing him into the sofa. That made it harder for him to breathe. He was already asthmatic.

"Talk. Talk. Talk!" was all that Shilpa would say. He tried to nudge Shilpa off of him. Shilpa got up. A moment of relief, or so he thought. Shilpa proceeded into the kitchen, filled a plastic cup with cold water, walked over to him, and poured the water over his neck and head. Some of it splashed onto the sofa. Triggered. He stood, grabbed the empty red plastic picnic cup, and threw it across the den while shouting, "Just leave me alone! Please. I just want to be alone!"

Shilpa's eyes lit up. She raised her finger and pointed at him. "See. You are just like your father!" In that instant, he felt shameful and apologetic for throwing the empty cup.

However, in Ocean Springs, he realized that his mother never harassed, berated, demeaned, and poured cold water on his father. Silence, his childhood response, always kicked in. Compartmentalize, bury, and pretend it never happened.

NO CONTACT – AN ANTI-HUMAN RESPONSE

He often listens to Dr. Linda Martinez-Lewi's podcasts as he drives. There is something very melodic, soothing, and comforting about Dr. Lewi's voice — her articulation of concepts and the importance of calming the nervous system. Shilpa knows he has left Culpeper, but she does not know where he is or when he will return. Boundary enforcement and the idea that he actually has basic rights are a novel concept that means rocking the boat. His initial attempts at personal empowerment were shaky, to say the least. Shilpa has to have access to him in order to know his whereabouts 24/7 and be able to keep track of him. An early-stage boundary, which seems unnoticeable to others, is for him to limit any phone communications. It is a tepid boundary during the legally required separation period that works 80% of the time.

He remains connected with Shilpa on Viber, allowing her to have access or the feeling of having access to him. Shilpa never follows any of the rules she placed on him. There is no equal reciprocity. He is not allowed to touch Shilpa's phones. He is not allowed to ask Shilpa questions. He is instructed on what to say and what not to say at family functions. If he didn't follow the rules, hell would follow. Anxiety. Panic. Exasperation. Hundreds and hundreds of messages. 175 missed calls. Insanity. Allowing contact through Viber only may seem like a small step to the world, but it is a tremendous first step for him. It is also strategic on his part. It allows him to collect data that might be required in the divorce, to demonstrate a pattern of communication, and to demonstrate his calm and measured responses. In a nutshell, his strategy is to collect a record of his crazy and manipulative world.

On March 13th in Mississippi, synched up with the timing of his "no turning back" divorce timetable, he would finally be able to fully enforce a total no-contact ban. Dr. Linda Martinez-Lewi has discussed "The Perfect Storm" of a marriage between a covert narcissist and an empathic individual. Dr. Lewi describes such a marriage union as "the ultimate nightmare scenario." It is a psychological nightmare, one that he has been living and had been entangled in for nearly 17 years since crossing paths with Shilpa. This traumatic bonding has trapped him inside of his emotional self, his weakness of being too sensitive and his weakness of caring about people. In order to begin breaking his traumatic bond, he would have to learn how to rip apart his emotional DNA from within every fiber of his being. He would have to learn how to block an addictive need for the push and pull mechanism that his mind has been conditioned to.

He stands at the edge of the bed in his hotel room. His phone is blowing up with messages from Shilpa.

Please. Please. Please. Please. Call me. Just for a minute. Please. Please. Please. Don't turn off your phone. Please. Please. I will do anything. You are my world. I love you. I'm sorry. I'm immature. Please. Please. Please. Just one more chance. One more chance!

He stares at the phone. He trembles. A cold sweat. Numbness. A tear in his eye. His heart beats rapidly as he switches off his phone.

FIVE

LOS ANGELES (1996-1998)

His life involved a series of slingshots. It was as if out of nowhere, the Universe would place his non-athletic, asthmatic, sensitive, complex, Yin and Yang energetic being, into a slingshot. It would stretch it back as far as possible, and then let it rip. Moving to Los Angeles to spend two years at film school was one of those slingshots. He wasn't born into a creative family. He wasn't a budding artist in high school. He watched a handful of films growing up, but he certainly could not recite dialogue. His parents had managed to save a little money for a decent in-State college but not enough for a super boujee private school in LA. Moving to California at the age of 20 was a head-scratcher. He blamed it on India. It was India's fault. Had he not been slingshotted to India at 16, he would not have begun to see the world in a more nuanced way, to see the world beyond small-town Big Red Culpeper.

Something within him was beginning to stir. Deep within his spirit, he felt as if he carried a message. The only problem was that he had no clue what that message was. It was just a feeling.

A local city bus headed down the boulevard — Bohemian storefronts and a few tall palm trees here and there. Blue skies. Inside, he sat near the back. He was not accustomed to using public transportation, but a semester without his car wouldn't deter him. It was a bit of a journey with a bus change at Alvarado and Temple. He was often the only White person on the bus that was filled with a sea of faces and cultures, a tapestry of America. He wore formal khaki pants and a nice shirt.

Finally, after an hour and a half, he arrived at 5555 Melrose Avenue. Paramount Pictures. He pulled the cord. *Ding. Ding.* He was the only person to exit. He made his way across the street and entered the main gate, always with a nod and wave to the security guards; it was the Southerner in him. He entered the compound. The Cecil B. DeMille building was just ahead of him. He turned left and walked past the fake blue sky and empty ocean-turned-parking lot all the way to the end of the studio. He turned right, passing George Jefferson (a.k.a. Sherman Hemsley), and both men shared a nod.

Straight ahead of him, up on the hill, was the Hollywood sign. He turned left into the Bob Hope Building and walked up a couple flights of rickety, but carpeted, stairs until he reached the top. He finally arrived at his office, the Xerox machine, located in the narrow hall next to the unisex bathroom. To his left, was the office of an Academy Award-winning producer, the location of his internship. To his right, was the head office of Paramount Casting.

He was known as the "Man Without a Face" and was, much to his displeasure, even referenced as such at a few industry events. Standing for hours at a time at the Xerox machine placed him with his back to the world. He understood that he was *just* an intern in an industry filled with bigwigs. However, he also understood that he was so much more than a bigwig's punch line.

His father and his best friend, Brian, spent part of the Christmas holidays driving his car cross-country so that he had wheels in Cali. He had requested for his family to not send him the Mercedes G-Wagon and instead, he opted for the '93 gray Chevy station wagon. It was also a "wagon." Freedom. His little Cavalier with Virginia tags, Carolina registration, and a Cali driving license, explored every inch of SoCal and beyond. 405. 110. 105. 5. 210. He was in deserts and mountains. He was in the Hollywood Hills and the Baldwin Hills. The gray wagon turned heads on Sunset Boulevard and Van Ness Boulevard. He found himself flying on eight-lane freeways and over towering flyovers that were built seemingly miles high in the sky. He could not help but be enamored by the large opulent mansions, the oversized entry gates, and the epic holiday displays during Halloween and Christmas outside of homes. He was enamored by the topography of it all, with its steep curvy roads and cliffside oceanfront homes. It was Hollywood. There were movie studios anchored in all parts of the city and celebrities driving Phantoms for mid-afternoon lattes. He felt no difference between 22701 and 90210. Just as deeply as he was struck by the indulgence of Beverly Hills, Brentwood, Pacific Palisades, and Malibu, he was equally struck by Inglewood, Pomona, Artesia, Cypress, and East Los Angeles.

His college life had commenced at George Mason University, in Fairfax Virginia, prior to transferring to the University of Southern California. In Virginia, there were times when he had trouble finding his car in the student lot since his wagon blended right in with all the other campus models — Ford,

Honda, Toyota, Nissan, and GMC. However, in California, he had absolutely no trouble spotting his car on campus. Many of his fellow students lived in other tax brackets and drove imports such as Mercedes, Rovers, and BMWs. However, there were a few modest classmates who arrived on campus in red or black Ferraris, depending if it were a Tuesday or Thursday class.

He had not relocated 2,500 miles across America to join a fraternity, pretend to be a sports fan, tailgate, or absorb campus life. The economics of the financial burdens his parents had amassed weighed heavily on him. He was grateful to be accepted, on the second attempt, into a film school with a 3%, Harvard-like, acceptance rate. He was even more grateful for the magic of his mother and how she managed to thread together a patchwork of federal loans and personal sacrifices to allow him, her only child, to follow his heart even when it made no sense to her and even when certain townsfolk ridiculed and lambasted his pursuits as not being "realistic."

The campus exuded opulence. Stately brick buildings. Large palm tree-lined walkways. Colorful flowers. A deep blue sky. He had just come from a middle-class college, which had felt very comfortable to him, so USC felt a bit extravagant. He had ridden in a first-class train in India, so he recognized luxury. However, India had taught him to see the totality, to see contrasts. Outside the compound walls existed a different America from his small-town life. Many store signs were in Spanish. Koreatown. There was a bit of graffiti and overflowing trash cans. Women pushed baby strollers and rolled grocery carts. The Burger King across the street served Whoppers without any meat. Huh? How could a Whopper be a Whopper without meat?

He was very close to South Central, the epicenter of the gangsta rap genre. Ice-T. Dre. Cube. Snoop. G-Funk. Pac. These were the sounds that vibrated and bounced their way into the heart, mind, and soul of a skinny White kid from Virginia who didn't rap or dance. Crenshaw Boulevard, to him, was more famous than Rodeo Drive. The energy, passion, and lyrical articulation of rappers like Ice Cube or Tupac had a deeply emotional element to their artistry. The social justice messaging connected with him.

When he first arrived in LA, he drafted a personal mission statement that read, "...*To bring about a greater understanding and awareness of culture.*" Through an intuitive inner download, he felt as though these words were somehow connected to his life purpose. However, he had no clarity on the next steps. Writing was never in his plan, but it was something that felt natural to him, and it was an endeavor that he greatly enjoyed. Writing also allowed him to tap into his imagination and allowed him to escape thoughts of his past, haunting thoughts of the willow tree.

He spent more time off campus than on, immersing himself in the movie-industrial complex. He shot a student film on the Court of Miracles backlot set at Universal Studios. He was humbled by the generosity of the operations team at Universal as he witnessed his little $5,000 student film title, written in Sharpie, on an enormous dry-erase board with each backlot and production listed. His teeny-tiny project was surrounded by multi-million-dollar studio productions.

Universal Legal required a $2 million umbrella policy to drive on the lot. USC provided him with a $1 million policy; hence, he was forced to hire an 18-Wheeler Semi-Truck from the transportation department to load up and move his gray wagon and two picture cars several hundred yards to the Court of Miracles. Throughout the day of the shoot, lawyers from Universal Studios would periodically drive by in golf carts to make sure "no one was driving." Therefore, he appointed crew members to be on the lookout for any legal suits and hoped that no one would realize that the vehicles were always in different positions. It was an action short, and the vehicles had to move.

He continued to develop his close and meaningful relationship with the Xerox machine. He estimated burning through 2-3 Sequoias per day. He xeroxed and xeroxed and xeroxed screenplays, double-sided and single-sided, page counts re-checked, Brad's fastened correctly. He had a window seat to all the action. To his left, he watched as normally polished film execs turned into little children, tip-toeing to the door of the Big Kahuna, to eavesdrop. Why? Because Al Pacino had just called in. When Al called, time stopped. To his right, there were often shouts and screaming rants. Woman-on-woman verbal assaults. The Head of Paramount Casting was a woman. Her assistant was a woman. Scripts would get thrown.

"I don't give a fuck about your grandmother. We're casting a movie!" ranted the head of casting. The female assistant, unable to take the abuse anymore, ran out into the hallway behind him as the Xerox machine hummed. She went into the unisex bathroom. He felt for the woman, who was crying hysterically. He later learned that her grandmother had just died and apparently the death conflicted with the casting of the film.

No day was typical. While answering phones, he would, at times, field calls from big shots, legends such as Robert Redford. He wandered in and out of backlot sets and sound stages. On more than one occasion, he would return to the Big Kahuna's office suite after hours. On Friday nights in particular, he would lay back on the sofa, pick up the phone, and dial friends and family in Virginia. He networked and networked and networked. He attended industry parties on Sunset, wined and dined, and went on weekend yacht trips to Catalina Island with friends in the TV world, Bob Loudin and Steve Grant.

He carried around his own Rolodex with XL spreadsheets of highly classified top-secret data, the personal numbers, office numbers, car phone numbers, beach house numbers, and entourage numbers for the Who's Who of Hollywood power players. He couldn't call anyone since that would be a major boundary overstep. However, he had the list and that was just dope.

He appreciated USC and was able to connect with one professor (Robert Brown), but he was generally disillusioned, financially strapped, and contemplated the sin of becoming an official college dropout. His new plan was to jump ship, leave academia, and work as a production assistant or a three-hole punch paper stocker at Staples. He was granted a meeting with his boss, the Academy Award Winning Producer, to pitch his Plan B. As an advocate for formal education, his boss advised him to finish school.

He graduated in '97 and marched across the Shrine Auditorium stage beneath the blaring music of the *Star Wars* soundtrack. His pursuits of getting hired on a Hollywood film as a production assistant were met with bolted doors. The legendary Clint Eastwood was shooting a picture that summer on the East Coast, and he felt certain that he could land a spot as a production assistant. The Big Kahuna was friends with Mr. Eastwood since they had made pictures together. He had two additional lines of contact with Malpaso, Eastwood's company, both in the office and a Second Assistant Director on the film. Three references. Three personal references for him. It was not to write the film, shoot the film, design the sets, design the costumes, or manage the production. It was three personal references for him to serve coffee, run errands, send a fax, and make a copy. Denied. Networking Fail.

A Day in the Life. Just as suddenly as life conspired to propel him to sunny California, unbeknownst to him, he was being pulled and stretched once again in that damn slingshot.

He was sitting in his studio apartment with a window view of the 110 freeway in South Pasadena when the phone rang. He was surrounded by mountains of rejection letters and their standard legal language discussing the refusal to take a peek at unsolicited material. In Hollywood, there were talent agencies, and then there was the Creative Artist Agency. CAA was the big shiny light on the hill. Mr. Martin "Marty" Baum was an agent, an institution, a big fish in a small pond. Back in the 1970s, Marty was the guy who the founders of CAA put all their eggs in one basket to rope in. Marty had a Rolodex. Marty represented the likes of Sidney Poitier, Richard Harris, Julie Andrews, Richard Attenborough, and on and on and on. God created the earth in 7 days. This phone call was 7 days in the making. 7 days. Marty's assistant had been scheduling and rescheduling the call with South Pasadena. His calendar was open; however, Marty's changed by the millisecond.

He looked at the phone. There was a bit of a nervous quiver. He trembled a bit but was eager and excited when he answered. Within seconds, his face turned to shock and awe.

Marty, screaming into a speakerphone, shouts, "You mind telling me what all this is about?"

He stumbled a bit in his response but reverted to his hometown Southern charm. "Good afternoon Mr. Baum. I was wondering if Mr. Attenborough had a chance to take a look at the script?"

He was met with silence at first, followed by a Category 5 response that shifted the San Andreas Faultline as Mr. Baum rants, "I'm not just gonna send Dickie your script! Who do you think I am? You get this funded by a studio and then you come to me!"

Click. Marty abruptly hung up the phone. It was apparent that Mr. Baum was not from the South. He sat back in the chair, feeling lightheaded, trying to process what just happened.

7 Days. 7 Days to coordinate a phone call in which there were no pleasantries, no mention of the sunny weather, no words of insight, no future brunch meeting with Sir Richard Attenborough, no feedback on the protagonist, nothing. It was a power call between a man sitting in a comfy chair in Beverly Hills and a guy with a story sitting in a tiny abode in South Pasadena. It could have been a form letter. It could have just been a standard industry rejection letter, but it had to be a phone call. People like Marty didn't just call them "little people" with gray wagons in studio apartments. It wasn't normal; therefore, 7 days had allowed his mind to fill with a bit of anticipation that perhaps the phone call was to be positive in nature. But it was so much more than a phone call, it was a slingshot. After three years in Los Angeles, he was packing up his wagon. Part of him felt that he was a failure, a failure at 23, and part of him was excited for the unknown adventure. He was relocating from the urban jungle to an actual jungle. He was moving from LA to the Himalayas.

SIX

HIMALAYAN FOOTHILLS

He exited the train in Dehradun, a small city with a population of 480,000, located in the Himalayan foothills, north of Delhi. He was wearing shorts and a T-shirt. He had a backpack strapped to him, and he carried a duffle-style suitcase. It was brutally humid, and he sweated profusely. The dark and dingy railway station was filled with locals. He was the only White one. He scanned the station as he walked, searching for something, like his name on a sign. He had been hired to teach English at a boarding school. In 1992, his own government had advised him against traveling north to see the mountains. Six years later, he was back on his own journey.

He had traded in the streets of Los Angeles for the unknown of India. His plan was to start a new chapter, live on campus in the Himalayas, absorb a new world, and use his downtime to write. His salary was to be 5,000

Rupees per month, about $250. His food and accommodation were to be provided by the school. He was instructed to travel to India on a tourist visa, which concerned him since technically, he did not think he was allowed to work under a tourist visa.

His first experience in India had left a romanticized vision of observing and experiencing culture from the cushy, though not boujee, confines of the U.S. Embassy — first-class train rides and private VIP Day Trips. As he stood at the railway station, he realized two things: one, his new employer had either forgotten or had not bothered to pick him up on arrival as confirmed and two, he had a sneaky suspicion that real-life India was not an American Country Club.

Pestle Weed College (PWC) was actually a primary and secondary school. It was a large campus with a security gate, cricket ground, administrative office, library, teaching block, and dorms. There were a couple of hundred students, from all across Northern India and Nepal. The topography was very hilly. The twinkling lights of the famous hill station of Mussoorie could be seen, high above, at close to 7,000 feet. Mussoorie was the front range and gateway to taller and taller mountains. PWC was surrounded by dense jungle. It was the monsoon season, and there were deluges of rain, inches per hour at times, for days.

The website, which had lured his mind, projected romanticism with horseback riding in the foothills. Upon arriving, he learned that the horses had died. No horses. The teaching staff, including himself, resided in small concrete dwellings, deep in the jungle. These were slabs of two-story flats with spotty electricity, slippery and steep moss-covered walkways, and monkey thieves lurking in the trees, waiting to steal any groceries or food he might be carrying. The principal/owner had a hacienda-style mansion being constructed on the main campus at the end of the cricket ground. A fleet of cars was parked just outside the hacienda gate. It gave off the vibe of a drug lord's compound in a Jack Ryan film. He was part of a pioneering group of teachers, an experiment for the school to hire international teachers. He arrived curious to meet the other foreign guinea pigs — three Americans and a Scottish woman. He learned that two of the Americans, a husband-and-wife teaching duo, had already checked out of Club Pestle Weed within five days.

He arrived at the dining hall that was still under construction. All the students had already assembled, and they were chanting and singing school solidarity songs and other dogmatic rituals. The breakfast was already sitting cold on the long tables. He took his assigned seat, exhausted from jet lag and wheezing from the hike. It was just after 7 a.m. and he was sitting next to the assistant principal. The man was an older Sikh gentleman with a very long beard and a large blue turban, who looked at him and said, "You're a lazy fellow!" He responded with silence and a stern look.

His sense of adventure carried him through the physical challenges of life in the Indian jungle. He mastered the art of taking a shower with a bucket of cold water and a scoop. He did this as more monkeys sat in the window above, behind the frosted glass. He learned that he must always pull his single bed and rock-hard mattress away from the wall at night; otherwise, the jungle critters might pay him a visit. One night, he was kissed by a spider. This resulted in a severe reaction that looked as if part of his neck was burned. He had trouble turning his head for a few days.

He learned that hitchhiking was part of life, especially when one lived seven miles out of town and had no wheels. One would just exit the gates of the school campus and begin walking down the mountain. Eventually, after a few minutes or an hour, one would jump into any mode of transportation that was available, whether it be a motorcycle, a tractor, a wagon, a bus, or a truck. Basically, anything with a motor would do. However, it was not advisable to hitchhike at night, in case one met up with a leopard.

Trips up the mountains to Mussoorie were magical. At times, he would be above the clouds or in the fog. It was always very cool. The small town was built right along a mountain ridge, and it had impeccable views of the snow-capped high peaks in the distance as well as the Dehradun valley below. He ate his first aloo paratha, piping hot and layered with melted butter, as he sipped masala chai, soaking in the world around him, always lost in thought. Mussoorie was more of what he had envisioned. It had the atmosphere for a writer.

He quickly developed close friendships with his roommate, a South Indian physical education instructor and cricket coach, and other local staff and their families. In them, he found the heart and soul of his primitive life, off-grid. Along with his roommate and a few teachers, he experienced his first Bollywood film, *Pyaar to Hona Hi Tha*. Superstars Ajay Devgn. Kajol. Hearts on fire love and romance. Zooming cameras. Exotic locales and an intermission.

The old movie theater was packed, the crowd jeering and humming along to the pulse of Bollywood songs. It was a roller coaster of emotion shared with hundreds of locals and one White guy.

Outside the theater, he sees a gorgeous and rather busty Bollywood actress on the cover of *Filmfare*, a publication similar to *People* and *Us Weekly*. He stopped in his tracks and picked up the magazine, feeling a bit lustful.

"Who's this?"

His roommate replied, "She's a newcomer. From Chennai. You like?"

He remained infatuated with the magazine cover. "Like? I'll marry her."

He had intended to remain at PWC for the two-year "teaching" assignment, but the vision of his decision was crumbling around him, and he found himself butting heads with management. He was fully prepared and focused on putting forth his best effort to teach English with his film degree, do his job, and utilize his downtime for personal pursuits and personal enrichment. However, he quickly ran into philosophical differences with a school.

School philosophy. Teachers were property. Available 24/7. Can't say no. Beholden to the whims and beacon call of a darling dictator principal wearing a safari suit and a Hitleresque mustache. His philosophy. Organization. Planning. Implementation. Focus. Human decency.

To him, it was a blur between living in a different culture and the personal needs of a madman. Teachers and staff were disrespected on a daily basis. Plans were changed at random. He was asked to hand over his passport so they could have it sent to change his tourist visa to a work visa. He didn't trust the process so he didn't comply with the request. Most of the staff did not know how to swim. He had the swimming merit badge, so he volunteered to be the swim coach. He marched with the young students down the mountain to the pool for the first day of swim class only to find eight inches of algae-colored bacterial-infected water and a small garden hose with running water. He advised his kids not to get in the water; however, most did not listen. He watched the kids who paid a handsome fee to fund the lifestyle of the principal run and splash around in the sad-looking pool with icky green water.

On a deeper level, he began to understand the value that was placed on his whiteness. He had been hired by the school, not for international exposure and enrichment, but to justify the fees charged to parents and to give the school a global feel. He, the White guy, was a diversity hire. He was also a puppet. There was a grand dinner on the lawn, in front of the administrative office. Delicious, warm, and spicy Indian dishes, not cafeteria food. The wealthy parents of a few students were present. The principal and the three White teachers — Debs, Sabrina, and himself — were also present. Noticeably absent were any Indian staff, who, by his calculation, were far more qualified to be there because they had actual teaching degrees and were great at their jobs. He enjoyed the food, but not the role in which he was playing.

Dead horses. A green pool. Cold food. Entry and exit permission requirements. He was still very much in love with India, but PWC felt like a prison. He had survived 42 days. Moving on would not be easy. It would have to be a covert operation, an escape mission since he would not be allowed to just quit and walk out of campus. He also hated conflict. Plans were made in secret, and his escape would have to be made in the dead of night. He had booked a hotel for a couple of days in Dehradun and hired an Ambassador taxi to meet him outside the gate at midnight. He had acquired a large aluminum trunk, rug, tapestries, and hand-stitched clothes from the market. In short, he had acquired stuff for his life that he wanted to take with him. The only other American, Sabrina, had already moved on up the road and into a Buddhist-run facility. The remaining holdout, the Scottish lass, Debs, who had taught English in Thailand, was also disillusioned and making quiet plans to leave.

He was always more comfortable expressing his feelings through written form than face-to-face sit-downs. He thought it was just a weird quirk. He had written lengthy letters to his parents informing them of his decision to abandon all sense of reality and apply to film school. He had written a lengthy letter to his parents outlining, explaining, and justifying his intention to reroute from LA to India. He saw no reason not to continue his tradition by composing a handwritten resignation letter, in very poor penmanship. It was to be typed, but, go figure, the power was out. He didn't possess Thomas Jefferson's writing contraption, which would simultaneously print a duplicate copy in the 1700s. Nope. He wrote two. One for management, and one for his personal HR file.

On August 25, 1998, he wrote:

I feel it is no longer healthy for me to continue my affiliation with Pestle Weed College; hence, I am resigning from my post, effective immediately. I shall move forward to pursue other interests. Had the campus facilities been functioning properly, this letter would be typed. My sudden departure is based on the following: 1. My philosophy and the school philosophy do not work well together. 2. I remain uncomfortable with having a tourist visa, as opposed to a work permit. 3. I do not feel as though I am on equal terms with all the staff, in terms of duties, workload, co-curricular activities, and verbal abuse. I am under a different "contractual status." I also feel that the faculty are overworked and underappreciated. They deserve to be respected.

He stood at the towering black gate at midnight, surrounded by his luggage. The Ambassador car and driver were on the other side. His roommate was with him to help with the luggage. The night was still and the campus was quiet as two unarmed security guards refused to open the gate. His roommate requested for them, in Hindi, to open it. One of the guards placed a phone call, but there was no answer. He walked to the gate, put both of his hands on it, and looked up.

He turned to his roommate and said, "I'll climb it if I have to. You can hand me the luggage."

The security guards got even more agitated since holding a foreign teacher hostage had not been part of their training manual. He began to climb up the gate as his roommate begged the guards. They reluctantly gave in and eventually unlocked the chain.

He hugged his roommate. "You've been amazing. Thanks for your friendship, your kindness, and being you. Please give my love to everyone else. I will always remember our adventures."

As the prison gates closed, he drove away in the darkness of night, determined not to allow his Himalayan mirage to deter him.

SEVEN

SEPTEMBER 1998

An old beat-up black and yellow Fiat cab traveled down the Queen's Necklace. Towering skyscrapers could be seen on one side and the vast Arabian Sea on the other. Marine Drive, known as the "Queen's Necklace," followed the arc of South Mumbai. Thousands of old beat-up black and yellow cabs flew down the main drag. His new aluminum trunk from the Himalayas sat on top in a luggage carrier. He certainly was not a tall man, but the taxi seemed to have been built for children. He was hunched over, and the back seat was as soft as stone. His luggage was stacked around him. The taxi driver was a Muslim man. The cabbie wore a traditional kurta and kufi, or skullcap, and had a very long beard. The diesel taxi was loud, very loud. The gear shift was on the side of the steering wheel. The cabbie needed both hands to pull the crank down. The wind blew the humid and fragrant sea air inside the little black and yellow box on wheels.

Mumbai was a city of over 15 million, and it certainly felt like it. And on that day, the population was fifteen million and one. He had arrived to shake things up in Mumbai, the epicenter of Bollywood. Like another slingshot, Plan B had begun. His objectives were to familiarize himself with Mumbai, get settled into an affordable suburban apartment, begin networking in Bollywood, write a screenplay, and raise financing locally to produce himself without any assistance from Marty Baum. His plan to cover his living cost was to work three months annually at Merillat, a cabinet factory in Culpeper. It was a place he had worked at in previous summers. With three months' work, he would earn enough to live nine months in Mumbai on a tight budget, with minimal expenses. At the heart of his Indian Dream was his wish to connect these abstract slingshots in order to make his mother proud, to show that his unorthodox path in life had a purpose.

His apartment was on the fifth floor. No lift. Kandivali was a remote suburb located between the Western line railway station and the Western Express Highway. Middle-class Indian families lived in Kandivali and most of them spoke English. He was the only foreigner living in Kandivali, specifically the Police Quarters. It was a housing project in which the owners of the flats were all city cops. They purchased them as investments at reduced rates and rented them out. Thakur Complex was a sprawling neighborhood, with dozens of high-rise apartment clusters, one of which was known as the Police Quarters. The population of the Thakur Complex ecosystem exceeded that of his native place, Culpeper.

His studio apartment was leased for $85 a month. By this point, he had learned that everything in India was a concrete slab with baby blue paint that would brush off like dust if you swiped your hand across it. He had a small kitchen which had another slab of concrete. There was no gas, no burners, and no fridge. There was also no AC. However, there was a ceiling fan and a fluorescent tube light. The bathroom was split into two cubby holes. On one side was his concrete bath with a shower. It only had cold water until he purchased a geezer device to warm up the water tank. He had no Western-style toilet. His toilet was a hole in the floor with a ceramic bowl basin and an outline of where to place his feet. A toilet without a base to sit on... Performing number two or in the case of diarrhea, number three, would involve the art of squatting, aiming, dropping, and balancing. He was American, so he was familiar with Charmin Ultra Strong toilet paper. In India, toilet paper could only be found on tiny rolls, which he often hoarded. Tissue paper, as it was called, was the general term for both toilet paper and Kleenex. Trying to squat, balance, and utilize the thin paper in a hot and humid bathroom was a work of art. It was an art form that he had to master.

Aside from the toilet, he loved the little apartment. It was enough space to call his own where he could decorate, bring in color, and give it his flare. He rented an AC, got a tiny fridge, had rods installed in the kitchen to hang his clothes up, bought a two-burner stove, had a gas cylinder delivered, got a simple cot and a very soft hand-stuffed mattress, purchased a nice chair... and finally, bought the centerpiece to his little world, a new desk to organize his thoughts — to write and to maintain his detailed Indian Rupee expense account. While his apartment may have lacked material comfort, it was a space that was filled with hope, love, inspiration, and the noble pursuit of a dream.

Bollywood, like Hollywood, wasn't just a place — it was an image, an idea, and a myth projected and exported around the world. Bollywood films were typically large, colorful musical productions — love stories with oversized sets and hundreds of background dancers and film shoots in exotic locations across the world. Film City was the largest movie studio in Mumbai and incorporated thousands of acres, a few remote villages, and a great deal of forested land. Heroes and heroines in Bollywood were ranked daily and annually, and one had to have the last name "Khan" to make it in the top three. Shah Rukh. Salman. Amir. Bollywood films were seen globally by the Indian diaspora, but they were popular across the Gulf, North Africa, Asia, and Europe. Star Trailers on sets were known as "Vanity Vans." The Mumbai suburb of Bandra was the Beverly Hills of India. Bandra, and the surrounding suburbs like Juhu, were home to actors, directors, producers, writers, and musicians. In the days of silent films, imported films from America and Europe were the most popular and profitable. However, once Indians were able to hear the rich sounds of music, dance, and culture, Bollywood was born and actors were transformed into idols who were worshiped by an entire nation. Many films at the time were financed with bundles of cash. There was absolutely no corporate structure, just bags of cash, black money. Wealthy diamond merchants from South Mumbai often funded these films. In India, producers equaled financiers, and the producers perk was personally selecting the heroines.

The days when he remained home, writing and thinking, would only cost him a few dollars. He maintained a large cloth-bound ledger expense account, tracking every single rupee spent. He had to pace himself for the nine-months stretch. He was surrounded by dozens of local restaurants and quickly developed a taste and craving for bhindi masala, chicken tikka masala, palak paneer, malai kofta, paneer tikka masala, jeera rice, naan, roti, chapati, and most things on the menu. And for a few more bucks, he had a maid come daily to clean and hand wash his laundry. Several days a week, he had a cook who would come and prepare a gloriously delicious Indian delicacy on the concrete slab called a kitchen. At 24, he was living abroad and pursuing his vision with an entourage all on a meager budget. It was his kind of boujee.

SERENDIPITY

OCTOBER 2, 1998

He found himself sitting in the Gazebo Restaurant in Bandra, on Linking Road, having lunch and enjoying the frigid atmosphere of a powerful air conditioner. Gazebo was a place he had discovered when he first arrived in Mumbai and lived for a month as a paying guest. He was a regular patron, well-liked by the manager and staff.

On his table was a book on Gandhi. It was a book he had randomly purchased a few months earlier. It was a mix of pictures and general history, not a wonkish deep-diving biography. By October, monsoons had generally subsided in Mumbai, so it was unusual to see dark storm clouds rolling in and a deluge of rain falling from the Heavens on that afternoon. Linking Road was a river. To him, another oddity about the day was that many stores were closed and there was very little traffic. He had finished eating, but he could not leave because of the storm.

Sanjeev, one of the friendly waiters who he chatted with often, stood nearby. He asks, "What's up with today? Another holiday? Everything's closed."

Sanjeev's eyes widened in disbelief. "You don't know? It's this man's birthday. Gandhiji!" Sanjeev said, pointing to the book.

It was the definition of serendipity, an accidental discovery. Trapped in a restaurant. Epic monsoon flood outside. Random book on Gandhi. Gandhi's birthday. It was the first of two revelations that day. The second, being, the identity of Sanjeev. Sanjeev was an actual nephew of acting legend Om Puri. One of his favorite films was *City of Joy* with Patrick Swayze and Om Puri. It was released in 1992, the year of his first trip to India. At USC, his professors would go around the room on day one with favorite film inquiries. *Star Wars* was the response uttered by 95% of his classmates. Not him. His response was always *Gandhi* and *City of Joy*. He spent the next five hours reading at the table.

ME & GANDHI

The title of his little indie film story. A guy and a gal. Contemporary love story. A drama. Cross-Cultural. A wise old village tailor. The concept of past lives, being a bystander, a face in the crowd during a brush with history. In trying to read the tea leaves of his future, he felt that perhaps this was his message.

Mani Bhavan. Mumbai. The name of the building where Gandhi resided during visits to the city was now a museum and heritage site. The two-story home was tucked away on a quiet side street, shaded by palm trees and beneath the sounds of the Asian koel — black birds the size of a crow with loud and distinct calls. Inside, there was a film room to watch old movie reels, a museum downstairs, and a research library upstairs. He seemed to make instant connections everywhere he went and always believed in the goodness of humanity. He sat in an old wooden chair that creaked in the research room, surrounded by books as he took notes.

The head of the museum stopped by to check on the foreign guest. "Are you finding what you require?"

"That and more! I keep getting sidetracked," he responded.

The museum director smiled. Before leaving, the man said, "Did you know that Richard Attenborough sat in that *very* chair? To do research."

His eyes glazed over with childlike wonder. "Really?"

He grabbed both arms of the chair and looked down. Marty may not have scheduled brunch with Dickie, but he was sitting in the same chair that Dickie sat in... in the house where Gandhi stayed. And that was dope. Just a small-town village kid from Virginia experiencing possibility.

He wasn't in Mumbai to pursue girls or a relationship. Marriage was not part of his life plan. 1.7 children. Suburban house. Minivan. He was on a different path, and he knew it. Yet, in an instance, a trip to Mani Bhavan would change the trajectory of his life path. An innocent conversation would set the foundation for darkness to enter. As he was departing Mani Bhavin, a small group of college students stopped him. Curious. Eager. Both boys and girls. This unusual foreigner. American. Many questions. Several students asked for his contact number. Naturally, he had his business card with him. Taj Entertainment. Without any hesitation, he handed out the cards, always thinking of networking. Shilpa was not in the group, but her older sister was. The card made its way back to Shilpa. Soon after, he received a phone call. He was cordial, but he wasn't interested in talking. Shilpa claimed she wanted to improve her English by talking to him. He had left Pestle Weed and was no longer an ESL teacher. However, Shilpa was persistent. She'd call a few times each week, seemingly respectful. He was more annoyed than interested. But after six weeks of regular incoming calls, he decided to meet Shilpa.

From their very first meeting, something felt *off*. It was odd. Shilpa seemed overly nervous and timid. Shilpa seemed anxious, always looking around with eyes darting back and forth. Shilpa always walked very far ahead of him. It was not love at first sight. It was not lust at first sight. He was not particularly drawn to Shilpa, but on an energetic level, there was an unusual comfort. Shilpa tended to dress in a black long-sleeve shirt and jeans. She'd tie her hair into a ponytail. She possessed a childish quality that was very whimsical. Shilpa hailed from a strict Maharashtrian family. Her father was an Assistant Commissioner of Police, a lofty post.

On a subconscious level, Shilpa energetically tapped into his extremely sensitive emotional wiring, not his heart. Shilpa quickly latched herself to him. She wanted to know all of his movements, and she became jealous if there were any girls around him. Shilpa would lose her temper quickly, with a sudden pivot back to remorse for her actions. Shilpa was argumentative, and she blamed it on cultural differences. He once had a meeting with an acquaintance and model coordinator regarding networking links for his film. A Nepali model showed up at the office followed by Shilpa. It was an office meeting, yet Shilpa's eyes became evil. He ushered Shilpa into another room to deescalate the drama when she threw a hardback book at his head.

At the same time Shilpa was pursuing him, she was also in communication with a local Indian cricket player as well as another foreigner from Australia who was in Mumbai for a medical school program. It was all a bit sketchy, and no details were ever provided. Shilpa deflected when questioned. Shilpa shared a story with him of being abandoned by her family for several years when she was a child. Shilpa was the only sibling out of five to be sent away to live with a very poor grandmother. The story tugged at his heart and made him feel sorry for Shilpa. Surprise visits to his flat. Ripped-up pictures. Broken gift items. Stomping fits. None of it phased him much since he grew up around emotional outbursts and thought that was how people were. Growing up, he learned that maintaining calmness around him meant he needed to prioritize his father's emotional well-being. He was clueless to the psychology of it all, to the reality that his mind was a target and that he was being groomed as his sense of self slowly chipped away.

HALLOWEEN REDEFINED

The American Consulate was having a rooftop party at one of the foreign service residential buildings, and he was invited. He was connected with folks at the Consulate. He had pitched and promoted the concepts of bilateral relations between America and India through the arts. He immediately knew what he would be, a maharaja — a weed-free maharaja. He rented a head-to-toe outfit from a Bollywood costume shop. The party was a blend of diplomats and wealthy locals. The U.S. diplomats lived in grand flats the size of a house. His tiny writing abode out in the burbs could have fit into one room of the American hardship post flat.

He was the only maharaja. He wore a burgundy and gold turban with clip-on earrings. He wore a long golden robe with a maroon patterned printed shawl. He wore loose white baggy kurta pants and curled traditional flat shoes which were very flamboyant. He was ready for his close-up. As he mingled, he was befriended by a man, perhaps ten years older, and a woman, perhaps his age. The woman was tall and voluptuous with long curly hair and striking features. A model perhaps. An actress perhaps. No. No way. Really. The magazine cover he had seen in Dehradun. The Bollywood newcomer.

Starlet. The gorgeous heroine from the magazine cover was standing in front of him. The man was shorter, friendly, inquisitive, and wealthy. To him, it seemed natural. Organic. He was invited to join the actress and the rich guy at a new club named Fire & Ice. He wasn't really a clubber. This wasn't Culpeper. This wasn't Los Angeles. He had never received an invite to any Holmby Hills party. Marty slammed the phone down on him. Without hesitation, he said yes.

The innocence of a moment in time...

THE NEXT MORNING

His eyes slowly opened. His mind was foggy. He floated in and out of consciousness. His body felt numb. He was on his back. He had no idea where he was. He remembered club music and the hot Indian starlet. He hadn't been at the club very long. He remembered a drink. Being handed a drink. His eyes closed once again. And opened.

The room was blurry. He heard a sound. A rhythmic sound. He couldn't feel anything. A figure. A man. There was a man on top of him. His mind tried to engage with the moment, to figure it out. A haze. The man from the Halloween party. The man who invited him to the club. The man who handed him a drink. This was the man on top of him. What was happening? He felt lightheaded. He realized he was naked in a very large room with lots of marble and large windows. Arabian Sea. Queen's Necklace. His mind was short-circuiting. He remembered sitting with the man in the back of a car. They were leaving the club, and he was desperately trying to stay awake. So sudden. It was all so sudden. He was frozen. Frozen on the inside. Frozen on the outside. What was happening?

He rode the local train back to his tiny dwelling. His maharaja costume was stuffed in a plastic bag. He was numb. He was shaken. He was withdrawn. He was sad. His soul hurt. Back in his apartment, he sat in silence at his writing desk. His internal light was now dimmed. He wondered how an innocent Halloween party could turn into another nightmare.

He began to question all of his choices and decisions from the night before. He began to beat himself up internally. He hated himself. He wondered why he didn't run. He wondered why he didn't punch the guy in the face. He wondered why he stayed. He wondered why he allowed himself to be taken to breakfast with the man and the actress who had slept in another room. His mind tried to rationalize that spending time with the actress was worth it. She seemed to be flirtatious with him so maybe if he stayed longer and had the opportunity to sleep with her, it would somehow erase what had happened to him. He realized he had been drugged and that he was physically unable to move. His body had gone into shock.

Ultimately, he did the very thing that he had been conditioned to do as a child — take what happened to him and bury it as deep as he could within his soul. Tuck it away, hide it, put on a smile, and act as if nothing ever happened. Remain silent and move on with life. These were the survival skills he had learned in his treehouse.

EIGHT

A FEW MONTHS LATER...

The sounds of thousands of birds broke the silence as he walked across the sandy ground beneath the towering trees to approach Hriday Kunj, the residence of Gandhi. He saw a very simple structure — white and burgundy with terra cotta-style roof tiles. He removed his shoes and walked a few steps up, stepping into Gandhi's home office.

A small wooden desk a few inches off the ground. That of a school child. A hand-woven cushion. On the ground. Simplicity. Famed spinning wheel nearby. The charkha was used for spinning cotton to make clothes. He looked around as beads of sweat dripped from his forehead. He stood across the sandy front lawn and near the dried-up Sabarmati River, which flowed about as much as the creek in the backyard of his own childhood home. So many thoughts crossed his mind. It was overwhelming. He was standing in the room where leaders, diplomats, and artists from across the world had sat with Gandhi. *What did they talk about? What did they laugh about? What did they think of one another?*

As he continued to explore, he heard the sounds of children laughing and talking in an unknown language. Captivated. His energy was drawn to investigate further. He walked behind an old building and saw dozens and dozens if not a hundred, Indian children laughing and playing in an open courtyard. They appeared to be very poor. Happiness radiated from the children's faces. A light. The innocence of childhood. He took a few steps closer and felt an overwhelming sense of connectivity.

From behind him, someone asked, in a very heavy Indian accent, "Would you like to meet them?"

He turned to see Jayesh, male, early 30s, mustache, wearing a simple white kurta. Jayesh was barefoot.

"I'm sorry. I just heard the laughter and ended up over here."

"From where are you?" Jayesh inquired in broken English.

"Virginia. America."

Jayesh was very relaxed. "Welcome to Manav Sadhna. Come, let's go inside."

It was his first trip to Ahmedabad. It was a city of nearly five million, the largest in the State of Gujarat. An overnight train ride from Mumbai. A 45-minute flight. A research trip for the little film project, *Me & Gandhi.* Sabarmati Ashram, a thirty-six-acre campus, was established by Gandhi in 1917. It served as the incubation center in the pursuit of non-violent resistance from British Occupation and the dream of an independent nation. He was just a small-town kid from Virginia. No biological ties. No ancestry. Serendipity. Once Again. Slingshots.

Manav Sadhna, a new and fledgling NGO, meant "Service to Mankind." Inspired by the teachings and life of Gandhi, Manav Sadhna began outreach just across the street in the largest slum community in the city. The open courtyard was part of a youth hostel for kids to learn and grow in a structured environment where they would attend a day school on the grounds of the Ashram. Jayesh and his wife, Anar, were trustees along with Jayesh's father, Ishwarbhai Patel. Ishwarbhai was an actual Gandhian who was dedicated to improving sanitation conditions in slums and villages throughout India. Viren Joshi. Joshi Sahib. The inspiration and catalyst for Manav Sadhna. Viren, originally from Ahmedabad, was an engineer and lived in Chicago. Unmarried. Unattached. Authentic. Real. A Rare Soul dedicated to serving others. Viren was living the American Dream but had a much different dream. In India. Manav Sadhna. Gandhi Ashram. The essence of it all had captured his heart.

MARCHING FORWARD

For 24 days, from March 12, 1930, to April 6, 1930, Gandhi led The Salt March. Gandhi was joined by 79 trusted volunteers who walked ten miles a day from Sabarmati Ashram to a small village named Dandi in southern Gujarat to protest the British Salt Tax. The act of picking up handfuls of salt was in defiance of the law. The Dandi March was designed to be a strong symbol of the Civil Disobedience Movement — a symbol of non-violent resistance that served as a catalyst to inspire growth in the movement. Pre-social media optics. Pre-algorithm. Pre-like, subscribe, and share. The Dandi March drew worldwide attention to the Indian Independence Movement through newsreel and newspaper coverage. Awareness that crept into the mind of a young American pastor in Atlanta... Dr. Martin Luther King Jr.

He was on a tightly organized research mission with limited funds. He walked, but he also wheezed. Thus, he hired a Tata Sumo. Not a Japanese wrestler, but an Indian SUV. White in color. It was a rental that came with a driver. His goal was to retrace the Dandi March with air conditioning. His little off-the-grid road trip wound its way through the small towns and villages of Gujarat. His new friends at Manav Sadhna had hooked him up with a free overnight stay at a local hostel and spiritual center in Navsari, just a few kilometers from Dandi.

Bright and early the next morning, dressed in jeans and an Indian kurta, he found himself walking the last stretch of the historic march. He walked alone, stopping to photograph the water buffalo and rural farming scenes he witnessed along the way. Every now and then, a tractor or a two-wheeler would pass him. Each time, a local Gujarati would stop to offer a ride, but he graciously refused. 70 years. It had been nearly 70 years. A simple, quiet, solo walk. He was walking into the past, into the future, into Y2K. There was an energy about the place that seemed to vibe with his soul.

The Dandi March had long been forgotten. Living in India, it often seemed that Gandhi had also been long since forgotten. An oversaturation of images perhaps. Gandhi's image was on every single Indian Rupee note. Postage stamps. Adorning the office walls of powerful and truthful (pun) politicians. He didn't feel the same level of reverence and respect as say, Lincoln, King, Jefferson, Washington, or Rosa Parks. Much of modern youthful India seemed to reject the idea of Gandhi. He often wondered why the nation had only seemed to promote and elevate one name only, instead of including other defining historical figures. He was often told in Bollywood that he must remove the name Gandhi from the title of his film. The reason being there would be no audience and no interest, just an image of boredom. He was told numerous times that his title gave the impression of an art house film with zero commercial appeal. India was a young democracy, created in 1947. Culpeper. Taj Mahal. South Pasadena. Himalayas. Mumbai. Dandi March. He could not put his finger on exactly what he was feeling, but he felt like he was getting warmer to understanding his message. Energy. Vibe. Inspiration.

MUMBAI HUSTLER

Sleeves rolled up. Focused. On a mission to raise $350k for his production. He often found himself at the boujee JW Marriott, a brand-new luxury resort in the heart of Bollywood. There were flames of fire greeting guests at the entry gates. Bellman suited up as maharajas. Expansive lobby. Live music. Gourmet eateries. JW was a magnet for the who's who of Bollywood. It was not uncommon to find the wives of local billionaires stretched out on an oversized sofa with their sandals off, cocktail in hand, wearing designer shades. If Norman Rockwell had painted a portrait of "A Day in the Life of Bollywood," the easel would be at the JW.

He was indeed a bit of a novelty. Folks were curious. An American in Mumbai. Reverse migration. He developed several local friendships — Jaideep and Priya Verma. Vivek Paul. A close neighbor, Yashendra Prasad. And a middle-aged diamond merchant in South Mumbai. Raju Joshi.

With the Joshi family, it wasn't about the film, it was about the friendship and perks. On a typical weekend, he would take the train into the city and meet up with Raju and a few of Raju's friends at a local hotel bar for a few drinks. This was the reason why he had absolutely no hesitation or second thought about leaving the Halloween party and going to a club. He was accustomed to the hospitality of India. After drinks, all the families, kids included, would meet up for a fancy multi-course dinner at a chic restaurant. There were also weekend trips to the farmhouse which were out of the city in a hill station named Lonavala. All in good fun. All harmless. All free. He never paid a bill! The art of being a novelty. INFJ social skills.

He was surprised to learn that there existed a RED book, known as Film India, which listed the addresses and contact details of everyone. All he had to do was simply open the book and scroll down to find the name, Om Puri, and jot down the home address of the legend. The idea of a RED book could never exist in Hollywood. Nope. Not even a big-time agent like Marty Baum could stop him from boarding an auto-rickshaw and traversing the Western Express Highway — loud roar and occasional backfires on the way to Om's house — with his script in hand.

He was anxious as the rickshaw approached the high-rise tower. He motioned for the driver to stop away from the building. He didn't feel as if the loud and obnoxious rickshaw was the best method of arrival, but it was the cheapest and he was on a factory budget. He exited and then walked toward the entrance. A security guard stopped him. He explained, with matter-of-fact confidence, that he had come to meet Mr. Puri. Just like that. His own subconscious White privilege card. Without any pushback, the security guard nodded, smiled, and let him proceed. His heart rate increased. He started to sweat. He was already tongue-tied and hadn't uttered a word. What confidence? Where did it all go? He was wilting and withering. Abort mission. No. He had to get his mind together. He passed by three men without looking. As he neared the lift, he heard shouts.

"Sir. Sir!" shouted the security guard.

He turned.

The guard was pointing to a man. "Sir. Puri Sahib."

FACE TO FACE

He had just walked past Om Puri. Imagining a moment and living that moment was often completely different. He and Om stared at one another. Om was taller than he thought. Momentary awkward silence.

He finally uttered a few words, somewhat intelligible. "Mr. Puri. Hi. I'm Brad Baldwin. From Virginia. I have a film project for you," he said in broken English.

And just like that, Om's response blew him away. Om changed course. Om was on his way to a business meeting. Canceled. Om sent the other two men in the waiting vehicle off. "Come. Let's go up and have a chat!"

Huh? A chat? His mind was trying to process the moment. Om Puri had just canceled a business meeting for him, the "Man Without a Face" intern, the anxious kid from Virginia. It was anything but a normal day. Inside Mr. Puri's 7th-floor residence, Om offered him a drink, listened to his pitch, and agreed to read his script.

Huh? His mind raced again. Mr. Puri actually wanted to read a story he wrote. In Hollywood, there were year-round allergies where everyone was allergic to reading. In Hollywood, execs sought stories, but nobody read anything. Doors were bolted shut. Legal clauses. Form Letters. Lots of Attitude.

AN EVENING WITH OM

Not only had Om Puri agreed to read his script, but Om had also invited him to a small social gathering with a few friends. It was his introduction to Old Monk, a brand of Indian rum. Old Monk and Coke. He was not a heavy drinker, but Old Monk Rum became his favorite. It was special. It had meaning. There was a story behind it. He and Om sipped on Old Monk as they mingled with guests and shared laughs. Priceless.

The evening reminded him of his visits to Screen Gems Studio in Wilmington, North Carolina. Wilmington was an hour's drive from his paternal grandma's house and after his 1992 trip to India, he had become focused on making a movie. He randomly went to Screen Gems' head office and bumped into Frank Capra Jr., the son of the great director Frank Capra. Frank Jr. ran Screen Gems. Frank Jr. took an interest in him. Frank Jr. always took him to lunch, in Wilmington, whenever he was in town. All through those lunches, folks in the eatery would smile and acknowledge Mr. Capra. He never understood exactly why he was invited to be Frank Jr.'s only lunch guest. *It's a Wonderful Life.* Indeed, it can be.

FAMOUS WORDS

"Read the script. Love it. I'll do it!"

He was sitting at his official desk in his 250-square-foot global headquarters located in the far-flung suburbs of Mumbai with his bamboo-inspired artwork for Taj Entertainment when he received an incoming call from Mr. Puri. Om was in South India and was calling him from a movie set. A range of emotions would be an understatement. Thrilled. Shocked. Speechless. Nervous. Confused. Unsure if it was real or not. He thanked Om and hung up. Afterward, reality hit like a train. He had only one problem. A bit of a doozy. He had an esteemed actor attached to his film, but had no money...

RAISING CAPITAL

He joined the Producers Guild of India, complete with his ID card and photograph. He pursued diamond merchants, business tycoons, and Bollywood. At a meeting with the National Film Development Corporation (NFDC), a government enterprise that invested in the arts, he submitted a proposal for production funds. NFDC tended to fund what was deemed as art films in India — those that were not song and dance with a wild camera zooming love stories. It was at NFDC where he, once again, crossed paths with the shadow of Attenborough. He learned that "Dickie" had been seeking financing for *Gandhi* for nearly two decades. Mr. Attenborough had even approached NFDC for funding. When told the entity had limited funds and could only provide seed investment, "Dickie" was gracious and said, "I'll take it!" His face lit up with possibility. He knew his factory job and personal finances wouldn't last him twenty years, but perhaps NFDC could provide a seed too.

Yashendra, who was his neighbor, friend, aspiring guru, geographer, historian, and Bollywood art film director advised him to go to the media. "Run your story. In all the papers. Investors will line up. Money will come pouring in!" Yash claimed.

His gut told him it was a bad idea. His gut told him it didn't make any sense, but he still decided to give it a shot. He hired a PRO, Public Relations Officer, to set up his interviews. And off he went, playing the role of somebody who was successful at something. He dressed the part and met with journalists in five-star and boutique hotels — Marine Plaza. Oberoi. Taj. His Hollywood resume was a bit thin. Yet, he sat on sofas and corner rooftop tables, sipping chai or freshly squeezed mango juice, wearing his goggles and articulating his vision. He did have a verbal from Om. Journalists took him seriously. It was the whole reverse migration thing. No one doubted him. Days later, newspapers all across the city of Mumbai ran his story. Newsstands. Flats. Bungalows. Businesses. Every nook and corner of the city. And then it happened... Nothing. Pin drop. Silence. Crickets. Total failure. The line of investors pouring in money never materialized.

His networking had connected him with a DJ in a tiny club. It was owned by a man named Mohan, who was a business dude slash film producer. Mohan, a large and boisterous man with a deep voice, had a genuine interest in *Me & Gandhi*. Mohan wasn't turned off by the name. Mohan believed in it, and saw potential for audiences in India and abroad. Mohan was connected with a group of venture capitalists who were establishing a corporate structure in order to finance a group of smaller independent films. For the first time, it felt as if the universe was aligning, even if it was only for a second. *Me & Gandhi* was to be the first film produced until it got bumped to second place.

He was bumped by a local Indian actor. The actor had name recognition and value and wanted to direct a pet project, a passion project, as a first film. The venture investors bet on the guy with the resume and it backfired. The film was a total bomb. It was a financial loss that also took *Me & Gandhi* off a cliff. No more venture funds.

NINE

SUMMER 2000

He walked through the narrow and unpaved lanes of the slum. There were small brick and concrete dwellings, thousands of them in a maze of networks all with tin roofs. He saw a bustling and industrious community. Men sat in small stalls, selling grains, vegetables, and cleaning supplies. Wooden and woven cots dot the lanes in front of homes or in the middle of the lane as the elderly — women and men — sat praying, chatting, and watching time. Children, in matching school uniforms and little backpacks, carried thermoses as they walked in small groups. They were arm in arm or holding hands as they navigated the uneven road surface with the fresh cow dung or the dog diarrhea covered in flies. Housewives, in brightly colored blue and green and beige and yellow traditional dresses, pounded grains, chopped vegetables, and rolled out atta, Indian flour, to make fresh roti for the night's meal.

He walked past a small medical clinic, located adjacent to a large Hindu temple, and saw stacks of sandals just outside the temple's entrance. He heard the hum of life. He heard the ringing of bells. He heard laughter. He heard babies crying. He heard the sound of dogs barking. He heard a loud auto rickshaw maneuvering through the lane, pulsating the contemporary hip-hop sound of the latest Bollywood song. He followed Ishwarbhai, Jayesh, and Anar into Ramapir No Tekro, the largest slum in Ahmedabad, located across from Gandhi Ashram.

Ramapir No Tekro was a community of over 150,000 human souls, including rag pickers, rickshaw drivers, and daily wage laborers. They were all part of a social structure that had labeled them "Scheduled Caste." These were the men, women, and children known as "The Untouchables." It was the first time he had journeyed deep within Tekro. He had returned to Ahmedabad for a few days, nudged by the universe, to meet with the trustees from Manav Sadhna to understand their world and operation more. He thought back to his teen days spent at the U.S. Embassy in New Delhi and how he was sold a narrative of fear — fear that it wasn't safe, fear that he might fall sick. But here he was, his soul was being drawn deeper and deeper into Gujarat.

He lay awake, eyes wide open, in his Ashram guest house accommodation. The noise of the ceiling fan oscillating back and forth as it spun was heard. A digital clock near the small single bed read 2 a.m. He possessed the exact facial expression as he did on the airplane as a sixteen-year-old. He was the only passenger wide awake, sitting in silence as he imagined what awaited him the first time he landed in India.

The next morning, he pitched an idea to the Trustees of Manav Sadhna.

He beamed. "The Awakening. That's the title. We will create a performance that links the lives of Mahatma Gandhi and Martin Luther King Jr. and we'll tour America. We'll cast children from the slum. Devise a show. And we'll tour America by road. Not just the cities. But we will travel to every corner and to the small towns. Peace. Love. Humanity. That's our theme. We'll visit American schools. Have our cast interact with American kids. We'll talk about the importance of India with the direct connection to the civil rights movement in America, led by MLK. I have it all in my mind. All we need is funding!"

The previous day, he had been asked by Jayesh to think of a project for the United States. Jayesh spoke about a recent trip with some of the youth from Ramapir No Tekro to Taiwan for a cultural performance. It was the catalyst for his mind. Wheels turning. Much to his surprise, the Trustees loved the idea. They offered him a small apartment to live in, free of course, within walking distance of the Ashram. A door was opening for him in Gujarat, an unexpected door in a world he never expected to find himself in. His Mumbai film project was not going anywhere. There was meaning, depth, and potential in this show. The icing on the cake was that a move to Ahmedabad would finally put the drama of Shilpa in the rearview.

TWISTED GOODBYES

He stood next to an old truck at the entrance of his Thakur Complex apartment. He was supervising as two movers loaded up his furniture, sweat dripping from his face. Mumbai was humid, but he was anxious. He looked at his watch. The movers were late. Go figure. India always ran on late.

Shilpa. His eyes were constantly surveilling his surroundings. He was a bit jumpy. He was hoping that Shilpa wouldn't show up. He had informed her that he was moving to Gujarat, and she had been unusually quiet. Whenever it was quiet, it usually meant an explosion was around the corner. Curious neighbors watched from various flats. The movers had brought limited packing materials for the 530-kilometer drive.

His worldly possessions were quite meager. Few chairs. His writing desk. Small fridge. Two burner tabletop stoves. Some clothes. But everything in India took time, lots and lots of time. As time ticked by, his heart rate increased. He was a bit fidgety. He ran his hands through his hair often, eyes constantly scanning his environment.

Damn it. Too late. Shilpa appeared and approached him. His anxiety skyrocketed as his heart rate increased. His breathing was more rapid. He tried to manage his mind and prevent it from spiraling out of control, into fear.

Shilpa was very calm. Shilpa appeared before him looking like a lost puppy. Shilpa had tears in her eyes. "You really are leaving me," she said.

Shilpa handed him a large bag of snacks for the road trip, a seemingly kind gesture. It was filled with his favorite Indian cookies, chips, and sweets. Hide & Seek chocolate chip cookies. Parle-G.

Shilpa looked at the old jalopy of a moving truck. And just like that, a passive-aggressive strike. Very calmly and void of emotion, Shilpa quietly said, "Who knows? Maybe you'll never make it to Ahmedabad."

320 MILES. 30 HOURS+

He wondered if Shilpa had cursed him or cast a spell on him as he stood on the side of the highway, just before dark, watching two drivers fidgeting with wires above the left front tire behind the headlight. The truck had no stable headlights and the wires had to be in just the right alignment for the light to come on. It was getting dark, and his lights were flickering. A flow of traffic whizzed past. Overloaded and tilted trucks. Cars. SUVs. He wondered why the moving company sent him a piece of shit on wheels. The only upside was that his anxiety had subsided. Just knowing that Shilpa could not pop out from around the corner was calming to his central nervous system.

11 p.m. He stood at the back of the truck with the tailgate down and two guys next to him. No English. No Hindi. No Urdu. No Punjabi. No Marathi. They were all parked in a crowded and filthy truck stop. In the shadows were dozens of trucks — many larger and many smaller. It was surprisingly very quiet. Well, quiet by Indian standards.

The driver jumped into the truck bed and took a dirty piece of cardboard and laid it down. The driver hopped off and looked at him. He looked at the driver. The driver's hand slapped the cardboard a few times before belting out, "Sleep. Sleep. Sleep!"

Huh? He was dumbfounded. He had not asked any questions beforehand. He had assumed they would drive straight through to Ahmedabad, but they left six hours late. And now it was nighttime.

"Sleep here? On this? Isn't there a room, a small hotel, hostel?" he asked.

The driver looked at him before slapping on the cardboard a few more times. "Sleep! Sleep! Sleep!"

The driver and the other guy headed to the front cab. They climbed in and settled down to sleep. They were twisted across the seat with their heads against opposing windows. He returned and looked at his little piece of cardboard, then he climbed in the back of the truck, brushed it off a few times, and laid down to sleep.

ENTRY CHECKPOINT - AHMEDABAD

He was a Boy Scout. He survived the night sleeping on a ratty piece of cardboard on the floorboard next to his luggage at the dingy truck stop. The next afternoon, he found himself surrounded by local Gujarati police. An official building. A checkpoint. The group of officers wore olive uniforms and navy-blue berets. They were inspecting the content of his life. Cross-checking with the manifest from the moving company.

"A tax!" he firmly says. "A tax. For my stuff," he says in a raised voice. He soon began to realize it was a shakedown attempt. It was a little travel game called "Fleece the Foreigner," and it was played in every country. He hated games. He was informed that he needed to pay a very hefty import tax to enter the city. His items were hardly worth much, but they were sentimental. They were items connected to his Indian Dream. In his mind, they were not taxable.

He was pissed, agitated, angry, and determined not to pay a single rupee! He was a dirty, smelly mess. He had dried crusty salt rings on his shirt from his body's exhaust system. He was in a philosophical stand-off with the Gujarat police. Cue Edison, he had a lightbulb moment. He searched through his daypack and a stack of business cards, hundreds of them, until he found it — an official Indian Government card with gold emblems. The name was Anandiben Patel, Minister of Education, Gujarat State. Anandiben was the mum of Anar, a Trustee at Manav Sadhna. He loosely knew her. He was learning how to navigate India. He boldly presented the official government-issued card to the chief. With great confidence and a touch of sarcasm, he said, "Why don't you call Anandiben and ask her how much tax I need to pay?"

The chief looked at the shiny gold card as if it was kryptonite. The man gave a head bobble and was wide-eyed, in shock. The chief looked at the dirty little American and motioned for him to go. He returned to the truck. Not a single rupee. Justice came in small steps.

A NEW LIFE

His new home in Ahmedabad was an upgrade — a double-wide, two whole rooms, a large kitchen, and a ground-floor unit in a three-story middle-class complex.

He was the first foreigner living in the building. No surprise. First foreign (non-Indian) volunteer at Manav Sadhna. He was thrilled to have a second room to turn into his production office for the show.

And there it was... big sigh... the bathroom. It was always the bathroom. He often struggled to understand the bathroom designs in India. There was an art to figuring out which knob to turn and in which direction. Did the water flow or not? Wet floors. Flip-flops. Ventilation issues. Electrocution hazard of water and dangling cords from heating units. Being a man helped a bit, except for 2 and 3.

His Ahmedabad bathroom should have won an award for "Best Airflow." Awkward was an understatement. Tiny and dark. Dark tiles. While standing, he noticed a window with slats in it. He also noticed that on the other side of the window was the kitchen of the adjoining flat. He could see and hear his neighbor's kitchen. India wasn't American frozen meals and processed foods, heat and serve. Indian kitchens were 24-hour food factories with complex dishes for all three meals, afternoon tea, and guest visits.

So many thoughts. He was already extremely self-conscious since birth. By nature, he was a private lad. The noises. What about the noises his neighbors might hear? The scent. The fragrance. The aroma. He imagined himself cooking in the kitchen as the Gujarati jet stream brought in a whiff of pungent air. They were human after all. Everyone did it, but perhaps they might think differently of him.

The light. He would have no privacy at night once he flipped on the bright yellow light. Everyone would know he was in the toilet. He learned to perfect his technique. In Ahmedabad, that meant sneaking into his own bathroom, maneuvering in the cover of darkness, and perfecting stealth missions to drop untraceable bombs.

It's A Wonderful Life.

JANUARY 26, 2001

It was early morning. He sat in a plastic chair, on the sandy ground, beneath the tree canopy at Gandhi Ashram. Republic Day. It was an annual function of speeches, songs, national pride, and in India, always a dance program. Suddenly, the ground began to shake violently. He was in the best possible place, outdoors. An unnerving feeling. A jolt to the heart. A violent earthquake had just struck the city. Magnitude 7.8. A physical act of tectonics. 20,000 dead across the entire state. 340,000 buildings were destroyed. Aftershocks. Fear of tremors.

His new life in Ahmedabad, immersed in pre-production for the international Gandhi/King stage production, had already been facing earthquakes. They were human in nature, quakes with an epicenter being Shilpa. A twisted goodbye no more. It was now a twisted nightmare.

Shilpa was relentless in the prior months. She did not want him to settle into a new life. She did not want him to speak to another women. She did not want him to be happy in life. It was a constant struggle between an attempt to move forward in life and an attempt to manage Shilpa and his internal sense of anxiety and occasional panic attacks. He was trying to move on from a parasitic relationship. He changed his phone number. Shilpa enlisted locals in Gujarat to "keep tabs" on him and "keep a watchful eye on him." His movements. Who he talked to. Who he spent time with. Human intelligence. He received a very angry letter from Ishwarbhai about cultural norms and philosophies in India and that he needed to depart immediately. He was being kicked out of Gandhi Ashram. Shilpa had planted seeds of evil. Defamation. Character assassination. False narratives. He was the American. The black sheep in the Gandhian family. The manifestation of corrupt foreign culture. The dirty American who ran from Mumbai, leaving girls pregnant. Once, Shilpa actually flew to Ahmedabad, showed up at his flat, and chased him around the city in an auto-rickshaw. She did all this to "win" his love back and blow up his budding friendship with a local Gujarati girl who also was connected to Manav Sadhna.

Severe panic attack. To escape the endless black hole overwhelming the spiral of a panic flare-up, he once hired an Ambassador tank to travel to Porbandar, the small coastal town where Gandhi was born. Suddenly, without warning, he fainted in the street and was carried into his nearby motel by local street vendors. Concerned and compassionate locals had rushed to his aide. Everyone in Porbandar blamed it on the heat, not knowing the root cause were the waves of crushing anxiety from an altered mind. It was collateral from a parasitic infection named Shilpa.

PRODUCTION DELAYS

He sat, squished, in the far back of a burgundy Toyota Qualis on a remote road. The Qualis was a 7-seater SUV and with him were 12 people, also with hand luggage. Outside, the land was arid and dotted with scrub brush. Camel caravans could be seen in the distance. The CD system blared with Indian bhajans, prayer, and devotional songs, which lasted for hours. The male and female vocalists were melodic, and there were drum beats and bells. Everyone, except him, seemed to know all the words to every single bhajan as the entire overloaded Qualis flew down the road.

The Republic Day quake was an enormous natural disaster, which meant that the Gandhi/King show was to be delayed a year. Manav Sadhna had adopted a small village named Ludiya near the epicenter of the quake. It was in a dry desert region, close to the Pakistan border. He and the team were on their way to spend several months living in the remote desert village. They were going to build Bhunga-style homes — traditional mud houses with thatched roofs that were quake-resistant. It was a disaster site with the heartbeat of humanity. Kutchi was the local language. Villagers were artisans. Men crafted ornate wooden furniture. Women designed unique colorful blankets, quilts, and clothes, often with tiny mirrors embroidered. Days were hot, with temperatures often surpassing 115 Fahrenheit. Dust storms were intense. Every star in the universe was visible at night. The locals were gracious and friendly. Small-town vibes. Food was limited. He survived on aloo (potato) sabzi daily. A pack of Parle-G glucose cookies with chai. There was an endless parade of VIP guests, politicians, business tycoons, and social workers. One such guest was none other than Arun Gandhi, the grandson of Gandhi. He was introduced to Arun and pitched his little peace project. He had a request for Mr. Gandhi. He had a working title for the show but asked Arun to come up with a name, something short and simple for the American market.

"How about *EKTA*, the Hindi word for unity?" declared Mr. Gandhi.

It fitted. It was perfect. The name and the project now had an even greater meaning.

THE HUMAN LANGUAGE

His least favorite guest was a little rich business tycoon from Mumbai who was considering a large donation to Manav Sadhna. Perhaps it was the attitude he was first introduced to way back in 1992 on that train ride to the Taj Mahal. Perhaps he was just exhausted from a day of working in the field. He was different. He was the only White dude in Manav Sadhna in Ludiya Village or within a 50 km radius. All the foreign aid workers, the ones with training, skills, and equipment, were set up in larger urban areas. The short little tycoon crossed paths with him as he returned to the organization office, surprised to find an American in the tiny village. The man turned to him and inquired, with a heap of attitude and a condescending tone, "How do you communicate? With *these* people."

That tone... It rubbed him the wrong way. The body language. The eye rolls. These poor villagers were also Indian, they weren't aliens. He simply turned to the tycoon and replied, "I speak the human language."

All the staff and overnight guests slept outside, under the desert sky, on traditional cots. He wasn't always a fan of early mornings, as he often laid awake at night thinking. The next morning, he found out he had company. The wealthy tycoon also wasn't a fan of early mornings. Eventually, the tycoon sat up, hair a matted morning mess, and uttered two words, "human language." Words did matter and something had connected in the mind of the tycoon. He felt a bit remorseful that perhaps he had been a bit curt with the man the day before. However, hearing the man utter those two words and sensing that perhaps the man might look at the world a little differently was a great way to start the day.

ONE OF A KIND PHONE CALL

There was a buzz in the air. Anticipation. Prime Minister Atal Bihari Vajpayee and a high-level delegation were visiting. A security team arrived in advance and set up an emergency satellite phone located inside a Bhunga he had been building.

Cue Edison. An idea. He thought how dope it would be to call his parents in Virginia using the Prime Minister of India's emergency satellite phone, from a remote desert. He was used to being told no. In India, everyone's first response was always no. No. No. No. No. No.

He wasn't about to create a diplomatic seismic event just by picking up the phone. Naturally, he had to ask. Therefore, he was totally speechless when the security team gave him the green light with no real restrictions or time limits. No one had bothered or thought to ask such a question. No one, except him. He made his way to the satellite phone, thinking he was going to surprise his parents. Instead, he was the one in for a great surprise. His father, in Culpeper, answered. His father was emotional and in tears. His father never got emotional. He learned that earlier in the day, his mum had just moved out. His beloved mother was not at home. The only world he had ever known no longer existed. He was no longer a child, but it did not matter. It was still a jolt to his entire being. He hung up the Prime Minister's phone, slid down to the ground, and wept.

TEN

MARCH 2002

Himangini. Falgini. Reena. Meena. Dipika. Tejvanti. Parvati. Ravi. Sandeep. Kamlesh. Barot. Upendra. Kiran. Bharat. Seven Boys. Seven Girls. He watched with immense pride as the artists, fourteen beautiful souls from the slums of Ramapir No Tekro, had just completed a final dress rehearsal. The teens took a bow. Standing ovation. Packed auditorium. Gujarati working class. Business class. Political class. After over two years, the team was ready to fly. Two years. Focus. Training. Practice. Personal challenges (Bharat lost his father). Two years and an earthquake. The least likely faces to represent India on an overseas mission. Soft diplomacy tour. Journey of the heart. The sheer fact that these thirty cast and crew were granted visas to the

United States was nothing short of a miracle. Section 214(b). The most common word in the vocabulary at the U.S. Department of State seemed to be "denied." This particular miracle included a months-long old-fashioned facetime diplomacy between him and the American Consulate in Mumbai. U.S. Consul General David Good was *EKTA's* Jehovah Jireh. It was a blessing that he and the team were immensely grateful for.

EKTA had faced many headwinds and a great deal of resistance, especially in regard to raising funds. He had written hundreds of grant applications, all denied. Air India refused to provide discounted air tickets. He and the Trustees of Manav Sadhna hatched a plan to source funds from wealthy HNIs (High Net Worth Individuals) in Gujarat and the United States. Manav Sadhna had the contacts. He had the vision. The dog and pony show began. The power of politics opened doors. A typical dog and pony show consisted of, a) Political heavyweight Anandiben Patel had a donor meeting set up; b) Viren, Jayesh, Anar, Anandiben, and the Little American dined on a multi-course vegetarian Gujarati meal at a long table in an opulent surrounding at a boujee bungalow; c) Everyone shifted to an oversized living room, doors were closed, 4-5 split air-conditioners were turned on, and everyone focused on him, the Little American pitching his vision for *EKTA*. Meeting after meeting, each time Jayesh and Anar were enamored by wealth. Viren was irritated at the hypocrisy of wealth and would rather be at a project site in the slum. As for him, he was just trying to get his project off the ground and not complain about the free meal and the nice furniture.

He was in California shortly after the tragedy of 9/11. He was on a fundraising trip. He was at the office of an Indian-owned aerospace company in Orange County.

"Why take them from the slum? It's too expensive! Why take them from the slum, show them America, and then put them back into the slum?" barked the have-an-answer-for-everything rich man.

Pride. Attitude. Ego. Tone. "Build a medical clinic. It will serve thousands!" the man continued to opine.

He wasn't annoyed with the difference of opinion. Different viewpoints were normal. It was the condescending tone that triggered him. Defensive mode. He leaned in across the desk, looked the owner in the eye, and asked, "When was the last time you actually visited the slum? Any slum?"

Total silence. Crickets. Suddenly, the man that knew it all had no response.

AN EPIC MOTORCADE

Bigger than the Prime Minister of India. Bigger than the American President. *EKTA's* motorcade extended for a mile on the way from Gandhi Ashram to the airport. Three luxury coach buses. The Qualis. Tata Sumos. Ambassadors. Fiats. Rickshaws. Police. Politicians. Parents. Relatives. An impressive sight. It was late in the night, nearly midnight. He stood inside the lead bus watching the anticipation build on the faces of the cast. Kids that had never left the state now had brand-new passports, flashy visas, and airline tickets to Chicago. The children were dressed for winter in their *EKTA* embroidered navy blue sweatshirts. The motorcade turned heads at the airport. The public had no idea what was happening and which VIPs were arriving. Curiosity. The bus pulled up. Side door opened. He grabbed his leather briefcase, the one with his nuclear codes and his CIA mission objectives, and exited.

It was a Bono kind of moment. A frenzy. He was overwhelmed. He was a producer, not a rockstar. Parents and relatives were vying for his attention, pushing and shoving. They were thanking him, blessing him, and throwing flower petals at him. Mothers of cast members placed flower leis around his neck. Another. And Another. And Another. Red tikkas on his forehead. Grains of rice were stuck to it. A sense of slow motion took over his mind and perception. He saw the weathered faces and the hope in their eyes and smiles. There was an outpouring of love and compassion, like nothing he had experienced before. A love that was palpable. A love that was authentic. A love that was genuine. Across the crowd, he saw Viren watching him with a grin. With a tear in his eye, he smiled at Viren. He entered Sardar Vallabhbhai Patel International Airport wearing eight flower leis around his neck.

THE PLAN

Chicago. Terre Haute. Memphis. Atlanta. Culpeper. Washington DC. New York. Los Angeles. Tucson. San Francisco. He was very organized, structured, and a bit stubborn. He had a packed itinerary. It included performances but also visits to public and private schools, historical landmarks, host families, religious service visits, and social service projects. He designed an itinerary that would take the young artists to both rural and urban America, mainly by road. There was a heavy weight and responsibility on his shoulders. A message. A theme. But most importantly, young lives, fourteen of them. They rented an RV motorhome and two fifteen-passenger vans. The *EKTA* team would see more of the United States than many Americans.

In addition, the team included social workers and trustees from Manav Sadhna as well as two choreographers and a technical director (TD) from Darpana Academy of Performing Arts, a co-partner in the production. The kids mainly spoke Gujarati with a wee bit of English. Having a bilingual support staff of seasoned social workers was essential to assist with language barriers as well as the health, safety, welfare, and emotional needs of the youth. There were many different worlds, personalities, and philosophies in the cast and crew alone. It was the prime breeding ground for behind-the-scenes tension between that of Gandhian Thought and a much wilder-free spirited production crew from Darpana.

Seema. Rajeev. Seema. Rajeev. Seema. Rajeev. One more time. Seema. Rajeev. Two Indian Americans from California that became pillars for *EKTA*. Seema Patel, from Mission Viejo, opened her home and heart to the mission of *EKTA* long before the team landed in Chicago. Rajeev Virmani, from the Bay Area, was an aspiring educator. Rajeev was able to teach the kids in a way that great teachers can about the places they were visiting in the States. Seema had organized a volunteer base of supporters across California. Both Seema and Rajeev dedicated their lives to the mission of *EKTA*. It was heart-warming to witness.

THE MAGIC OF FLIGHT

He walked up and down the aisle of the Air India cabin. He was somewhere over the Mediterranean. A little mid-flight wellness check for the team. Sleeping. Snacking. Watching a Bollywood movie. Stretching. Smiling. The faces of 30.

It was their first time on an airplane — not only for the 14 youth but for most of the adult crew as well. First flight. First take off sensation. First experience and a doozy at that. 24 hours of travel from Ahmedabad. Layover in London.

He was learning something about himself. He was learning how much he enjoyed observing others experiencing an event for the first time. Their facial expressions. The energy they radiated. The sense of watching others grow and learn... He loved that. He made his way back to his seat, tossed the blanket over himself, and shifted into INFJ thought mode. His little ragtag production was finally happening. He grinned and shook his head as he reflected.

10 RUPEES

He never looked for a fight. He hated conflict. Daily, he and the kids would board a couple of auto-rickshaws and make the 10-minute journey from Gandhi Ashram down to Darpana Academy for rehearsals. During one of those early trips, the auto-rickshaw driver attempted to charge him the "foreigner rate" which was 20 rupees for a 10 rupees ride. No one liked to be cheated, and he wasn't the exception. He raised his voice to lecture the driver in English, in a way that only self-righteous Americans could. A few kids went into the dance academy. Others stood by, watching him. He held up the 10 rupees note in front of the rickshaw driver's face and tore it in half. He threw it inside the rickshaw and proceeded into the dance academy.

The next morning, at Gandhi Ashram, Viren and Jayesh pulled him aside to have a word. "We heard about the 10 rupees," Viren remarked.

He felt a bit embarrassed by his actions.

"Everybody's watching you. All the kids, they learn from you. This is Gandhi's Ashram. Please, you keep your mind cool. Find another way," Jayesh calmly explained.

IN SEARCH OF KING

In a creative meeting with the heads of Darpana, Mallika, and Mrinalini Sarabhai — a mother-daughter duo of world-renowned Indian dancers

— the idea of an audio-visual element was discussed to be projected on stage. The video clips would bring to life recreated images of Mahatma Gandhi and Martin Luther King Jr. that would be timed according to the particular musical sequence and performance on stage. Dressing up an Indian to play Gandhi wasn't a problem, but the suggestion of dressing up an Indian to portray Dr. King didn't seem like the best course. Cue Edison.

"Wait. At Gujarat University, there are three Black Guys. Sitting. On the corner. Having chai. Always. When I pass by," he eagerly proclaimed.

Ahmedabad was a city of millions. Diversity was non-existent. One White Guy. Three Black Guys. Out of five million people. Within moments, an old white Premier Padmini Fiat raced across the city. It was chauffeur driven, of course. He, the producer of *EKTA*, sat in the back as the Padmini zigzagged through traffic around camel carts and stationary cows in search of Dr. King. Mrinalini had sent him in her personal car. It was just a hunch, just a gamble, and purely speculative. As the Padmini neared the famous tea stall, located at the campus entrance, he saw them. Three Black Guys! Divine light. Destiny. Keen observation. He jumped out of the car, hoping not to startle the three Kenyans who were enrolled at the local college.

"Ah, excuse me. My name is Brad, and I'm searching for Dr. King." It worked and one of the three volunteered to play the role. The man was cast on the spot. He and the young Kenyan Dr. King returned to Darpana in the chauffeur-driven Padmini Fiat, much to everyone's surprise.

A ROUGH START

It was *EKTA's* first scheduled event. A visit to a public school on the South Side of Chicago. It was an inner-city school of primarily Black youth and staff. They were eagerly anticipating the teens from India. *EKTA's* base camp was out in the burbs. Hanover Park. It was an Indian group. They were already late. A second van hadn't been picked up yet, as it was supposed to be. He drove a van, packed with kids and a few adults. Seema drove a local host family's car with the rest of the cast. It was the definition of ragtag. Oh no. He got a call from Seema as they rolled down the freeway. Her tire felt wobbly. Emergency pit stop. They pulled off at the first gas station.

He sat in the van. It was cold and cloudy. He hung up his cell phone, having just informed the school that they were running late. The passenger door was open. The double side doors were also open. He glanced at his watch and the group. He liked to be on time. He got a bit anxious. He reached his hand into the left pocket of his jeans to make sure the petty cash was still there. When he got stressed, he tended to check and recheck and check again. There was $3,000 in his pocket. The arrival had been so chaotic that Viren just handed him a wad of cash for expenses.

He noticed a cop car with no lights heading slowly down the road toward the gas station. No big deal. What? A glance into his rearview revealed two additional Chicago police cars, no lights flashing, creeping up. Side mirror. Cop car. Driver's side mirror. Cop Car.

He began to get a little nervous. Perhaps there was trouble at the gas station. The *EKTA* kids were talking and laughing in Gujarati. No one, except for him, was aware of anything unusual. What? Oh, no. What the hell? He saw two officers approaching the van. His eyes shifted back and forth to every mirror. He counted eight. There were eight cop cars surrounding his rental van. His heart began to pound. Sweaty palms. He was much more nervous than before. He didn't do anything but tell that to his anxiety. He began to think. Seat belt laws. What if he was arrested and hauled off to jail? The school on the South Side. What a nightmare... Then he remembered something... A man. A suspicious-looking older White male at the gas pump earlier. The man was on a cell phone just staring at the van.

Time seemed to stop. He was frozen. His mind began to go into that spiral. He didn't have a rap sheet, only three speeding tickets — Culpeper, San Francisco, and Western Pennsylvania. He never had a mugshot. Wait. It was unofficial, but once in Los Angeles, Burbank police detectives showed up at his downtown apartment and took a Polaroid snap of him. He agreed to the unofficial mugshot as he didn't understand his rights. Burbank detectives were actually investigating his roommate, a White, wealthy, USC college student from an affluent family in Texas. The detectives were investigating a theft at big-time producer Joel Silver's office at Warner Brothers.

He never stole a thing in his life, but his wealthy roommate had some kind of addiction to lifting props from television show sets for the black market. He just paid the rent, never asked any questions, never hung out, and never really saw his roommate much. He was waiting for the lease to be up. It wasn't soon enough, however. Months later, he returned in the gray wagon from the Bay Area at 2 a.m. At 5 a.m., he had LAPD officers banging on his bedroom door — not his front door, his bedroom door. It scared the shit out of him. He stood in his underwear answering LAPD questions as his wealthy Texan roommate was escorted out. He later learned that his roommate was arrested in Beverly Hills. His roommate was caught in the act of stealing, not winning, a Grammy after sneaking onto the estate of an elderly acquaintance. WTF? Foreal? Big-time felony. It never made sense to him. His roommate led such a privileged life with family trips to Wimbledon and five-star resort vacations. Addictions, they came in all shades, and they came in all tax brackets.

A REALITY CHECK

His overcrowded van headed down the freeway. Chicago skyscrapers ahead. No interrogation. No arrest. Nothing. He simply told the officers what they were doing and where they were going. The man at the gas station had called the cops. Confirmed. He was not only thinking about the cop's response to him, but he was thinking about the man at the gas pump as well. The "good Samaritan." What was suspicious about kids in bright colored traditional outfits? What was suspicious about kids smiling and laughing and being happy? Kids being kids. The energy of it all. Not a nefarious vibe radiating from any corner of *EKTA*. He realized that he was the only White person in the group. He was also the only one with three thousand dollars in his pocket. As he neared the Southside school, he wondered if the color of his skin had erased all suspicions by the officers.

EKTA: THE UNTOLD STORY

On the surface, there were lights, cameras, stages, happy kids, and messages of peace and love. The mission. However, below the surface was the increasingly agitated and hostile technical director, a middle-aged man and an integral part of the crew. The TD handled all aspects of lighting and sound. On one side was Manav Sadhna — Gandhian. Pure Vegetarian. Simple. Every decision was a family decision. Circle Time. Group sharing time. Meditation time. Prayer time.

On the other side, there were the Darpana creative souls, the choreographers, and the TD. Sensitive. Needy. Feeling Unheard. Trapped. Isolated.

Homesick. In addition, the technical director was desperately seeking non-vegetarian food, hard liquor, and women. He was in the middle — Referee. Counselor. Unpaid American Diplomat.

The group had arrived in Memphis and were staying in bunks at a local church. Arun Gandhi and Christian Brothers University were hosting them. Earlier in the day, they had visited the Lorraine Motel where Dr. King was assassinated. The TD joined him on a late-night run to 7-11 to gas up the van. Within moments, the TD emerged from the 7-11, drinking a 40oz malt liquor out of a paper bag in the parking lot. He purposely took the long route back to the church so the technical director could finish up the 40oz, and they disposed of the evidence prior to reaching the church parking lot. Things heated up again, and by the time they reached New Jersey, the TD threatened to quit and was packing to go stay with an uncle on Long Island for the rest of the trip. Crisis mode. He called the TD into his hotel room for a heart-to-heart, a man-to-man, a soul-to-soul. They were in Jersey and so Indian food was available on speed dial. He ordered the best chicken dishes on the menu and had them delivered. Tandoori chicken. Butter chicken. Mughlai chicken. They feasted. He counseled. They feasted. He listened. They feasted. He executed International Butter Chicken Diplomacy, and the TD decided to continue pushing forward and stay with *EKTA*. Crisis averted.

SPOTLIGHT ATLANTA

Ebenezer Baptist Church. MLK Historic Site. Gandhi Statue. Sold-out overflow shows at Morehouse College. CNN Interview. School visits. It was all thanks to the groundwork and coordination of Joan Thomas, Educational Telecommunications Specialist for Atlanta Public Schools and Manager of

Atlanta Public Broadcasting Channel 22. He had connected with Joan two years prior. He was sitting at a small cybercafé in Ahmedabad, one with reliable and fast net speed, for days and days sending out hundreds of cold mails. No social media, just old school R & D outreach city by city. Those efforts paid off big time connecting with Joan.

MLK Urban Learning Center, April 4, 2002. He sat in a metal chair on a small stage in an open forum inside the school. He was dressed in a formal khaki shirt and dress pants. The audience was filled with young Black youth. A podium and mic. Spotlights. He sat next to Reverend Al Sharpton and Martin Luther King III.   He wasn't sure of his qualifications. All he had was a boujee-ass film degree from a boujee-ass college on the West Coast. Lots and lots of people had made *EKTA* happen and yet he was sitting next to the son of Dr. Martin Luther King, Jr. A bit of a head-scratcher. The mysteries of life. The winding journeys. The roads less traveled. He tried not to become too lost in thought as he was supposed to get up and speak in front of people. Symbolism. Synchronicity. Depth. The irony of the moment was not lost on him.

He was an observer of life and people. He was astonished at how laid back, casual, and relaxed King and Sharpton were. Multi-tasking. Both men were talking to each other; however, they were also sending messages on their phones while engaging in the program. He was a bit anxious, hoping he wouldn't forget his name at the podium. Public speaking. The art of it all. He observed Mr. King and the Reverend — the organic shoot from the hip flow. Elongating words. Dramatic pauses. Tonal changes. Rhythm.

Here was an example: Mr. Sharpton said, "As we gather here today, with these young children from India..." Most people's delivery would be straight-forward, but Mr. Sharpton would engage in a slow rollout of "as we gather here today." This was followed by a dramatic pause, then with a powerful rise in tone and inflection, Mr. Sharpton said, "With these young children." This was followed by another dramatic pause, a look to the left, a look to the right, and then the closing, full of emotion, "from India." At that moment, he thought to himself maybe one day he could be a preacher too.

HUMBLED

EKTA was a catalyst. EKTA was bigger than Self. He was humbled to witness Americans whole-heartedly embrace the cast and crew of EKTA — to welcome them into their communities, to share parts of themselves, and to learn. He was surprised to see principal after principal, teacher after teacher, standing up, after he had spoken to address crowds of students and highlight the link between India and America through Dr. King and Gandhi. Most were unaware that Dr. King had traveled to India or that Martin had once been introduced in India as an "Untouchable" from America. Atlanta Public Broadcasting produced a short documentary that was aired the following year in every public school across Atlanta.

One single event encapsulated the very heart of EKTA. The cast and crew were dinner guests of a wealthy Indian American family in a suburban New Jersey mansion. Fourteen shining lights, the heart and soul of humanity from simple one-room dwellings were seated in such a grandiose and well-furnished home. After dinner, the mansion owner threw out an open question: "If you could have anything in the world, what would you want?"

The room became quiet as young Bharat stood up. Bharat's father had died of tuberculosis early in the production. He had sat outside Bharat's small home as relatives wailed in great sorrow. He had walked with other men behind Bharat as the body was carried through the streets of Ahmedabad to the funeral pyre for cremation.

With humility, sincerity, and authenticity, young Bharat replied in Gujarati, "Sir, if I could have anything in the world, it would be for other kids from my community to have the same opportunity like us, like *EKTA*."

The room was silent and many had tears in their eyes. Bharat didn't ask for anything for himself. Bharat didn't ask to win the lottery. Bharat didn't ask for a job. Bharat didn't ask for a green card. Bharat didn't ask for new clothes. Bharat didn't ask for a designer watch. Bharat didn't ask for a phone or a fancy car. Instead, Bharat had asked for others to have similar opportunities. At that moment, all the challenges, the roadblocks, the battles, and the earthquakes seemed worthwhile. Inspired. Humbled.

ELEVEN

MEXICAN HAT, UTAH (DAY #18)

He holds his black tripod, which is partially extended. He flips open each of the three clips and extends the legs to their maximum length. He then sets the tripod down into the reddish dirt.

He wears sturdy low-cut hiking shoes with thick soles. The ground is so dry that a burst of red dust is created as soon as the three tripod legs hit the ground. Even his beige-colored shoes are now a dusty red. Very red. It is as if his road trip has taken him to Mars. He reaches down and grabs his Canon SLR out of a black bag. It is also covered in red Martian dust. He fastens the camera to the tripod and makes sure the level is balanced. He then removes the lens cap and switches the camera on. He is wearing a black Columbia fleece jacket with his boujee Kohl's Henley underneath. He lowers his head, closes his right eye, and presses his left eye up to the viewfinder. "Wow. There are no words," he says out loud.

Through the camera lens, he sees an epic landscape. The first rays of early morning sunlight are behind him. The gigantic red sandstone towers light up in a deep glow of red hues. Behind the rock towers is a large mesa, perfectly sculpted over thousands of years. In the foreground of the frame is an expansive red valley filled with yucca plants and Russian thistle. He presses the shutter button and fires off a couple of shots. He raises his head and adjusts the camera timer. He presses the button and then scurries out several yards in front to a pre-selected marker. He is hoping to capture the perfect memory, an original selfie. As he looks out across the landscape, he wonders if John Wayne will pass him at the helm of a stagecoach. He looks around, curious as to where John Ford may have stood. Could he be standing in the same spot?

He had weeks of practice shooting himself with his camera setups. Sometimes, he would face the camera. Sometimes, he would be seated on the ground, legs crossed, with his back toward the camera. Sometimes, he would be framed — to the left or right, side profile — looking off into the distance with an American landscape taking center stage. Selfies had their purpose and while his iPhone selfies were quick and at times, enter-taining, he was off-grid, essentially disconnected from his life. No likes. No subscribers. No shares. No desert dances. No filters. Only the quiet rhythm of framing a shot. Alone, in a far-flung corner of America. A dude. A camera. A tripod. And a personal battle.

The southeastern corner of Utah had a special place in his heart. He had driven through briefly once before. Little did he know that a traumatic bond would be the catalyst to send him back to such a magical place.

He loves humanity. However, he also loves the feeling of being the only person in nature. He loves places that challenge his perspective of who he is in the world, a universe that dwarfs him. He is but a few grains of sand, of red Martian sand. To him, his struggles and battles are very real and all-consuming; however, standing alone in the vastness of the desert makes him question them.

The land itself possesses a healing quality. It soothes his mind and fills it with a sense of calmness. As the travel distances in the west increase along with the driving speed, he knows he has to cover a lot of ground if he wants to stick to his 48-day schedule. However, he has been looking forward to this part of America so much that he wants to squeeze every ounce of every second out of the place. He drives the entire 17-mile loop in Valley of Gods as well as the entire loop of Monument Valley.

Driving in from Durango, he had stopped along a side road in the middle of nowhere with the yellow lines of the road meeting the edge of the horizon. From that perspective, it surely looked as if the world was flat. The way ancient sailors feared sailing off the horizon... It was quite a fearful thought. He set up his shot — Tripod in the middle of the highway. Private shoot. Perspectives. *Click. Click.*

He walked away. He walked toward. Walking man. Thinking man. Broken man.

Four corners — Utah. Colorado. New Mexico. Arizona. He had visited once as a child. Decades later, the place had changed a bit. It was more commercial, with more people. He set up his tripod and waited for a clear frame, a shot without any people in it.

"I was gonna ask if you wanted me to take your picture. But you look like you know what you're doing!" said a friendly tourist.

He was appreciative of the gesture. He wasn't Ansel Adams, nor was he trying to be. However, he wanted the shot just right with him in it. No baby strollers. No dogs. Nothing growing out of his head. Crooked frame. Feet cut off.

In reality, in a world in which he seemingly has zero control over life, the art of taking a photograph was one small step, one aspect of his life, in which he feels as if he has ownership over. He is quite protective of those little moments, those tripod set-ups across America. It is so therapeutic.

ADX Florence. The "Alcatraz of the Rockies." The United States Penitentiary Administrative Maximum Facility (USP Florence ADMAX) located near Florence, Colorado is the most maximum-security prison facility in the United States of America. His mind can qualify him for a cell at ADX Florence. He never learned to share his feelings with anyone. He possesses a series of internal belief systems only known to him. He interprets the world and his experiences in it through survival. He survives. He is surviving. His mind is a supermax prison that prevents him from being his True Self.

ADX Willow Tree — the code name for his mind. He is ADX Willow Tree, an image of Self that had very rigid walls. First, is the belief that he is unlovable, that no one in the world, except Shilpa, loves him. Second, is the belief that Shilpa will never abandon him. Third, is the belief that he deserved the path he has been on. Fourth, he believes his soul is damaged and that he can never be good enough. Fifth, euphoria and shame are two sides of the same coin. Sixth, anything sexual in nature is not love and has no emotion. Romantic love and intimacy are separate train tracks. Seventh, he will never have children, biological or adopted, because he will not be able to protect them and does not want to risk his own child suffering in silence. Eight, divorce isn't an option due to the cultural and social burdens he carries. He has taken a certain path in life and has to face the consequences as he does not want to disappoint society or his world at Gandhi Ashram. It is an idea that he must adjust at any cost. And ninth, silence. Remain silent. Don't rock the boat. Minimize Self. Focus on making others happy and catering to their needs.

ADX Willow Tree is a self-imposed life sentence. As a young boy, he loved holding large key rings, filled with keys of all shapes and sizes. Perhaps one of those keys could have freed him from ADX Willow Tree. He never had a chance to find out, as he threw them out the treehouse window and had no spare.

Mexican Hat has two hotels, two restaurants, and a gas station that is Native American owned and operated. Mexican Hat is smack dab in the middle of Valley of the Gods and Monument Valley on the San Juan River. He is very hungry after a day of gallivanting, so he moseys on over to The Swingin' Steak for some grub.

He is a modern cowboy. He doesn't have the boots, the spurs, the belt buckle, or the Stetson. He has a fleece, a USC baseball cap, his specs, and a mind that he is working to reprogram. While he does have a love-hate relationship with his alma mater, he does, without thinking, often promote the boujee brand. The cap. Deep down within him, he is proud to have a meaningless degree framed and hung on the wall next to his high school diploma and Eagle Scout certificate. "Fight On." "Lifelong and Worldwide."

Mexican Hat has put him in the mood, the mood to indulge a bit in a Gujarati Gandhi-inspired dinner consisting of steak, potatoes, beans, salad, and Texas toast. He is a bit of a hybrid being. He goes all out that night, guns blazing, and even splurges on a beer or two. After all, that's what cowboys do.

And then it came. Out of nowhere... Confusion. The ping pong match. Images. Memories of the life he is fleeing. On one hand, it seems that Shilpa did care about him. Over the years in India, he would fall sick from time to time — Asthma. Bronchitis. Food poisoning. Shilpa would rush him to the hospital, seeming worried and concerned with the doctor, and collect his medicine. But on the other hand, in private, Shilpa was cold to him and offered no affection. Shilpa refused to kiss him since she deemed it to be "dirty." Confusion.

On one hand, Shilpa always talked highly of him in front of others. She'd compliment him, boosting his ego. She'd say nice words to students, parents, maids, the flat owner, and folks at Gandhi Ashram. But on the other hand, in private, Shilpa would pick on him, demean him, belittle him, and instruct what he was allowed to say at his own family functions. Confusion.

On one hand, Shilpa would spend hours and hours counseling others. She was friendly with exchange students and their parents, providing advice to the poor family working in the building where they resided. But on the other hand, in private, Shilpa never had an in-depth conversation with him. She never had time since she would regularly spend 3-4 hours a day on secret phone calls with mysterious men. Confusion.

His mind is trained to bury the bad stuff, the stuff that makes him feel alone, empty, and sad while cherry-picking the good times and only saving those in the hard drive of his mind. It creates a skewed reality in his mind.

He starts to realize that from the very beginning, he had been a High-Value Target. The very core strengths of who he is as a human being have been used against him, to keep him locked up in ADX Willow Tree. He isn't Superman, but he is always stubborn, fiercely independent, and willing to sacrifice comforts and convenience to pursue something that he believes in, something bigger than himself. He possesses empathy. He thinks about others and cares about their well-being. It is as simple and profound as that. He is a challenge. His mind is a challenge to crack in such a way that a puppet master could exert a powerful hold over his emotions, to render him defenseless.

He is not a physical boxer. He is a mental boxer. The emotional and verbal boxing matches that Shilpa subjected him to for nearly eighteen years have worked its way into each of his broken pieces, each and every childhood wound, each and every rigid self-belief system. It is as if Shilpa knows things about him on a subconscious level, like his triggers, without him ever having a single conversation about them. It is a play of energetic forces. It is the pathology of Shilpa's mind.

Shilpa viewed him as a High-Value Target. She had the intention to break his mind, to turn his mind into mush, to turn his mind into a rag doll, and to render a hold over him. He was nothing more than an endless source of narcissistic supply to her. It left him feeling as if he were a forgotten toy, sitting on a shelf in a darkened closet. He and Shilpa were magnetic forces that had nothing to do with love.

The effects of attempting to break free from a traumatic bond are like being caught in a strong riptide. His mind is being pulled far out to sea. He now has situational awareness as the land disappears. He knows that all he has to do is swim a little to the right or swim a little to the left to get out of the current of the riptide. However, his mind is often in the mode of drowning in anxiety, in fear, in chaos, and in a heavy fog of helplessness.

Even though he knows how to swim, even though he knows he has to get to shore, it still seems impossible. His mind has been rewired and programmed to provide full-time compassion, empathy, and care for Shilpa despite the physical and emotional toll on himself. He is often lost in the riptide of his emotions, drowning in his natural inclination to see other points of view, to see the point of view Shilpa is projecting onto him.

In the chill of the desert evening, he walks back to his hotel room. He is a little buzzed. He is a thinker, not a drinker, so he has a very low tolerance. He is very much a Libra and has always sought balance in his life. Balance is especially important to him as he has often pursued adventures that were well out of his comfort zone.

While he has a habit of driving off cliffs metaphorically, he needs an internal mechanism to offer stability and a feeling of safety to him. The red Martian landscape of the great American West provides him with a feeling of emotional stability at a time when he most needs it, at a time when his mind is in constant battle with itself.

TWELVE

NOVEMBER 2004

He stood drenched in sweat in an overcrowded and smelly administrative office at a courthouse in Bandra. It was the Beverly Hills of Mumbai,
the place where Bollywood resides. He was jittery. He was exhausted. His
stomach was in a knot. The ceiling fan was hanging extremely low, and he
could feel the blades within centimeters of his hair. He was constantly being
pushed from behind, shoved by a crowd of locals who were all vying to get
their papers signed and work done.

It was hot, sticky, and humid. His profuse perspiration was not only
from the muggy Arabian air but from his own anxiety. Shilpa stood next to
him in the courthouse. She was dressed in a traditional Indian kurta which
was out of the norm for her.

An administrative officer, an older female, sat behind the counter. The woman handed both him and Shilpa a little scrap of paper with smudged purple ink and asked them to both write their names. The woman instructed both of them to read the overly simplistic marriage vow, "I, blank, take, blank, to be in lawful union."

The battle was over. Shilpa had won. Shilpa had captured his mind, not his heart. The drama of four years — the harassment, the stalking, the gift bags, the constant forcing him to answer the question, "Who's your wife?", the loving threats that he would be arrested by the Indian Police at departure or arrival immigration checkpoints, the apologies, the Jekyll and Hyde outbursts — had taken a great toll. The cumulative effect was that his mind was taken hostage. The deception was that his mind didn't understand it. There were romanticized visions of India in his mind and then there was the reality of daily life. He had imagined that if he ever did get married in India, it would be a grand event, one fit for a maharaja. He imagined lots of colors, elephants, camels, sumptuous Indian food, and JW Marriot flames.

He didn't imagine courthouse filled with sweaty folks. His dramatic courtroom wedding was not the wedding of his dreams nor was Shilpa the bride of his dreams. He felt as though he was on a fast-moving bullet train, unable to stop it, unable to flee.

He made the decision to get married for two reasons, and none of them were traditional or fairytale-like from any angle. It was a decision that put his personality on a collision course with his trauma. As an INFJ, he was hell-bent on pursuing a dream, to make a film in India. He absolutely loved India. He had a vibration with India. He loved the food and the culture. He appreciated the people. He enjoyed the challenge and uniqueness of living in a place where everything wasn't polished and robotic. His heart drew him to places like Gujarat. He succeeded in producing *EKTA*, a play that changed his life in many ways.

India was his grand adventure, and he was learning about the world and himself. He felt that his intersection with India was somehow, some way, connected to his mission — his inner purpose, a message he carried with him. It was the very unorthodox part of his mental hardwiring that presented Shilpa as a challenge to him, a challenge that needed to be managed. His mind had convinced itself that perhaps if he got married, Shilpa would change and calm down. Perhaps, he was overreacting. Perhaps, it was just Shilpa's Indian cultural background. Shilpa would no longer have to pursue him and create drama. His primary goal was to pursue his mission, not a marriage; therefore, he had to find a way to "manage" the Shilpa problem.

The second reason was internal and due to his life at ADX Willow Tree. His pursuits of the heart when related to women were few and far between and always crashed and burned. He wasn't just left brokenhearted, he was left confused. He was either abandoned for reasons he did not comprehend or his inner sensitivities birthed in the treehouse wreaked havoc with his emotions. There was the middle-school cheerleader girlfriend who resembled Brooke Shields. She was the girl in which yearbook messages were written about futures, sunsets, white picket fences, and 1.94 children. He never understood why they broke up, but he always blamed himself, his triggers, and his brokenness. The trials and tribulations of teenage love...

His second relationship was in high school, and it was much shorter than his first. It went south when lust reared its head within him, and college was on the horizon. In Los Angeles, he developed a relationship with a beautiful Mexican-American woman. She was a few years older than him, and she was a woman who was actually capable of providing him with authentic love and emotional stability. She was a woman who was invested in him. These were all foreign concepts that were "uncomfortable" to him. He had no frame of reference for "healthy" and was unable to appreciate her actions and compassion. In California, his mind was focused on the big picture with a series of failures propelling him to India. It was his inner calling that superseded any relationship.

He pursued love on two additional occasions, both in response to heart activation. It was the energy, butterflies, and giddiness that made him feel like a teenager again. He was enamored with a local Gujarati girl who volunteered at Gandhi Ashram. She was from a very large, wealthy, and boujee Indian family that lived in a massive bungalow. In his mind, he could have seen himself getting married to her despite the trappings of her boujee family. It was an innocent love, a love based on friendship and mental chemistry. It wasn't a physical love, and it never made it to first base. The cold reality was that he wasn't Gujarati enough; he wasn't Indian enough to be taken seriously. And then there was the missile fired from Mumbai...

Just to make sure the budding romance between him and the socialite did not mature, Shilpa organized a daytime soap opera-style plot to blow it up. Shilpa recruited local intel operatives in Ahmedabad to track him and secretly plant a low-grade cheesy softcore porn flick in a video camera bag he had borrowed from the rich family. He had been shooting footage of the earthquake rehabilitation for a documentary project. He had no idea that a cheesy porn video was in the bag. He had no idea where it came from. He hadn't seen it.

Nonetheless, it was discovered and he was vilified as the "Evil" American Man, a deviant culture who had no place in "pure" Gujarat. The wealthy family viewed him as someone who attempted to corrupt their innocent daughter. He had a sit down at the mansion with the girl's father which went nowhere. Nothing he did or said could change the way in which he was viewed. It was a gut punch because he was innocent. He didn't do anything except love. He had been framed. Upon exiting the gates of the Ahmedabad bungalow, just across the street, waiting for him, was Shilpa and the alcoholic womanizing brother of a prominent local Gujarati social worker. Shilpa's intel operation had provided her with information about his planned meeting with the boujee family that morning. Shilpa had flown into Gujarat State from Maharashtra State, at that very moment, to watch his life implode and "save" him. Happiness Sabotaged.

His final pursuit of love was very organic, and he made sure to keep it under the radar. He had met an Indian-American lass. She was a volunteer assisting with the West Coast portion of the *EKTA* tour, and she caught his attention. Once again, he had fallen off the wagon. He was head over heels in love with his mind racing 100 miles per hour. It was a brief relationship that never fully took flight. He lived in Ahmedabad. She lived in West Covina. It was another innocent pursuit of love that only consisted of phone calls and letters. He would receive love letters mailed from California to India, sprayed with lots of perfume.

EKTA was over. In his mind, he was prepared to pull up stakes in India and move back to Los Angeles for love. His mind was very Bollywood-like. Suddenly, it all crumbled. He wasn't Indian enough. He wasn't Gujarati enough. A few friends had gotten in her ear. The expectations of Indian-American parents. The expectations of society. That whole interracial marriage drama. Once again, in matters of the heart, he was left holding a broken one.

In his mind, as crazy, as dramatic, and as over the top as Shilpa was, he was her main focus; he was the object of all her attention. His romantic heart pursuits had failed. He had failed as a writer. Catalysts. A shift of his mind. Change of perspective. Acceptance. Perhaps he was not worthy of love or deserving of love. After all, he was a broken man. Maybe Shilpa was what he deserved. A slippery slope. Once the human mind was set on a new course of thought, there would be no turning back. Perhaps he was viewing the world wrong. Perhaps Shilpa's pursuits were not stalking, but actually love. Perhaps he misunderstood Shilpa's childlike qualities. Since he failed at heart-based love and romance, perhaps a mind-centered relationship was more suitable. If he had really been loveable, then those other women would not have abandoned him.

Red flags. Storm clouds. Warning sirens. His close friends in Mumbai warned him against marriage to Shilpa. His friends in Ahmedabad had no idea he was getting married until after the fact. His neighbor advised that Shilpa had psychological issues and that her behavior was not indicative of Indian tradition and cultural norms from any angle. His best buddy, Jaideep, agreed to be his witness at the Bandra Court, but Jaideep didn't understand what he saw in Shilpa. His mother had her concerns, but she kept them private. She was not one to poke around or interfere in her son's off-the-beaten-path journey. His mother had sensed in his voice and his emails that he was not happy, that those emotions one would expect to be present on the eve of such an auspicious occasion were simply not there. His mother did not see or sense a glow in him. He barely spoke of Shilpa to anyone.

Even his soul was sending him warning signals. A nuclear reactor meltdown. Something was off. A darkness in the energy. But his mind... that slippery slope. The walls of ADX Willow Tree, thick internal prison walls. He was operating out of alignment. His mind was not in coordination with his heart or his soul.

With jittery confidence, he signed the little paper and stepped into a black hole.

THIRTEEN

THE NEXT
TEN YEARS

Sturgis, Michigan. The winter of 2005-2006. A snow-covered parking lot. Afternoon. He sat behind the wheel of a borrowed family SUV. His mind, his soul, and his being were under attack. He was agitated, angry, empty, frustrated, and hollow.

Shilpa was seated next to him. She was berating him and yelling at him with raw vitriol. It was unusual since it was in a public place, as Shilpa preferred closed-door private attacks.

"What kind of man are you? Don't you have a brain?"

"She's in high school for God's sake! She's our student," he sternly responded.

Shilpa began to twist the knife and taunt. "You enjoyed it, didn't you? You liked it when she touched you. Hugged you."

He got defensive. "It was a hug. You were there. How was I supposed to know Janvi was..."

Shilpa raised her hand. She was very animated, and she gritted her teeth. Shilpa appeared to tremble with hatred. "You don't know anything! Janvi is Gujarati. They will sell their own daughter to get to America!"

A car passed by. The woman driving it seemed to stare and pick up on the hostility radiating from the SUV.

Shilpa immediately calmed herself and flipped the script. "I'm protecting you. It's not your fault. You don't know how Indian people are. Baba, I'm protecting you."

Janvi was a J-1 exchange student who was living with a host family in Michigan for a year while enrolled in the local high school. Months prior to getting married, he established his first entrepreneurial effort — a small Ahmedabad-based student exchange business with a local Gujarati partner. He was in the United States for the holidays and was making site visits to host communities to meet with students and host families as well as shoot some videos for promotional material. A wellness-check. At the moment, he had zero knowledge of projection, gaslighting, or depths of covert narcissistic abuse. Not a clue.

The truth was he loved Gujarat. He loved the people of Gujarat. He certainly felt a deep connection to that particular part of a very diverse India. Shilpa knew that. Shilpa understood that his heart was in Gujarat which was why she perceived it as a threat to her emotional control. Therefore, Shilpa had to work very hard to create a wedge, to create doubt in his mind, to build a narrative that despite her anger, she was somehow his well-wisher. The brilliance of the 'con' was that Shilpa had to manufacture drama, take bits of truth, weave a believable narrative, and present herself as the 'only one' who could fix it and protect him. Shilpa did this in order to train his mind to become dependent on her for his well-being, a trauma bond.

TAJ GLOBAL UNDERSTANDING

He packed up his dreams. No more indie film. No more writing. No more starving artist. No more starving social worker. His mother, while always supportive, always had a phrase: "You just can't live on air." Perhaps his mum was right. He certainly tried to live on air, to live and experience life. To pursue his internal guidance.

But now he was married. He had a wife to support, and the cookie-cutter American dream to pursue. He had a suburban house in a nondescript neighborhood. Bills. Grass cutting and trimming on Saturdays. Church on Sundays. A few weeks of vacation per year. 30-year retirement planning.

To him, the idea alone was drab and dreary. It was the antithesis of his off-the-beaten-path existence. His version of the American dream was different, and if he could no longer write, no longer live on air, and no longer produce international stage plays with kids from the slums, then he would need to design his own life. He would need to set up his life in such a way that he could bring depth, meaning, and creativity into his work. He closed the company in India and birthed Taj Global Understanding. It was a Virginia-based non-profit organization created to build bridges between India and the United States through youth sector educational exchanges and volunteer programs. It was different. It gave his mind a focus. It was intended to be life-long. Perhaps his detour to Los Angeles was a mistake. Perhaps his idea of pursuing writing was a mistake. Perhaps it was all just an escape. Perhaps TGU was his message, soft diplomacy. He was willing to put his heart and soul into finding out.

WARDEN SHILPA

ADX Willow Tree had evolved from a mental prison to a physical one. He wasn't married to a loving and caring wife, he was married to a Warden. Shilpa was his warden at ADX Willow Tree.

Shilpa seemed to have changed since the days in Mumbai. She appeared calmer and no longer broke things. Shilpa always set up her little Ganesh religious idols and would periodically light up some incense.

His anxiety and fear seemed to wane, although he did not understand the real reason why. His mind was no longer fighting, no longer fighting to be free of control. It was that slippery slope, that black hole he had entered. He was following the rules. He was living in isolation. He was building a business. He was a full-time caretaker of Shilpa. Even his mother had become a full-time caretaker of Shilpa, placing her on a pedestal and giving, giving, giving. Subconsciously, his mind was self-medicating itself from mental trauma, from PTSD, from panic, and from anxiety by simply being a model prisoner. He didn't rock the boat. He no longer challenged Shilpa or attempted to flee. His mind accepted Shilpa as his Warden.

THE BIG LIE

His mother had gotten remarried and was truly living her fairytale. His mother and his second father traveled to India twice to see him, to support him, and to attempt to better understand what exactly it was about India that had captivated him. They visited once before his marriage and once afterward.

On that first visit, Shilpa introduced his second father to her parents as his biological father. Shilpa's reasoning to him was that India was a very traditional nation and that marriage was taken very seriously; therefore, her parents may not agree to her marriage to a foreigner based on the fact that his mother was a divorcee. At the time, what seemed to be a relatively harmless exaggeration was in fact bold deception.

Shilpa emotionally cornered his mother and wove together a story in which his mom would need to privately inform her father that he will "never leave Shilpa when they get married." His mother was overwhelmed and quite shocked to be placed in such a position, especially one that could not be guaranteed. His mother used her PhD in compassion to have a private talk with Shilpa's father. Although details of that conversation would never be known, he was quite sure his mother would have used her diplomatic skills rather than lie.

During the trips back and forth to America, he and Shilpa would have dinners with his father in Culpeper. His father would often eagerly ask many questions about Shilpa's family, especially her siblings, with genuine curiosity. Shilpa would share and laugh while he remained silent. Shilpa's web of deception was tested when his father traveled to India to visit. His father was keen to travel to Mumbai to meet Shilpa's family. However, his father had no clue that in the eyes of Shilpa's family, his father did not exist. He was caught in Shilpa's lie. He listened to Shilpa's fabricated stories about why his father could not meet her family. He listened in silence. He didn't say anything. He was sad and ashamed of himself.

CHILDLIKE PHILOSOPHIES

"Money goes and money comes," that was Shilpa's mantra to him whenever he was stressed and overwhelmed with bills, payments, and keeping the business afloat. Life didn't work like that. Money did not just come. Shilpa refused his attempts to go over financial statements. Shilpa refused to look at the mortgage, the car payments, and TGU's balance sheets.

"I trust you," Shilpa would reply as she walked away. Shilpa did not spend money, had no expensive clothing habits, or demanded things "like American wives!" There were always subtle inferences, little nuggets for his mind. In India, Shilpa would take a train or bus to "save money." Thriftiness, a wise attribute, was simply a part of the game, the ruse, the deception.

"No. I don't want. You'll kill me!" Shilpa would quip in a whimsical fashion at the idea of a life insurance policy. He was simply crossing out the "I Am a Responsible Adult" checklist and planned to buy a State Farm life policy for himself and the exact same one for Shilpa. It wasn't some random million-dollar policy on Shilpa taken 24 hours before a cruise. The kind of policy articulated on *Dateline*. It should have been simple. A pair of equal 250K policies. Shilpa made such a drama about the policy that it made him even suspicious of himself. He proceeded with only one life policy, his. His value had increased to 250K.

Refusal to carry ID. Refusal to drive. Shilpa never carried any sort of purse. During a trip to the MedExpress for a summer cold, when asked for ID and insurance, Shilpa looked at him. What? Why would he have her documents? Shilpa was not a child, she was a woman approaching forty. Annoyed, he drove back home to collect Shilpa's documents. From that day forward, he just decided it was easier for him to carry Shilpa's license and medical card in his wallet. She was his Warden after all. He was in solitary. He was the responsible one.

His mother was always trying to encourage Shilpa to be more independent and to learn how to drive. His mother weighed heavily on him that he needed to get Shilpa a car. "Mom, she's not going to drive. I'm telling you, we're only here like 5 months a year. It's gonna sit in the garage."

At that moment, his mum had selective hearing. "Shilpa needs a car," she said.

He was already stressed. He was already spinning the hamster wheel to pay for a home in America and a flat in India. He was also paying for international travel and for a small office staff in India, so he just didn't feel like buying a car for Shilpa was the best thing to do.

However, his mother had spoken and that was that. He loved and respected his mother. And days later, a $10,000 pre-owned car was sitting in the garage. And, just as he had prophesied, the PT Cruiser sat in the garage. Annual miles driven: 250. Mainly by him, to keep it running.

Shilpa had essentially transformed her life from a Mumbai Street Hustler to a Queen. In India, married life had provided her with a large leased flat, a maid, a cook, and a black Mahindra Scorpio (Indian SUV) with a driver. In the United States, married life had provided her with a nice house, a car in the garage, and two full-time waiters and assistants — he and his mother.

There were many pitfalls to being empathic and caring for others. Shilpa refused to do any laundry, claiming she might break the machine. Shilpa refused to do any grocery shopping since she was too afraid to drive. How about cooking? Why bother? He certainly wasn't sexist, nor did he have any notion in his mind of a woman's "duties."

His mother had always cooked with love and affection. His grandmother had always cooked with love and affection. Homemade dishes. In

India, cooking was a national pastime. Indian cooking was a full-day affair. Shilpa's mother cooked. Shilpa's mother cooked so much that each meal was customized to various siblings' tastes and eccentricities. However, Shilpa did not cook. Imagine that...

He never mentioned or expected anything. His mother often tried to encourage Shilpa to learn one or two of his favorite dishes to surprise him. It didn't work. Shilpa's own mother often tried to encourage Shilpa to learn a favorite Indian dish and that didn't work either. He was too burdened with life to add "chef" to his plate. In America, his mom often prepared gourmet meals and invited him and Shilpa over at least three days a week. The rest of the time, he oscillated between fast food and Nutrisystem diet meals. Living the dream.

THE DARK SIDE OF A QUEEN

One might think that being placed on a pedestal, with the opportunity to live a carefree life and having all needs attended to, might be grounds for perhaps a ray of appreciation. Well, not with Shilpa. Even with everything, even with American citizenship papers in process, Shilpa was unable to mask her true unvarnished self.

"As fat as you are, you're lucky I'm still married to you!" Shilpa would say. An overwhelming amount of stress and those fast-food meals had not treated him so well. He had gained some weight since those early days in India.

"When are you going to be successful? Buy lots of properties. Take me out of this village. This isn't the real America!" Shilpa would say.

He had friends in slums and families who lived in one room. He was proud that he had established a business, one that was self-reliant. He loved small towns, his town. He was a small-town guy at heart. However, nothing was ever enough for Shilpa. One night, deep in his sleep, he was abruptly woken by a sharp kick to his back. One kick. A second. "You were snoring!" Shilpa shouted.

Shilpa curtailed and controlled his freedom. It wasn't worth a fight. His visits and interactions with Shilpa's family in Mumbai were tightly scripted and choreographed. They happened 2-3 times a year. Just enough, but not too much. Shilpa's mom was a simple and humble woman with a 9th-grade education. She had a genuine and compassionate heart, but she was a woman trapped in her own world in many ways. Shilpa's mom, who only spoke Marathi, would cook him fabulous meals, dishes he loved. Shilpa's mother was caring. Shilpa's older brother owned a security business and was a part-time model who often wanted to take him out for drinks or to a club or to social events in Mumbai. No. No. No. Forbidden. He wasn't much of a party guy anyway, but Shilpa made sure that those family connections never happened. He was forbidden to have any of Shilpa's family on his Facebook list or in his phone contact list.

Shilpa had an uncanny ability to understand his psychology on a subconscious level. Shilpa could read him — his emotions, his triggers. Shilpa could observe him and take note of his reactions. Shilpa learned his vulnerabilities in order to exploit them.

STEWART DETENTION CENTER

U.S. IMMIGRATION AND CUSTOMS ENFORCEMENT

The sky was blue. The air was muggy. A black Chrysler 300 meandered its way through the single-lane roads and peanut fields of South Georgia. He was at the wheel, and he was focused. It was his first nice car — always washed, shiny rims. Shilpa sat shotgun.

They drove through tiny Plaines, Georgia. They passed Jimmy Carter's house. An autographed copy of the *White House Diaries* sat on the back seat of the Chrysler. He was wearing formals — dress pants and a buttoned-up shirt. He was on his way to a real prison, an I.C.E. facility in Lumpkin, Georgia. One of his exchange students, a J-1 Summer Work & Travel middle-class male Gujarati kid, had been unjustly persecuted by the American legal system. The United States vs. Rishi. Rishi was accused of being a visa overstayer. It was an in-house court trial followed by a planned deportation back to India. Mayday.

Rishi had been picked up and flagged in the system. Myrtle Beach, South Carolina. Rishi was secretly transported by the U.S. Government to multiple jail cells across the Southeast, and there wasn't any information being provided on those exact coordinates. Rishi's family in India was frantic.

Rishi had been in Lumpkin for three weeks. He reached out to the Indian Embassy for support, but there was no answer. He reached out to Immigration lawyers in Atlanta for assistance. $10K retainers. Bullshit. He seemed to be the only person who moved without money. Rishi's parents in India had agreed to pay TGU $1,000 to cover the cost of travel to Georgia, hotel, and trial prep costs. He was traveling to the Stewart Detention Center to represent Rishi and argue against the United States federal prosecutor. It was a little stressful. He had a film degree, not a law degree.

He sat in court, seated next to Rishi. Rishi was wearing a blue prison uniform. Rishi was scared and wanted to be deported. To his left was the prosecutor, an older gentleman. The judge was in front and seated behind him were fifty other detainees in different colored jumpsuits.

"Your Honor, Rishi is part of an exchange program, created by Congress, set up by the Department of State. The J-1 Summer Work & Travel program has an automatic 30-Day grace period for students to travel across America and learn things. Those are the rules. Those are the parameters. If the court finds Rishi to be in violation of the J-1 visa, then the court must apply the same to all the other 100,000 international students who are currently in America, but not in prison."

Crickets. The deportation plane was ready until he showed up. Confusion. The judge had never heard of the J-1 program. The prosecutor had no idea either. However, something made sense. Within hours, the United States of America dropped the case against Rishi. It was a sudden and surreal twist to the ordeal. Rishi exited the prison, walked down the lengthy corridor with high fencing and barbed wire, and to the waiting black Chrysler 300. Free at last.

He didn't have much time to ponder ADX Willow Tree or the antics of Warden Shilpa. He was busy running a business and often battling his own government. Ever since he was sixteen and was bumping heads with the Embassy in Delhi, he had hoped his own country would have been more supportive of his soft diplomacy efforts, the bilateral programs he was building in India. Over the years, there were stellar diplomatic standouts. Consul General Michael Owen was the only State Department bigwig he encountered in ten years who rallied and advocated for the mission of TGU. Foreign Service work was a revolving door with officials flying in and out every couple of years. TGU averaged 50% of visa issuance rates. At times, it might be as high as 80%. At times, only 5% of students were issued visas. He lobbied senators and congressional leaders time and time again. Letters were sent and meetings were held, but the status quo remained. There was often a disconnect between the nicely worded diplomatic statements from Washington and the actual reality. The programs he developed and promoted took many months and up to a year to cultivate; however, they often were shut down in an instant by visa denials. Section 214(b). A denial paper was handed to applicants from the Almighty Uncle Sam. TGU's economic stability and growth were always stunted by uneven adjudications that were quite often unfair. Is 30 seconds really enough time for a visa applicant interview?

Nothing in his life came easy. Nothing.

MOTHER EMANUEL AME CHURCH

Charleston. 2015. He was on another American road trip to visit students and meet with host communities. Shilpa was being chauffeured. The Chrysler 300 made a detour to South Carolina. He had reconnected with an old high school friend who was living in Charleston. A Black woman. He reached out to see if she'd like to meet up and walk over to the church together to say a prayer for the nine lives lost. A ray of light in a tragedy. He didn't have many Black friends, not since grade school. He lived in India and knew thousands of Indians, but not Black people. His high school friend was super excited. They all met at Starbucks for lattes and to catch up. He, his friend, and Shilpa walked down to AME Church. He isn't sure what Shilpa did, but he and his friend stood beside one another, bowed their heads, and prayed. The intersection of hatred, ignorance, and America's unique niche claim to fame, gun violence.

"You just wanted a chance, didn't you?" Shilpa snidely remarked as they traveled toward Florida.

"Chance for what?" he asked.

"To spend time with her. Who was she? Your girlfriend?" Shilpa was already scanning her iPhone for Facebook pics of his high school friend.

Shilpa was smug. He could sense that Shilpa was pissed. "What kind of character does she have? See this picture!" Shilpa's tried and true tactic when she felt threatened was to trash talk, tarnish, and defame a person.

He reacted angrily. "Enough Shilpa! Why are you talking about her like that?"

Shilpa's mind morphed into detective mode. "Why are you defending her? I knew it. I knew there was something there. You like her, don't you?"

He knew what would follow was an endless mental game. Pick. Pick. Pick. Pick. Pick. He turned to Shilpa and said, "Everything's not about you."

The truth was Shilpa hated women, especially attractive women. His high school friend was attractive. Shilpa had this all-consuming jealousy which was uncomfortable to witness.

TROOP 1992 – MARK TWAIN

At times during his marriage, his heart rebelled against Shilpa. He fondly remembered the innocence of his days roaming the slums of Ahmedabad, EKTA, and his former life at Gandhi Ashram. He missed it terribly and had an idea. He collaborated with the Gujarat State Bharat Scouts & Guides organization to formally establish the very first volunteer troop in Gujarat. In India, unlike in America, scouts were set up through local schools. Viren Joshi and Manav Sadhna supported his vision once again and provided the meeting space, selection of the local youth, and the humanitarian guidance.

Troop 1992 was born in the slums of Ahmedabad. 1992 was a nod to his first visit to India, and Mark Twain was a nod to the fact that both Twain and Baden Powell had visited India. It was intended to be a cross-over troop with elements of an American scout program along with Indian formalities.

Troop 1992 rooted itself in the community. Kids beamed with excitement. Parents witnessed personal growth and changes in their sons. There were weekly meetings. He organized swimming classes and high adventure camps for the scouts. He attended every scout meeting when he was in Ahmedabad. He was always joined at the hip by his Warden who was keeping tabs on him to make sure he didn't wander off.

He loved Taj Global Understanding. It paid the bills. However, in many ways, Troop 1992, his little ragtag creation with poor kids and his Gandhi Ashram family, were the highlights of his married life. His heart sang. His heart was filled with love. There was an innocence to it all, a simplicity that he longed for.

ZERO AFFECTION

The Willow Tree had conditioned him to separate love from intimacy. His Willow Tree conditioning allowed his mind to accept the idea of living in a platonic marriage. With Shilpa, any prior physical relationship ended the day he was married at the court in Bandra. He was living in a different kind of fairytale, a bit abstruse.

Shilpa had zero interest in him physically. He never had to tell Shilpa "No." He never had to push away her advances. He never had to make excuses that he was "too tired" or "too stressed." All of it left him even more confused. He felt that if there was a God, he was getting what he deserved, which was Shilpa.

Hundreds of hotels and motels across the world, budget and luxury, and still zero intimacy. In fancier, more boujee hotels, hotels that could have been deemed romantic, Shilpa would always instigate a fight to agitate his mind, extort the life out of him, and ensure that he did not get any idea of wanting to be intimate. Sofitel, West Hollywood. The Venetian, Las Vegas. A boutique lodge in the Swiss Alps. An anniversary cruise through the Caribbean. Zero intimacy.

He was married to a nun. He lived in silence. He had no barometer. Every now and then, he would do a web search on "sexless marriage" to try and find out if anyone else in the world was stuck like him.

All of it left him confused and empty.

THE WHISPERS

The most devastating aspect of his marriage were the secret phone calls to other men, an outpouring of emotional energy. He spoke English. He understood a little Gujarati and a little Marathi. Mastering another language was on his lifelong to-do list. Shilpa exploited this. Shilpa was obsessed with the phone, with social media, and with talking. Attention.

Shilpa did make business calls, student calls, and calls to her family. However, she had a subset of hushed and secretive calls that were made daily, often on a routine, and would last for hours. He was not allowed to touch Shilpa's phone or ask any questions. If he did, he should prepare for a mental beatdown and a long-term battle. Mob boss Shilpa. He would do anything to avoid the panic attacks, the anxiety, and the sweats of years prior. Shilpa had stories for everything and everyone. She would often say to him, "Trust me, baba. I'm your wife."

He may not have been multilingual or possessed great fluency, but he was immersed in India for a long time. He was very familiar with the sounds, tones, and words of various languages, of conversations, and he knew if he was being talked about. His INFJ personality was wired to cue in on all of the nuances of tone, expression, body language, feelings, and emotions that would radiate from conversations. He could absorb the emotion of the situation with great specificity.

He understood very clearly when Shilpa was conversing with her family in Mumbai, in Marathi, and the various ways in which she expressed herself. He understood very clearly when Shilpa was conversing in Hindi with a student or a parent, which had completely different tones, dialogue structures, and emotional vibes. He could feel and sense when the calls were off, when the calls were suspicious, and when the calls had different tones and different emotions.

His inner child craved it. His adult husband Self, craved it. Just a little. He wanted a fraction of that attention, a fraction of that emotion, to be directed toward him.

At times, he felt suffocated, trapped, and helpless in pain. He would hear Shilpa engaging in a flirtatious conversation in the bedroom. He would become overwhelmed with hurt in his heart, and he would walk outside the flat into the hot and humid night air. He would then sit on the steps and cry. He cried and cried. He cried until he was numb again. Then he would stand up, walk back inside to his office, sit at his desk, and search for his next escape.

DUBAI

As Shilpa became more self-assured of her dominance and complete control over his emotional state, as his puppet master, she became bolder. Shilpa developed an online relationship with an Algerian man named Imran.

Imran had recently moved to Dubai for work and to be near a sister. Shilpa proclaimed to him that Imran was gay. At times, she would even coerce him into speaking to Imran.

He wasn't happy with the friendship. He found it odd, especially when Shilpa casually mentioned, from time to time, going to Dubai to see Imran and the sister. Shilpa was persistent and somehow made it seem acceptable for her to go to Dubai. He was reluctant, but he agreed under one condition: He also wanted to see Dubai. The plan was for him to fly out a few days later and for them to both return to Ahmedabad together. He had scoped out a deal at the JW Marriott and was excited to travel. When he arrived at the airport in Dubai, Shilpa was a no-show. Shilpa was not waiting for her husband at the airport. He checked into the Marriott. He called Shilpa but there was no answer. Shilpa remained missing and unreachable during his entire first day in Dubai. The excitement of being in a new place and a nice hotel evolved into a deep sadness. It was an emotional sadness, an emptiness that he could not hide on his face.

That night, he sat on a large couch, tucked away in a second-floor hallway. Shilpa finally arrived... with Imran. A man who was younger than him. Taller. Imran had sharp features and a lean muscular build.

Shilpa was giddy. Both Shilpa and Imran were giddy. His heart began to hurt. He wished he never boarded that flight. He felt invisible. He felt like a third wheel.

Shilpa said, "There's a posh club nearby. We want to go. Can you come?"

He tried to smile, but his emotional infrastructure was taking over. Sadness, deep sadness. "No. I think I'm okay. I'm a little tired from traveling. I'd rather stay here."

Imran totally ignored him. Imran looked directly at Shilpa and asked, "Do you want to go?"

Shilpa gushed, "I'd love to."

Feeling emotionally winded, he couldn't bear it anymore. He stood up and said, "You guys do whatever. I'm gonna head up to the room."

In the room, he stumbled across a motel receipt in Shilpa's bag. Shilpa was supposed to stay with Imran's sister, not at a motel.

Shilpa returned soon after, not having gone to the club. He was empty, not angry. Shilpa denied, downplayed, and brushed off the receipt. "That's nothing. I was going to tell you, but didn't want you to worry. Her flat didn't allow guests. I had no idea what to do baba. Don't you *trust* me? I'm your wife."

With an aching heart, he climbed into bed and held on to the hope that perhaps tomorrow would be a better day.

FOURTEEN

BANGKOK, THAILAND

In America, the city of Las Vegas had a slogan that was known all over the world: "What happens in Vegas, stays in Vegas." The same could be said for Bangkok. In fact, he could have used the same slogan for many cities across the world.

In addition to his noble and lofty pursuits, his dreams and his life at ADX Willow Tree had provided him with a vice, an outlet for his pain. His own shadow self. His own coping mechanism. His own inner demons. His tug-of-war with shame. His inner wrestling with worth. It could have manifested itself in any direction and taken any form. He rarely drank. He didn't smoke. He never did drugs. He was a weed-free gangsta. He didn't cut. He wasn't suicidal. He didn't hate. He had no track marks.

He had one vice, lust. No emotion. No feeling. No love. No romance. Just lust, plain and simple.

The air was trifling. It was noisy. The street was filled with tuk-tuks, buses, cars, and mopeds. Night had fallen over the massive city. Street vendors sold all kinds of local delicacies. He wore shorts, a Henley, and running shoes. He wished, in many ways, that he could run from himself. He was in Bangkok on a work-related trip; yet, he was deceiving himself.

Split personality. He would spend his days promoting his organization and building education sector programs, and he would spend his nights wrestling with his demons. Innocence no more. Years earlier, he had visited and even stayed in the seedy Patpong district. Bars. Women. Clubs. Women. Everything was for sale. But these days, as he had matured in life, he preferred a quieter side street in another part of the city. His focus wasn't to party or to drink. His focus was to be touched, to feel loved by a stranger who he was on a collision course to meet.

As he walked down the sidewalk, he glanced down each side street. Residential. Commercial. He often contemplated turning around and returning to the hotel. Staying focused. But then, like a magnet, he was pulled to the flashing lights. The neon lights of a non-descript parlor at the end of a street. He turned right. His heart started to beat faster.

On this night, timestamp unknown, the demons had prevailed. He lay naked on a small bed in a tiny room. The yellow light was dimmed. Three white towels lay on the floor as drops of water ran down a nearby glass shower door. To his left and his right were two girls, Asian women, nationalities unknown. Both were busty. His preference. One natural. One silicon. Both girls were in their 20s. He was in his 30s. His face was somber. Both women, strangers, appeared to be very much at ease with him. Perhaps they were feeling his energy and calmness. He was not wasted. He was not stoned.

He was not angry, not violent. He was empty.

One girl reached over to the nightstand to grab a condom. She began to tear open the package as he gently placed his hand on hers and shook his head. "No. It's okay. No sex."

Surprise. Shock. Both girls understood that this encounter was different. He ran his hand across his chest. "Just touch me. Touch me. Please." He closed his eyes as the women began to caress him.

In his world, shame was indeed married to euphoria. He longed to feel affection. He longed to be touched. He was desperate to feel loved. And he found love, in brief moments, with strangers in transactional relationships. None of it was about sex. His escort escapades were a reflection of his perception of Self, a perception of the little boy trapped in the treehouse without a voice. Black women. White women. Asian women. Latin women. He found love in soapy massage parlors, apartments, motels, and shady places from Shanghai to London to Singapore to Mumbai to Atlanta to Reno. Superficial. Meaningless.

He knew that it was not okay. He knew that the world would think less of him. He knew that he was fighting shame. He knew that God would not approve. He knew he tried to be a good person. He knew he was an Eagle Scout. He knew that if he just never had a treehouse, then he would not be wrestling with the demon of lust.

His own father had built the treehouse out of love. What child wouldn't be excited to have a private treehouse, high up in a willow tree? His father had no idea, no inclination that the loving gesture for a son would become a trap.

His mind swore to him that it wasn't an addiction. His mind swore to him that he was in full control of himself. His mind could compartmentalize the hour or two spent in the parlor and then tuck it away as if it never happened. Detachment, it was an art he had perfected.

THE FIRST TIME

Knoxville, Tennessee. He was 23 when he paid a woman to "love" him for the first time. He was on his cross-country drive from Los Angeles back to Virginia, before moving to India. He had driven away from an actual relationship with a beautiful soul who actually loved him, and he had detoured into a new world of hookers. He had attempted to reach out to a counselor to open up about his pain and his struggles, only to find the door closed.

In high school, his mom hired a counselor to try and fix her marriage. His mother had set up some private sessions for him and the counselor in order to find out what was happening in his head. He was so private. He would not share his emotions or feelings. His mother knew that, but his mother didn't know why. It was his one and only experience with professional counseling. Years later, he called the same counselor from Los Angeles and conveyed that he needed an outlet. He hinted about his abuse. However, there wasn't much appetite on the other end of the phone to discuss it. Perhaps, he wasn't clear. Perhaps, it was a misunderstanding. He had received a glowing recommendation letter to USC from the counselor. In his mind, his tepid outreach for help had failed.

He had no idea why he responded to a little ad in Tennessee that night. He certainly had no business spending $150. He certainly knew it wasn't one of the 10 Commandments, a pillar in the Boy Scout oath, or an approved activity by local law enforcement. He knew that spending an exorbitant sum of money was wasteful. But at that moment, he needed an escape. The White girl, with dirty bleach-blonde hair, arrived. He sat in a chair in the room. He sat and sat. He sat so long that the girl asked him what he was waiting for. He responded, "Can I touch you?"

It was an awkward moment for sure. His introduction to his shadow self. It was a seed rooted in pain. A seed that had remained dormant much of his life until he crossed paths with Shilpa. It was a relationship that would create explosive growth in his own darkness.

THE MAN IN THE MIRROR

The truth was that every time he took a shower, no matter how much time he stood there, he was never able to wash away certain feelings. He was never able to feel clean afterward. Comfort came in writing. Comfort came in imagining. Comfort came in social endeavors, being immersed in a project. However, the man staring back in the mirror... was not comfort. His life was busy. His mind was always processing. Even alone, alone as an INFJ, his mind was processing and thinking and creating. It was rare for him to not have anything to do. It was rare for him to not be busy. It was rare for him to sit in a room with himself. He avoided those moments at all costs. He never liked what he saw in the mirror.

His truth was, it didn't matter how many women walked in and out of his hotel room because it would never have been enough. He was feeding, medicating an empty void. Life at ADX Willow Tree did not provide him with many opportunities to be by himself, away from his Warden Shilpa. Perhaps a couple of weeks in a year. It was in those moments, those glimpses of freedom, that he felt he needed to overcompensate.

At one point, in Thailand, he had three different women scheduled at different times on the same night. One after the other. They bumped into each other in the hallways. A true model in self-worth. A true model in self-love. The sadness of the man in the mirror.

In his preparation for his prison break, one of his goals was to read and research. He wanted to study psychology, to connect the dots in his own life. Ross Rosenberg, a Chicago-based psychologist, with books, blogs, and a well-established online presence had specific concepts that spoke to him. Light bulb moments. One after the other. Mr. Rosenberg articulated a crucial and profound link in the relationship dynamics between covert narcissism and sexual addiction. He was riveted by Mr. Rosenberg's concepts and correlation. It was as if Ross was speaking directly to him and had lived in his world, lived in his mind. At the core of the dysfunction was a deficit in self-love, the ability to love oneself. The toxic nature of the hidden codependent relationship with a covert narcissist directly worked to create a secondary manifestation in the mind of escapism, of becoming an actual addict. The pathology of each and every psychological avenue was traced back to childhood trauma in the treehouse. In his mind, he thought of his marriage as a garden. In a healthy relationship that was watered with authenticity, compassion, and love, the seeds of one's true identity and true Self would be able to grow and flourish. But in a toxic relationship dynamic, especially one in which childhood trauma had been brought in and was untreated, the water which was poured into the garden activated the seeds of the shadow Self. Thus, allowing the manifestation of an addiction. The more he ran on the hamster wheel of blindly serving the needs of Shilpa and unknowingly coping with severe emotional abuse, the more he ran on the hamster wheel of escapism lust. Both cycles were interconnected and fed off one another.

FIFTEEN

DAY #21

His Land Rover sits parked in an empty lot in Pahrump, Nevada. It's mid-morning on a Sunday in March. It is church time for many but not for him. He sits in his car at the Chicken Ranch, a brothel Northwest of Las Vegas. There is only one potential client at that time of day. Most of Vegas isn't awake yet, but he is on a schedule, 48 days.

He had a good night's sleep at the Candlewood Suites and even got his laundry done. At least he's clean on the outside. His face is pensive. He contemplates. He should just drive away. Is attempting to break a trauma bond really worth it? A new direction is almost unbearable. A new Self is hard. There's comfort in the old. Maybe ADX Willow Tree really isn't so bad... His mind is at war. His emotions are at war. He is anxious and a little jittery. He is confident he is making the right decision to break free. He is confident he is making the wrong decision to break free. He's terrified of the unknown future. An overwhelming stress. When he is stressed, his mind magnifies his perceived human flaws. He is uncomfortable with himself. He feels that he just needs a hit, a release, to feel better.

He feels that perhaps the tall busty Eastern European woman he's scheduled to meet can be that release for him, that her transactional "love" will be the fuel to push him onward. The inner demon always seems to be percolating beneath the surface. Maybe this is the last time. Just one more time... At this point, what's one more sin? Perhaps there's a Chicken Ranch outside the Pearly gates.

He makes his way into the main lobby. Pin-drop silence. Vegas is still hungover at 10 a.m. Most of the professionals are sleeping. His presence at that hour signals to him that he is the epitome of emptiness and desperation. Loser. Failure. Worthless. That man in the mirror.

He is led to a smaller room where he waits for his European companion. The woman, early 30s, arrives. There is no bait and switch. She's tall and looks just like her online picture. He feels bad because he realizes she woke up and got ready to meet him and he is doubting himself.

"I'm really sorry for waking you up," he says.

"It's okay," she replies, not exactly wide-eyed.

They begin the super romantic art of price negotiations and services. An hour. 30. Even 15 minutes. 15 minutes! The thought of 15 minutes feels just a tad bit desperate. The addict within him is undressing her with his mind. The prison escapee within him begins to question what in the hell he's doing there. He's an Eagle Scout for Christ's sake. Does this stranger really have the magical healing powers of touch? Will his life be better? For the first time, he stops himself.

"I apologize for your time. But I can't do this," he says.

He exits the brothel and drives away.

Day #21 is by far the longest single-day drive of his trip. He isn't a tourist. He's an off-grid escapee and on the run. Day #21 is essentially a logistical repositioning day to get him from Vegas up to Corning, California. The winds in the high desert along the spine of Nevada are brutal. The gusts are so strong they make his car swerve. He crosses the Sierra Nevada outside of Reno late at night as heavy snow falls, creating additional hazards. He is a natural loner, but on this day, he is lonely on the inside.

Self-worth has no boundaries. Self-worth doesn't care if one is born on the north side or the south side of town or to the east or west of the railroad tracks. Self-worth doesn't have a zip code. Self-worth doesn't care if one lives on Wall Street or Main Street. Self-worth doesn't care if one lives on the Upper West Side or in a trailer park. Self-worth doesn't have a skin color. Self-worth doesn't have a religion or a culture or a country. Self-worth doesn't speak only English or Japanese or Arabic or Hindi or Swahili. Self-worth doesn't care about bank balances. Self-worth is simply the feeling evoked within when one looks in the mirror.

CRATER LAKE

He loves snow, always has. There is something about the innocence, the purity, the dreamlike blanket of pristine snowfall that makes him feel like a child. He is fortunate to learn that the road to Crater Lake is accessible and open. He makes a slight detour on the way to Bend, Oregon. He needs Crater Lake at this very moment in time as his entire inner-self was running on empty, on fumes.

He is a broken shell of himself. The images of snow seem to help him escape. The intrinsic beauty that is nature... He has never seen so much snow in his life. The snow banks, sliced out, are well over fifteen feet tall. He has only seen pictures of such snowfall in photos and news reports. He drives up and hangs a right toward the fancy lodge hotel. It is closed for the season and buried in snow. He grabs his tripod and walks up a snow bank, revealing the deep-water volcanic lake. It is cold, but not frigid. There is no wind. He isn't dressed for winter survival and is cautious not to get too close should the snow collapse and send him off of a literal cliff. He sets up his tripod for a very low-angle shot. He wants the frame to have his back facing the camera. He wants to be seated cross-legged on the snow, looking out over the majestic American West.

The depth of the snow has an inverse and proportionate relation to how he is feeling inside at that moment. He has never seen so much snow. He has never been so utterly empty. He doesn't stop the tears that begin to stream down his face as he hits the timer on his Canon. He walks over to sit in position and then captures the moment. *Click. Click.*

He continues to sit in the snow as an emotional dam breaks. He looks across the lake, closes his eyes, and utters in a mumbled tone:

"Dear God, Help me. Show me. Please. Show me how to love myself. I don't know where to begin. I don't know what to do. I have no clue. Please, God. I need help."

BEND, OREGON

He arrives just before dark at the Days Inn in Bend. He is at an emotional rock bottom. Numb. Cold. Everything is a blur. He moves slower. His body physically aches. He checks into his room in slow motion. He has been the one to ask questions his entire life, questions that no one had answers for. He opened his MacBook and sent a one-line mail to Stephanie, his energy healer. He writes, "Question. How do you love yourself?" He then closes the computer and crawls into his bed. He lies there, under the blankets and covers, shaking and trembling. He wonders if these were the kinds of withdrawal symptoms an addict felt.

He has been so conditioned to checking his phone, to hearing from Shilpa all the time, to being tracked, to dealing with passive-aggressive behavior, to walking on eggshells, to being comfortable suppressing his unhappiness, to being a caretaker, to absorbing all of the burdens in life, and to making sure everyone else was happy that his mind just did not know where to go or what to do. His mind didn't know what to fixate on. He lies in bed, trembling, and shaking. His throat feels dry. He feels nauseous and physically ill. He isn't a suicidal person. Never in his life did he have those thoughts. No matter what, he always held on to hope, hope for tomorrow. He has never lived in a world devoid of all hope. Hope has become an escape mechanism. But on that night, in Bend, the hollowness and soul-crushing emotional pain of wanting to have his mind free again, to have control over his own emotions, caused him to let go of hope.

DAY #23

The clouds have lifted in Bend. The late morning sun illuminates his white Evoque in the parking lot of the motel. Most guests have checked out. A housekeeping trolly cart, loaded with cleaning supplies, noisily rolls along the walkway outside the rooms. Inside his room, there is darkness, except for one shaft of light beaming through a crack in the curtain. The large lump beneath the covers begins to move a little and then a little more. The noise of the housekeeping trolley is loud. The walls are thin. The housekeeping staff is loud.

Whoosh. The mass of blankets and covers are tossed back to reveal his face. It is the face of the middle-aged maharaja, from the Kingdom of Culpeper. One eye opens and then the other follows. He squints and looks around. He is a little disoriented. To him, it doesn't look like Heaven. The cart outside squeaks and squeals as it rolls by. It doesn't sound like Heaven. He stretches a bit, body and face. To him, it doesn't look like Hell or what he imagined as the final resting place for sinners. No. To him, it looks like the same Days Inn.

The computer system hard drive that is his mind begins to light up and function. The hard stubborn head of his, made out of concrete, realizes he made it through the night. He woke up. His body is calm. He doesn't shake or tremble. He is not anxious. He is peaceful and rested. He begins to remember what he had said the night before, his little prayer to God. He begins to feel like the drunken friend who maybe was a little too chatty the night before and said something they regretted. He realizes he had been drunk on shame, drunk on self-loathing, drunk on not being perfect. He also realizes that he has no hangover, that all hope is not lost, and that he is excited to find out what Walla Walla, Washington is like — whether it is rural, rural boujee, another west coast weed joint, or Washington chic.

God begins to speak to him as he dodges flying tumbleweeds traveling across the dustbowl of Northeast Oregon. God speaks to him in a very strong and boisterous Indian accent. "Bredbhai!" "Bredbhai!"

His official name, per his birth certificate, is Brad. It isn't Bradford. It isn't Bradley. It is Brad, just four letters. However, in India, he was primarily referred to as "Bred." Gujarat is very warm, friendly, loud, and a bit flashy. Everyone's first name had "Bhai" or "Ben" added to it. "Bhai" means brother and "Ben" means sister. "Bhai" and "Ben" are even included on official documents, like passports.

Names are identities given to souls. Some names have great meanings. Some names are inspired by ancestors. Some names are inspired by places of conception. Some names are generic. Some names have a flare. Some names are short. Some names utilize all the letters in the alphabet (South India). Language and the articulation of vowels and syllables are often tongue twisters.

He would quite often butcher the pronunciations of Indian names. Sometimes, when he would attempt certain words, he would completely alter their meanings because of his American English enunciation of a Gujarati name. Despite the fact that the name Brad only has four letters, it was seemingly impossible for many of his friends and those around him in Gujarat to pronounce. What emerged was "Bred," with a very powerful "b" and a roll of the tongue on the "r" followed by a flat "ed." For many years, people would always ask him, "Where is your butter?" Bred. Not Roti. Not Naan. Not Bajra Roti. Not Thepla. Not Puri. Not Chapati. He was simply Bredbhai.

He is in the middle of a midlife meltdown. He has spent most of his entire professional life, post-college, in India. He feels honored and humbled to be known as "Bredbhai." He has heard it tens of thousands of times, and it is always connected to a feeling of love, compassion, kindness, and generosity.

He is just a kid from small-town Virginia trying to navigate life, trying to find purpose. He remembers the simple action of walking through a crowded slum on his way to his scout program and hearing a random voice in the street shout out "Bredbhai!" He remembers the young *EKTA* teens, each with a different personalized nuance to "Bredbhai." He remembers walking into meetings at Gandhi Ashram, into the homes of the rich, into the homes of the poor, into the homes of the working class, and always being greeted with his adopted name, "Bredbhai."

India has given him the opportunity to experience humanity in a new way, with a new lens. His indie movie never happened. He fell into a few traps. But India, India, India, has given him so much richness.

SIXTEEN

DRIVING AND DRIFTING ACROSS MONTANA

He has been extremely sensitive his entire life, even before the treehouse, because of the fear of being abandoned.

Shortly after his birth, his father had planned a trip to the Caribbean. Grenada. Haiti. His mother felt sick to her stomach at the thought of leaving her only child, a baby, with the in-laws in North Carolina to go on a trip. However, she felt like she had no choice. Sure, he was with his grandparents, but he was a baby, and his mother disappeared.

A few years later, in 1980, his father departed for a solo vacation to South America. He was not yet five, and for some reason, his mother decided to memorialize a conversation on the family typewriter.

We both sat and cried after (his father) left for Peru. Then we both laughed at each other for crying and I tried to think of something funny to cheer Brad up. I told him he had enough money to buy some more Underoos. He wants to buy Aqua Man. I ask what they look like and he said they have bubbles on the front and I laughed. Brad said, I don't know why because Aqua Man can't blow bubbles in the sea! Then Brad said Mommy, we didn't cry too much, did we? We just can't help crying a little! I told him from now on, we all would take vacations together and this big grin came on his face. A few minutes later Brad came in the room with his teddy bear, stuffed dog, and another bear. He said, do you want a friend to help make you feel better? Then he gave me one, and tried to laugh again. He didn't know why he was laughing so hard! Brad keeps asking if you are flying yet?

There are many moments in life that appear as innocent and harmless as a solo trip to Peru, and then there are the moments that become roots in the mind of a child. The fear of being abandoned is one such root. These roots have manifested into wrong turns in life and limiting belief systems.

His mother placed him in a bubble, a bubble of unconditional love. His mother sacrificed everything for him in order to provide his mind and heart with the feeling that his life was normal. His mother sacrificed decades of her unhappiness internally, for him in order to raise her only child in union with his father. His mother was a mastermind at hiding her inner Truth, at hiding herself, to make him and everyone around her happy. His mother never wanted to see her son emotionally hurt or suffer. However, his mother did not know that he was already struggling. He was, in his own way, learning how to hide his inner Truth.

He and his mother were bound together by an energetic force. It was a light, a love that was so profound it did not ask any questions. It just was. His and his mother's subconscious minds, in a way, sought to protect each other.

His mother absolutely hated the film business and yet she would hide that distaste behind her generous smile and loving support. Truth be told, there were very few things that his mother disliked or had such a strong disdain for, which was why it was unusual. It wasn't rocket science. It was the fact that she hated seeing him invest all of himself into projects and creative pursuits that always failed. It was often as if he and his mother were two very distinct planets, each with very distinct orbits. At times, he felt misunderstood by his mother. His mother was focused on the present and the tangible — volunteering at the Humane Society, organizing church fundraising events, gardening, counseling others, holiday gatherings, creating change locally, and bettering the lives of those around her.

His mum lived and breathed and made a difference in Culpeper County. His mother knew everyone, could connect with anyone, and could help find a solution to any problem. If his family were a Norman Rockwell mob family, his mother was the mob boss. She was the decision maker, the connector. Everything and everyone reported to his mother for advice, insight, and a nod of approval. His mother made time for everyone. She listened, laughed, and made whoever was in her presence feel as if they were the most special person in the world.

He had a different planetary alignment. The gravitational pull of his trajectory was always focused on the big picture — big ideas, big purpose. Pushing boundaries. Outside the box. Human landscapes. His inner guidance system was pushing him toward a message, a purpose. It was an inner feeling, a calling; yet, it still felt very much like a mystery. His inner drive was not to settle on Main Street but instead to keep tinkering with his own spaceship. He hoped that eventually, he'd connect the dots.

His mother was living, in many ways, in her own version of ADX Willow Tree. It was an extent to which he would never know because she shielded him from those broken pieces. His mother had accepted her life as it was and pushed forward. She had two loves, her son and her job. She had a career of over twenty years as the office manager for Culpeper Family Practice. She oversaw a team of doctors, nurses, and admin staff. She effortlessly navigated an endless array of patient issues, insurance company drama, and staff issues as well as coordinating major holiday office parties and slogging through mountains of paperwork. His mother excelled at multitasking. She loved her job, and she loved the people. She loved being the captain of the ship. She excelled at any responsibility. She was gifted in soft diplomacy. She was a natural healer to others. Her million-megawatt smile sailed the ship for decades, and then she was fired... It was utter personal devastation.

The United States of America had a "Sheep in Wolves Clothing." Corporate Healthcare. The University of Virginia's healthcare machinery was in the process of ingesting small-town medical practices and brand-building in order to maximize profitability. The University bought out the medical practice.

America's other "Sheep" were lawyers. The heavily litigious culture in America ultimately was an overwhelming burden for the doctors/owners. Liability. The liability of being a physician in America was high risk. The docs sold out to the devil in disguise. Within weeks, his mom was canned. Collateral. God's plan?

The new corporate owners replaced his mom with another woman, a business major with fancy degrees and lofty titles. Double salary! How about them apples? His mother never demanded more money. In the eyes of corporate America, his mother was a Non-College Educated White. What the "educated" people failed to comprehend was the fact that his mother had a PhD in kindness, empathy, and compassion. She had skills that were quite useful in patient care and public relations. The real kicker was the fact that the new hire was only at the job for a few years. Stepping stones. Being fired in the middle of her life from a job she planned to retire from was in fact a slingshot for his mother. It was a catalyst.

After 30 years of marriage, his mom would walk away with nothing. By choice. Thirty years, and all his mom took with her was her clothes and her son's childhood toys — those GI Joes and Transformers. His mother stepped into her own unknown, a leap of faith.

HEIRLOOMS AND ANGELS

His mother was living as a paying guest in a small upstairs apartment in a house owned by a devout elderly Christian woman who played hymns on an old record player. It was a tiny apartment without air conditioning. She now worked at a low-wage hourly administrative job.

Within weeks of his mum's life-altering decision, course correction, a Bible came to her, an heirloom. His mother's family line was fairly small. There was an older sister, Peggy, and two half-sisters, Ruby in Mississippi and Lee in Maryland. Lee's career with United Airlines had provided "Companion Passes," almost free travel passes for friends and family. His pursuits were in India. His federal loans for USC were placed in Economic Hardship deferment. Yet, in the early days, he was flying back and forth to India once or twice a year in first class! He was even gifted a bottle of champagne once by a female flight attendant. This was all due to the gracious generosity of his Aunt Lee and those free "Companion Passes." Aunt Lee's side hobby was genealogy, connecting dots. Enter the Family Bible, which was being personally delivered to Aunt Lee, now living in Culpeper.

It was not a pocket Bible, not a Gideons, and not the standard print in the back of a pew. Nope. A dope ass Bible. Kimber And Sharpless' edition. Printed Circa 1820. It was the size of a small coffee table. Fraying dark hardbound cover. Illustrations. Hand-written maternal family tree. A two-hundred-year family heirloom. A time when America only had 23 States. The ancient, by American standards, Bible, came with an additional feature. An Angel. No exaggeration. No satirizing of the Word. A real-life angel. A second husband. A redo in life. A fresh start. A whirlwind of change that happened overnight. Billy, a relative, had been the one to deliver the Bible to Aunt Lee. Billy also brought along a best friend from childhood. His mum crossed paths with the stranger, along for the ride down to Culpeper. Within six months, his mom was remarried to a soulmate, a perfect energetic tuning.

When his mother got a second husband, he ended up with a second father. A man who seemingly fell out of the sky and was drama free. Her second husband was an accountant in a large Northern Virginia tax firm. No children. A first wife of thirty years had passed away from cancer a year prior. His second father was a Marine, a Vietnam Veteran. His second father drove a Harley on the weekends and didn't seem to have any relatives. His second father was a soul that just appeared in his mother's life at the right moment.

It was all very new for him. He had never witnessed his mother light up and beam in such a way. Her photographs were different. The frowns and expressions of heaviness were replaced by an inner glow, a light that jumped off the picture. It was a soul-level kind of happiness. His mom had sacrificed her entire life. She gave and gave and gave to others. And now, she was being rewarded big time. A dream. His mom and second father purchased a brick rambler on six acres a few miles outside of town with a small pond. Her country-girl roots were activated. Gardening. Growing her favorite sunflowers. Butterfly bushes. Dog adoptions from area shelters. First Dusty. Then Bree. Bird feeders. A hammock. Ice tea on the front porch. A private saltwater pool. A little country. A little boujee.

A DIFFERENT KIND OF RAINBOW

His mother stood alone in her newly renovated kitchen. Rays of light from a nearby bay window filled the space. The phone rang. His mother was pensive and anxious. She answered.

A very matter-of-fact male voice on the other end says, "Tests came back positive. Stage IV. Metastatic."

A blank stare. A flush of lightheadedness. The doctor, who was an hour away in Charlottesville and was part of the University of Virginia system, said without compassion, "Six months. You have six months."

His mother hung up the phone. A sudden hollowness. A dimmed light. She immediately called her best friend, Susan, as the tears began to flow. Susan rushed to her side.

The Metastatic Breast Cancer was estrogen positive and had spread into the lymph nodes and the bone. His mother had lived and worked in the healthcare industry. She was always vigilant. She had annual screenings and was a believer in medicine and doctors. Out of nowhere, Stage IV. A life sentence. Treatments but no cure. His mom would never have the opportunity to stand up and proudly say that she was a survivor, that she beat cancer. Stage IV. The last stage. His mother did what she always excelled at: minimizing and hiding her pain while focusing on others. She deepened her faith tenfold. She took concrete steps to divorce herself from anything related to the UVA healthcare system. A realignment to a better fit, the Martha Jefferson Sentara healthcare corporation. Better patient care according to her. Her opinion. Her choice.

CHRISTIAN FREE AGENT

For decades, his mother had been a proud member of the United Methodist Church. She would volunteer on committees, do fundraisers, organize an annual flea market, and religiously attend weekly service, both Sunday School and the formal service. The Methodist Church had a new pastor in town, one that wasn't exactly a fan of his mother. Churchy Politics. His mum ran a very powerful committee tasked with vision and budgets. The Lord spoke to the new Pastor in surprisingly very petty and human ego-driven ways. The Pastor had his mom removed from the committee as part of the church's compassionate outreach due to the fact that she was diagnosed with Stage IV cancer and may not live through the term. Glory be to God. Power of the Word.

Allergies. He was always allergic to hypocrisy. It didn't seem very biblical to kick a person when they were down, to mess with his mama. It was a cruel and heartless act done by an ordained theologian that triggered his mom to revoke her membership in defiance. His mom transitioned to a tiny Presbyterian Church, built in 1879, located several miles out of town in the middle of a farm.

Technically, he was still enrolled in the books at the United Methodist Church in Culpeper. It was the church of his childhood and the church without any Black people. Yet, he too was pissed. In solidarity with his beloved mom, in defiance, he too pulled his esteemed membership and became a Christian free agent. No more annual picture directories. No more free cookbooks.

THAT DAMN BUDDHA STATUE

His status as a free agent Christian secretly worried his mother. It was the kind of thing that kept her up at night. At the Methodist Church, at least he had roots, at least he had some connectivity. However, being a free agent meant he had no roots.

He had lived in India for many years. While his mom loved all people and was respectful of other faiths, she didn't want her son to drift too far into another lane. Perhaps India had influenced him. Perhaps India had secretly converted him. Perhaps Hinduism had taken root within him. Perhaps Shilpa had influenced him with her gods, her Ganpati statue. And then there was his damn, no offense, Buddha statue.

In the middle of his American home, the suburban small-town American dream, was this large Buddha statue in the foyer. There were no signs of Jesus in his house. No cross. No imagery. Only Buddha. His mother was afraid to ask him or pry into his life, thinking she may open a can of worms. Perhaps he would write her a lengthy dissertation as to the origin of the statue and articulate his case as to why he was not choosing to root himself at the Presbyterian Church. He had followed his mom's lead in uprooting but not in replanting. What soil was he now in? If any at all?

Naturally, as any parent would do, his mom launched an investigation. Pastor John was his mother's new guru at Mitchell's Presbyterian. Pastor John was unknowingly roped in for an investigation. Pastor John thought it was to be a simple flock request. The goal of the mission was to find out where his spiritual loyalties resided. Out of the blue, his mom mentioned that Pastor John wanted to meet to talk with him. His walls went up. His radar system flashed. Radicalization alert! Had the peace and love and silence of Buddhism radicalized him? Had his visits and invitations to mosques in India and Eid celebrations radicalized him? Had his visit to the Golden Temple and the heart of Sikhism radicalized his worldview?

"The world is a big and beautiful place. I know you've done so much work in India. And, you know there are just so many paths for people to choose in life..." Pastor John's lighthearted chit-chat had taken a sharp right turn. A heat-seeking missile. He knew where this train was headed. Respectfully, he interrupted the Pastor by cutting the man off mid-sentence. He sat back on the sofa and looked at Pastor John. With great conviction, he replied, "I was born in Culpeper. I was baptized at the Methodist Church. I spent my childhood at that church. Born and raised a Christian. Never left. And since I never left, there's no choice to make."

The meeting ended. There were no follow-up questions. His Buddha statue remained as art, as symbolism, as an appreciation of others, and of humanity.

SEVENTEEN

JUNE 2014

The dirt trail was narrow and steep. The late spring air was crisp, even more so at the high elevation. White Spruce. Lodgepole Pine. Trembling Aspens. These were towering trees in the Shoshone National Forest nestled between Cody, Wyoming and the entrance to Yellowstone in the Rocky Mountains. Multiple sets of hooves kicked up dust as a group of five horses maneuvered a switchback in the trail, carefully ensuring their footing. The open vista into the valley below was sweeping and breathtaking. An eagle soar's above. A young female trail guide sat on the lead horse, followed by his second dad, his mother, Shilpa, and him.

His mother's other best friend was HIPAA, the medical privacy law. For many years, his mother had relied upon her faith in God, the love and support of his second dad, and advances in Stage IV treatments, including oral medications. For nine years, the treatments were able to manage her disease, avoid harsh chemo, avoid hair loss, and maintain a somewhat normal life. For nine years, she beat the odds. Much of the cancer had been removed, though spots remained in her bones. His mother had issues with loss of taste, minor weight gain, fatigue, and other chronic ailments. But to the world, even to close friends and family, most thought she had beat cancer, that she was cancer free. His mother was skillful at hiding, at hiding her pain.

Questions put forth to his mom were always deflected. It was never about her. It was always about the other person in the room. Their life. Their story. Their struggle. Their need. His mother shielded him from the nitty-gritty of oncology screenings, tests, visits, and side effects. His mother never wanted to burden anyone with her internal fears and suffering. True grace. True humility.

He and his mother were city slickers from the rural metropolis of Culpeper and hadn't sat on a horse in thirty years. Being scrunched up in an economy airline seat and hitting potholes in an auto-rickshaw with no suspension was nothing compared to riding on a horse all day in the Rockies. His ass hurt. His legs were bowed out. His muscles ached. He had trouble walking and sitting in the rental car for the trip to Yellowstone. His mother was sore but fared better than him. While they both loved and respected the horses and were spellbound by the landscapes, they both decided to opt out of entering the local rodeo competition in Cody.

HIS SOUL SPEAKS

A year after Wyoming, he was traveling across the Midwest in his black Chrysler 300. He was back from India on an annual road trip to visit exchange students placed from Branson to Galveston.

His Warden, Shilpa, was in her default position, stretched out and asleep in the backseat. His face was very somber. He appeared to be in a bit of a daze as he drove. His soul felt exceptionally heavy. There was a sadness deep within him. He felt as though there was something off with his mother. It weighed heavily on him. His mother, the optimist, the projection of happiness, hadn't said a word to him but his soul felt something. It was his intuition.

"We always knew there would come a time when the drug would stop working," his mother said.

He and his mother were alone in her living room. They were next to the picture window, the pond in the distance. He had the same face he did in the car on the interstate.

"Where else? The liver and where else?" he inquired.

His mother sensed his fear and didn't want to upset him. She shook her head and minimized the diagnosis. "Nowhere. There are two spots in the liver. I'm going to have to start chemo. Probably lose my hair."

He knew his mom. He knew his mom was not telling him everything. They both had a habit of keeping secrets from each other, secrets meant to protect the other's hearts.

"Mom. You're not telling me everything," he said as a tear began to well up.

"I am," she replied, seeking to deflect.

His face began to feel numb, and he started to shake his right leg. He became sterner as he sensed that his mom's light appeared dimmer. "You can't stop fighting! It's been nine years."

His mother leaned forward with tears in her eyes and said, "I won't. I'll never stop fighting. We got this."

A MOTHER'S LOVE

Five months later, he pulled up to his mom's house. The magical essence of fall had turned into the gloom of early winter. The grass was brown and the trees were barren. The warmth of the sun was minimal and the wind blew harder.

It was around noon when he entered the home from the side door through the garage. It was the door that opened into the kitchen. His mother was in the kitchen. His mother was wearing a pair of jeans that once used to fit her but were now baggy and droopy. His mother was wearing a warm fleece and a stylish black hat.

"Hey, Bud!" his mother said. She was smiling as she stood at the counter.

He can't remember the first time his mother called him "Bud," but she had been calling him that his entire life. He walked over and hugged his mother. His happiness was subdued. His mother was very thin; she was frail. He took a seat at the kitchen table.

His mother turned to him and said, "Everybody just loves this hat!"

"Really? I know you hate wearing hats, Mom."

His mother was not a hat person, but her hair was very thin and fine. The stylish black hat was special because he had gifted it to her for her birthday, and she was receiving compliments from people even though she shunned attention.

"I really love this. It's perfect," she said.

He had concern, worry, and fatigue all over his face. "What's your weight now?" he directly asked.

His mother had committed to not hiding anything from him. "123."

"That's three pounds less than last week," he stated.

His mother needed a diversion. "You know Sharon, in Florida. Well, her weight is 117, and she's doing just fine. You want a sandwich?"

He shook his head.

"It's tuna! From Tom's. Sure, you don't want a sandwich?"

Tom's Meat Market in town always whipped up the best tuna salad with the perfect amount of mayo, salt, pepper, celery, onion, and pickles all mixed in. He and his mother were not boujee. They loved nothing more than the simplicity of a great tuna salad sandwich or a summertime BLT (bacon-lettuce-tomato) with fresh garden tomatoes — one slice was all it took.

His mother didn't wait for any further response from him. His mother began to walk slowly over to the refrigerator. "I'll make you one."

He was having a hard time watching his mother, in such a frail form, and not letting his anguish show on his face. He was emotional and sensitive, but he knew his mom was as stubborn as he was and that she wanted to make that damn sandwich no matter how much pain she was in. He watched as his mother slowly took the container of tuna the short distance to the countertop. She took out two slices of brown bread and began to spread the tuna. The simplicity of making a tuna sandwich for her was a monumental process. His mother was utilizing all of the energy within her to make him a special sandwich — one that had an extra ingredient, the unconditional love of a mom.

His mind wandered back to his childhood. His mind traveled back to the home-cooked meals his mom prepared. Chicken Tetrazzini. So many casseroles. His mind traveled back to all of the fancy gourmet home-cooked creations that she made in her second life, with his second father, in the brick rambler on her happy homestead. Waldorf salads. Tenderloin pork roasts. The most delicious thick chili. His mind traveled back to the countless desserts his mother had made for him, especially the new discoveries. His favorite dessert creation was a blend of dark chocolate devil food cake layered with more chocolate and oozing with condensed milk. It was topped with whipped cream, and she added Heath toffee crunch. It was a mouthwatering deep dish cake creation that tasted like Heaven, especially after being chilled in the fridge.

His mother finished the sandwich but had forgotten one thing. "You want lettuce?"

He felt as though he had already burdened his mother enough. "No. That's perfect."

His mother didn't listen and began to walk back toward the fridge again. "It's better with lettuce."

He watched as his mother continued to do things, as she always had, her way. His mother was determined, by hook or crook, to hobble around the kitchen and find every ounce of strength within her body to make that tuna sandwich for him, her son, her only child. Even though he was forty.

A SHIFT IN PRIORITIES

When he was with his mother in Wyoming, she had spied on him in a gift store when he was looking at a horse sculpture. It was a sculpture of a horse looking at its colt with a carved piece of fence and an inscription that read, "Blaze Your Own Trail." His mother had seen him pick up the sculpture. His mother had secretly acquired it and surprised him with it as a gift at Christmas.

He stared out the window into his own backyard. He had tried. He had given life all he could. He had indeed blazed his own trail into a seemingly endless wilderness of failure. He felt guilty because he had been so focused on blazing his own trail overseas in India that he had missed so many small life moments with his mom.

He had dared to dream. He had dared to take risks. He had not followed the crowd. He had traded the American Dream for an Indian Dream. He always swam upstream, trying to avoid normalcy. He had tried to connect the dots from Culpeper to Los Angeles to Ahmedabad, but he was out of time. None of that mattered anymore. His only priority, from that day forward, was to spend as many moments as he could with his mom, the PhD in compassion, kindness, empathy, and love. His superhero.

EIGHTEEN

DECEMBER 21, 2015

He rushed to the local cancer center in Culpeper. His mother had been unable to eat and speak all weekend. He had tried to get her to go to the emergency room, but she wanted to wait until Monday morning. His mother had been in and out of the hospital so much that year that her body needed a break. His second father had taken his mom first thing Monday morning.

Trouble. An abrupt change of plans. He learned that his beloved mom needed to be transported to Charlottesville, to Martha Jefferson. Just a few days earlier, his mother had endured a second treatment of a new FDA-approved drug, Ibrance. The first round of Ibrance went okay. The second bottomed out.

He rushed into the hospital. It was around 10 a.m. His mother was seated upright in a medical chair and was connected to an IV drip. She was wearing her favorite black hat, the one he had gifted her. He noticed a look on his mom's face. Coming from her, it was a look he was unfamiliar with.

His mother always hated for him to see her in the hospital. She didn't want him to "waste" time sitting around a room and "worrying" about her. A typical reaction from his mother would have been, "Go on home. I know you got things to do, Bud. I'm fine. Don't worry about me."

Not on December 21st. She was different. Her eyes were different. Her face was different. Love. Light. His mother's face lit up when he arrived. She was happy to see him and wanted him there. He could feel her energy. It was an indescribable feeling. No words. A stillness. An unspoken Truth. An unspoken love. His mind didn't have time to analyze it. He had no questions. He was happy to be next to his sick mama, to be next to his frail mama, to be next to his hero...

A nurse approached and he inquired, "What is it?"

"She's neutropenic. 104 temp."

He was confused. "But she wasn't warm. Her head feels normal. What does that mean? Nutra...?" Confused.

The nurse was not very *nursey*. The nurse seemed to have not passed the compassion part of the nursing exam. "Her white count is severely low. She's going to have to be transported to Martha Jefferson. Placed in a room with restricted entry."

His heart was beating rapidly. "When? Will she go by ambulance or do we drive her?" He was really not in the mood for an American attitude at this moment. Tone. Eye language. Condescending. He was really not in the mood for bitchy White attitude.

"You'll drive her. I mean, you waited all weekend to bring her in!"

Excuse me? Come again? He was not a doctor. He was not a nurse. He was irritated. He didn't have time or focus to google medical terminology.

Insinuation. The idea that somehow, he was to blame for his mother's condition, her fever, and her low white cell count. Her neutropenia. He knew he had tried to push and push his mother to go to the hospital over the weekend.

The nurse left. His mother looked at him, her eyes drifting off to sleep and then opening again. His mom wasn't able to speak much, only mumbles. It was enough for him to understand her language. That human language. That mama language.

"She's okay. I've had her before."

He was shocked. His mom understood that he was pissed at the nurse. His mom was engaging in soft diplomacy to refocus his mind.

"Well, I don't like her attitude at all! Mom, I told you all weekend we needed to come." Before he could finish his sentence, his mother had drifted off to sleep, breathing very heavily and loudly.

He ran his hands through his hair and looked across the hospital ward. Blinking hospital lights. A small Christmas tree. Twinkling lights. The faces of staff and patients were a blur to him.

He sat with his mama, his sick mama.

ROOM 121 – MARTHA JEFFERSON

He, his second father, and Shilpa stand and listen to the oncologist.

Dr. Boyer. Warm. Kind. Compassionate. Dr. Boyer had been her oncologist for ten years. His mum was lying on the bed, hooked up to machines and wearing that black hat. Near the bed was a small trolley suitcase.

It was the third visit in four months. It was somewhat routine. The life of a cancer patient. His mom's throat was very sore and swollen.

"The bad news is that your mom has neutropenic sepsis. An infection and the low white count mean that her body has a harder time fighting it off. The good news is that, with the antibiotic drip, we will get rid of this. The nurse will give tiny doses of morphine to relieve the pain."

"How long? How much time for the antibiotic to work?" he interjected.

Dr. Boyer was a bit hesitant and preferred to be conservative. "We should plan on three to four days. Hopefully, have her home by Christmas."

Christmas. Best present ever.

CHRISTMAS MAGIC

Christmas brunch. His mama's special homemade Christmas Breakfast Brunch. To him, Christmas wasn't necessarily about Jesus or presents. Those were second and third on the list. First was Christmas Brunch.

His mom also marched to her own drum beat. No turkey. No ham. No Chinese takeout. Thanksgiving was just weeks earlier. Christmas morning meant the famous eleven o'clock brunch with the most mouth-watering and delicious sausage, egg, and cheese casserole piping hot out of the oven. There was a mountain of dripping and oozing monkey bread, perfected and customized over the decades.

His mother was an addict as well. She was addicted to seeing others smile, especially that inner circle of loved ones. While his mother was always one to shun attention, she did enjoy food compliments and reactions to her cooking. Even brand-new dishes throughout the year, which his mother would claim did not taste very good, had already been perfected and taste tested by her. He caught on long ago and understood that his mom loved food compliments. However, they were sometimes difficult to give because he was too busy licking the plate clean.

Things had been different that winter. His mother had given him a Christmas card three weeks early. A card with money in it. Those little things bothered him. They ate away at his soul. They hurt his heart.

Normally, his mom was on Christmas radar 365 days a year. She picked up little gifts and big gifts for everyone all throughout the year. Like a squirrel, she would hide them in various places and then sometimes forget what she bought and where she put it. His mother was in the moment. She was a giver, a healer, and a listener, but she was not always the most organized. Scribble notes. A list here and a list there. In the end, it all came together with bags and bags and wrapped gifts.

His mother was not a frivolous spender. She was an intuitive shopper. His mother would always have a main anchor gift, where the money was spent. But for the optics, for impact, for love, there were a dozen other gifts and a fully loaded stocking. And a toy. Yes, a toy. It didn't matter if he was twenty or thirty or forty years old, Christmas came with a small toy. A spaceship. A little Hess 18-wheeler oil tanker. A remote-control sports car. Piles and piles of torn paper, bows, bags, and boxes would litter the floor.

Therefore, a Christmas card with money in it three weeks early was a shock to his system. It wasn't about the money or the thought. It was about the tradition. His mum had been so ill in 2015 that she was unable to shop or even buy the ingredients for Christmas brunch. Days earlier, she had given him a list of the sacred ingredients to pick up. The stuff was in the fridge at home since his mom had every intention of cooking and baking Christmas morning. Come hell or high water. No Stage IV cancer bullshit was going to stop Christmas Brunch. Signs of Christmas Magic were all around him. Culpeper. Charlottesville. Martha Jefferson.

However, a heaviness consumed his being. He tried to smile and pretend everything was alright, but his superhero was on morphine.

SICK AND STUBBORN

His mother hated for anyone to know that she was in the hospital. She never wanted a stream of visitors or to bother anyone. She wouldn't even tell her own sister Peggy. She didn't want to worry anyone.

His mother had a rule. No overnights. Not for him. Not for his second father. No overnights. It was a rule that was respected. Well, tolerated.

A hospital routine was in place. His second father would arrive early, at seven, and spend the entire day until around six. His second father would then drive an hour back to Culpeper to feed the dog, an Australian heeler rescue mix named Bree. Bree had six acres to roam, with an underground electric fence, but Bree had trained his second father that they must both walk together, at designated times.

As for him, he would often take care of work, manage what he could of his business in the morning, and arrive at the hospital around lunch or early afternoon and stay late. A tag team effort. Diplomatic. Approved.

Shilpa. Shilpa. Shilpa. Shilpa was hit or miss. Shilpa did not like to visit the hospital, especially long visits. If his mom was nearby in Culpeper, it was easy to drop in and out. However, Charlottesville was an hour away and Shilpa was a self-anointed Queen. She claimed to be afraid to be in the house alone in the dark. They had lights. He paid the light bill. In December, the winter darkness came at 4:30 p.m.

"Go or stay. Your choice. But I'm telling you I have no idea when I am coming back. Mom is sick. And I don't want you calling and texting a hundred times," he said very sternly to Shilpa.

It was a rare moment for him, but he was anxious. He was worried. He was focused on his sick mama. He was hoping to minimize collateral damage at home with the Warden.

Ultimately, Shilpa decided to go with him that day.

HER WAY

It was close to nine. His second dad had reluctantly headed back home. Shilpa was pacing around, bored. His mother was sedated on morphine and was drifting in and out of sleep. The room was very dim. The television was off. His mother's cell phone was sitting on a table, unreachable. He sat, watching her.

She opened her eyes and mumbled, "Go on home. You got things to do."

He saw Shilpa in the distance, rolling her eyes, pressuring him to leave. He ignored Shilpa. The hospital had lights. He stood to organize the room as he had always done for his mom.

"Want me to turn the TV on?" he asked.

His mother shook her head no.

He was a bit shocked. "*The Voice* is on. Your favorite!"

His mother shook her head no.

"Want me to turn the light on? The yellow light. It's really too dark in here."

His mother shook her head no. She looked at him. "Did you bring those cards?"

The cancer center in Culpeper had given his mom many handmade cards with messages made by local kids.

"Yeah. I put them in your suitcase." He grabbed the colorful Christmas cards designed by imaginative young strangers with heartfelt messages of hope and well wishes.

His mother tried to reach for the food tray but couldn't.

"What do you want, Mama? Here." He pulled the tray over and spread out the special cards. He realized that his mother was still wearing the black beret-style hat. "Take your hat off, Mama! Ain't nobody coming."

His mother smiled and shook her head no.

He was surprised again. It was very peaceful, but it was very unusual. "You don't want to take your hat off?"

His mother just smiled.

"How's your bed? You want me to raise it?"

She nodded yes.

He pushed the button and the clunky electronic bed tilted up just a bit, just enough for her to see the Christmas cards.

He grabbed her cell phone, a flip phone that was rarely used. "You want to call Dad? Tell him good night."

His mother shook her head no.

No. His heart sank. She always wanted to talk to his second father. Not tonight. He overruled his mama and pushed back. "Mom. Here, I'm calling. Just say something."

The phone rang. His second father answered. His mom, in her weak, frail, and feeble position, in numbed pain, chose to be light-hearted. She chose to joke, to project rays of light and hope to those she loved. "I'm coming home tomorrow!"

She hung up and looked at Shilpa. His mother handed Shilpa an empty cup and wanted her to go and get some ice. A distraction. He realized his mom was politely wishing to have Shilpa depart the hospital room for a moment, to give them some alone time. A boy and his mama.

She turned and looked into his eyes. It was a nurturing look. "I'm gonna to keep fighting." Code words.

He was filled with emotion. He stood and grabbed a hold of his mom's hand. "Love you, Mama."

She smiled, the biggest of the day. "I love you too!"

He gently squeezed her hand a couple of times before releasing it. "You get some rest. I'll be back first thing in the morning."

NINETEEN

DECEMBER 22, 2015

What? Where was she? What? Where was Mama? No. Who was that old woman? He stood outside of Room 121 at Martha Jefferson. He saw an elderly woman lying in the same hospital bed where, just a few hours before, he held his mother's hand.

It was the same room. The same room his mother told him she was going to keep fighting. A dream. A nightmare. Who was that old woman? Why was she in his mama's hospital bed? Where was Mama?

Wake up. Wake up.

He remembered his mother's final smile. The stylish black hat. The sounds of the hospital hallway around him began to blur, fade, and mute. He stood in the doorway of Room 121. Shattered. Empty. Frozen. Numb. Hallow. Confused. He wanted his mama back.

Her shoes. Her glasses. Her fancy black hat. The little earrings she was wearing. Her watch. Her clothes. Her little cheap-ass flip phone. The colorful Christmas cards designed by Culpeper kids. He stood in an empty waiting area, staring at her little suitcase. He was trying to comprehend the world in which he now lived.

Wake up. Wake up. Wake up.

Where was Mama? She had to keep fighting. His mother was at the hospital, in a room, in a place that had never crossed his mind. Hospitals were for healing. Get well soon. Flowers. Balloons. Trained professionals. Lifesavers. Hospitals were supposed to fix people. It was not even Christmas yet. All the ingredients for Christmas brunch were still in the fridge. He would prepare it. He would figure it out. Christmas was not Christmas without Mama. The doctor said she would be home by Christmas. Where was Mama?

Mama was dead. Mama died. Mama died, alone, in Room 121. His hero. His superhero. His little PhD. His unconditional supporter. His only audience that ever mattered. His mother was no more.

Time had stopped. The world was frozen. His mama was gone.

THE HOURS BEFORE

He had driven home the night before to wrap some Christmas gifts and finally went to bed around 2:30 a.m. His phone rang sometime after 5:30 a.m. He was jolted out of bed and disoriented when he answered the phone and heard his second father's voice on the other end.

Crying, his second father said to him, "Mama's gone."

He fell onto the floor, screaming. "What! What! What!"

He had never heard his second father cry before. Marines didn't do those sorts of things. He stood and aimlessly walked into the bathroom. Trembling. Shaking. Convulsing.

His second father informed him, "Dr. Boyer just called. He went to the hospital."

His mother, the PhD in kindness, compassion, empathy, and love had died at 4:07 a.m., seven hours after he last had seen her, seven hours after he was the last person to hold her hand, seven hours after she had told him she loved him. His mother had just turned 68. The light of his life was gone.

He arrived at his second father's house soon after. Shilpa and Pastor John were with his second father inside the house. It was an unusually mild December morning, warm enough to be outside in a light jacket. Daybreak revealed clouds, fog, and dampness from an overnight shower. He walked along the bank of trees in a far corner of the property.

His heart was in a million pieces. His hyperactive INFJ mind was blank. He was a shell of himself. In between tears, he would look up toward the sky and scream toward God. "Why? Why now? Why?"

His mouth was parched. He felt a sense of vertigo. He had no direction. He was lost at sea. His life had changed forever. Every second. Every minute. Every day. Every month. Every year. Every decade. For the rest of his life...

His mother would no longer be there. He wasn't prepared. Could anyone ever really be prepared? The jolt of loss. The jolt of unbearable grief. The finality of death. He wasn't prepared. Lost at sea. Lost in a wilderness. Lost.

HIS MAMA KNEW

His mother wrote the script. His mother wrote the last scene of the last chapter in the story of her life on Earth. His mother said she was coming home "tomorrow." His mother's final act was as simple as it was profound. She was, after all, true to character. The most genuine soul anyone could ever meet. His mother's final act was to protect the two people she loved the most from being present during her last moments. To protect him and his second father from gut-wrenching heartache. His mother orchestrated her last day on Earth, her way. Selfless.

He realized that his mother had died wearing his black hat. He realized why his mother did not want to take the hat off. He realized why his mother did not want the television on or the light or any routine that was normally done. He realized why his mother had refused to speak to his second father on the phone that night. He realized why his mother had told him the very words that he wanted to hear, "I'm gonna keep fighting." He realized that his mother knew that her time on Earth was nearing an end. He realized that his mother had had the final word.

His mother hated the idea of hospice. To her, hospice was a proclamation to the world that a person was dying. His mother did not want a trail of visitors coming to her little homestead to spend time with her because she was sick and nearing the end. His mother hated the very idea of having loved ones agonizing in a hospital room to watch her die. His mother wanted everyone, especially those closest to her, to live each day as normal as possible.

His mother had made peace with God. She did it her way. She wrote the script.

THAT SOUL THING. AGAIN.

Something unusual happened when he left the hospital the night before for that hour's drive back to Culpeper. His anxiousness. His stress. His worry.

His fatigue. All of it seemed to wane, if only for a moment. It was all replaced by a deep sense of calmness. An inner peace that radiated from his core being, from his soul. It was such a palpable feeling. Peace. Quietness. Stillness.

He had just spent the entire day with his mama. And as fucked up as it was — Sepsis. Words he had never heard before. Morphine drips. Warning signs. Physical discomfort. Hospital food. That bitchy nurse with an attitude — as fucked up as the day was on the surface, the Truth was it was a beautiful day.

He spent the entire day with his mom. There were rays of lightheartedness. Smiles. Jokes. Laughter. Wisdom. A different kind of Christmas. His mother had wanted him with her, all day, every moment, until late at night. Then, she wanted him to go. A beautiful day. Those were the images that rained across his mind as he drove home that night.

Until suddenly... just like that... a disconnect. A feeling he had never felt before. The cutting of a cord. A powerful disconnect at his soul level. Had his mind known his mother had hours left, he would have turned around and sped back to the hospital. But his mind was distracted by the beautiful moments of the day. His mind was protecting him. His mother had filled his mind with those images on her last day. But his soul was speaking to him. His soul was disconnecting from his mama, his nurturer.

A chapter was closing.

BLINDSIDED

At first, Shilpa seemed to have stepped up to the plate. Shilpa prepared the Christmas morning brunch for the first time. It was surprising. It was kind. It was unusual. Shilpa was scheduled to fly back to India in a week, in early January. His ticket had been booked for the end of February. Both were booked and paid for. It had not been a routine year. Planning was difficult due to his mom's health. He wanted to stay in America as long as he could to be with her, but he did have commitments in India for his business, most of which he could manage on his laptop.

A few years prior, Shilpa had lost her father. It was his first real up close and personal experience with loss and grief. Different cultures. Different belief systems. Different process. He didn't have a particularly close or warm relationship with his father-in-law. It was very cordial. His personal response to Shilpa's loss was to do what he could to be caring, supportive, and provide normalcy and continuity in life. He organized, hired vehicles, and paid for a trip for Shilpa's family to carry the ashes of her father back to the native place where her father was born. It was a picturesque small town in the lush green hills of Maharashtra.

He had organized an Indian police motorcycle escort out of respect for a career in law enforcement. The motorcycle cop led the vehicles to the river. He and the officer were the ones who actually spread the ashes into the river. He was doing what he could.

That year marked ten years since the Bandra courthouse wedding in Mumbai. He had taken Shilpa to Switzerland, a place she had wanted to see, only to be hurt again by the secret phone whispers in hotel lobbies. Later that year, a cruise was booked, a first-ever cruise to the Caribbean. He kept things normal and continued to check the boxes of life. Duties. Shilpa grieved for a minute. He wasn't judging. He had never experienced grief.

"I'm telling you right now. If you don't sponsor my family and bring them to America, I will divorce you!" Shilpa ranted.

His mother had been dead less than a week. He was lost, broken, and in unbearable pain.

"I will divorce you! Don't think I won't!" Shilpa stomped around the kitchen, angry, screaming at him.

She was kicking him while he was at his lowest point ever. It was out of the blue, out of nowhere. He was blindsided. He sat on the sofa, trying to process what Shilpa was saying. Her actions. Her anger. Her agenda. His mother was dead. Shilpa's antics, during a moment of his fragility, unlocked a door he thought had closed long ago. Anxiety. Irrational Fear. Those early days of the relationship. In Mumbai. He thought Shilpa had changed.

Shilpa immediately hatched a plan and began pushing her agenda. "I can't stay here, in this house. I want to go back to India right now!" exclaimed Shilpa.

His mother died. He was comprehending loss. He was blank. He was lethargic. The last thing he wanted to do was board a plane to India. His mother was dead. To appease Shilpa, he suggested a compromise. "Can you stay two weeks? For me. I'll change my ticket. We can travel back together. It's only two weeks. Dad is here. Everyone is here. I just can't rush to India right now. I need a couple weeks."

"No! Book my ticket." Shilpa refused. Shilpa refused to compromise, to suggest a counter-offer. Instead, Shilpa stonewalled him.

It was a simple request in an hour of his greatest need. It was his lowest point in forty years. As a husband, he simply asked for two weeks. He asked her to be an emotional support for two weeks, but Shilpa refused.

His mother was dead. The Celebration of Life was over. He was threatened with divorce and abandoned. He thought Shilpa had changed. He was confused. Who exactly was he married to?

Cracks in the façade.

TWENTY

A FEW
WEEKS LATER

The winter sun beamed down onto Calhoun's Country Hams, the official name of Tom's Meat Market. The shop was located on East Street behind the post office. It was around the corner from the Spanish super mercado, beside a Black Barbershop, near the micro-brewery, and down the hill from the gourmet eateries on Davis Street. It was close to the train station, the town "LOVE" sign, and the contemporary loft apartments.

Calhoun's main business was not tuna sandwiches, but since his mother had passed, he'd stopped by several times a week to pick up lunch — a tuna on wheat, toasted, with lettuce, a bag of chips, and a Diet Coke.

He had no idea what grief looked like or what it was supposed to feel like. He was moving a lot slower and noticed himself feeling things. He now took the time to feel things, time that he had never taken before. If his mind were a computer, grief was the reformat button. It was the reset to factory settings button, the one that erased all of his ideas, plans, goals, and dreams. He would pick up his lunch and drive nearby to the National Cemetery. He would park his car on top of the hill overlooking the rows of sharp and unformed white stone markers. Near the car was the flagpole with the black POW flag that often whipped in the wind. The sound of the rope and metal banging against the side of the pole broke the stillness and silence. On those cold winter days, he sat in his car eating his tuna sandwich.

The beauty of small-town life was the simplicity and the fact that everything was nearby. He didn't have to fight twenty lanes of traffic on the 405 to make it to Tom's before the tuna runs out and rush across the urban sprawl to the cemetery. He didn't have to wait for an autorickshaw, negotiate a flat rate or meter rate, and breathe diesel fumes at a crowded roundabout.

Culpeper had tourism for history, for the mountains and hiking, for the wineries, and for the boutique shops. There were upscale eateries on Main Street with European, Thai, and Indian cuisines. Or perhaps a sumptuous filet mignon supper in a notable landmark building constructed in the 1800s. City folks came to Culpeper to escape the urban jungle, decompress, and have some zen time in another world. Folks who wanted to be removed from the stress that came along with upward mobility, the larger paycheck, higher taxes, and chasing the American Dream.

Folks paid lots of money to experience the life his mother got to live every day. His mama lived and breathed Culpeper County. She dedicated her life to living and serving and being kind. His mother had a rich and abundant life, a life filled with human moments and human experiences. She never shot a gun. She never smoked. She rarely drank, if New Year's Eve counted as rarely.

She experimented with Facebook but hated it. "Just get rid of this. How can I get rid of this? I don't want to see it!" His mother was not a fan of the newsfeed, the ego drama, and the pettiness of posts.

His mama personified the best spirit of America. She welcomed all. She was open-hearted. She was willing to learn and grow. She lent a hand to those in need.

WHAT ARE THE ODDS?

His mother had just died. He still resided in ADX Willow Tree. His "compassionate" Warden had abandoned him. He was alone in every sense. Deep within his spirit, he always knew that his childhood experience in the Willow Tree would never see the light of day as long as his mother was alive.

He knew his mom. He knew that she would not show it but would blame herself. It was a burden he refused to let her carry. She was his hero. His secrets were his only. No one knew. No one knew what was in his mind, these secrets that were locked away.

And then it happened... just like that. A nudge. Two serendipitous synchronicities that were so profound, so jarring to his mind, that a door would begin to open to the possibility of God's existence.

THE VISITATION BOOK

There had been a Celebration of Life service for his mother. Hundreds attended. An overflow crowd. He stood and greeted mostly everyone. Others had made eye contact with him, to send condolences through an expression.

He stood alone at the funeral home for as long as it took to meet everyone who was in line.

Weeks later, he was in a reflective mood. He sat on the floor of his home office with the visitation book. He opened the book. What? He froze. What? Confusion. Was this for real? Shock. He looked up to the ceiling. "Are you kidding me?"

The very first name in the book. Number one. First. Out of hundreds of names... It was glaring back at him. Adam's Father. Adam. The same Adam who had stolen his innocence and stripped away his childhood. The same Adam who had planted the seed in his mind that would grow into ADX Willow Tree and influence his choices, decisions, and self-worth. His heart was beating fast. He looked around the room. His mind was racing.

He knew that Adam was dead. He had heard, through the small-town grapevine years ago, that Adam had died of a drug overdose. Confused. Why would Adam's father show up at his mom's funeral? Odd. Maybe, maybe not.

He hadn't seen Adam's father in over thirty years. Confused. He thought back to all the people at the funeral. He scanned through all the names in the visitor book and remembered virtually everyone. He remembered either shaking hands with them or seeing them from a distance. But not Adam's father.... the first name. Did Adam's father come early and leave? Did Adam's father stay for the service? Confused.

Adam and Adam's children were living at Adam's father's house, the place where Adam overdosed. What kind of house was it? Those kids. Those grandkids. He hoped they had not suffered. Confused. Why did Adam's father not greet him or wait in line to see him? Overthinking. Triggered. Perhaps.

THE LITTLE COUNTRY CHURCH

Curious, he decided to go online to see if he could find Adam's obituary. His jaw dropped. Adam was buried at the little country church next to the cornfield outside of Culpeper. The same little Presbyterian church his mother had transferred to years earlier. A second coincidence.

He knew the world was small but not that small. All the little dots were connected. What were the odds that his mom would get cancer, get ticked off with the Methodist Pastor for rather less-than-churchy behavior, pull up decades of stakes, and relocate to a tiny ass church in a cornfield? The same church he attended a little to make his mom happy. After all, he was a CINO. He had always run away from God. He felt he wasn't worthy. He was burdened with shame and guilt. He thought those days in the treehouse were buried within him forever. His mom died and his past showed up.

"God, is that you?"

REACHING OUT

"I lost my mom about six months ago. I think I'm a narcissist (self-diagnosed). I don't know which way is up or down. I have no idea what is normal and what is not normal. I'm forty and I've never spoken to anyone, my entire life, about what's in my head."

He sat, for the very first time, in a warmly decorated office studio. A splash of artwork on the walls. A small bookshelf. A few plants. A large window. He was dressed in his trademark jeans and a Henley. It was his very first meeting with Elaine, a professional clinical social worker.

He was filled with heaviness. He had already begun to diagnose himself. He figured perhaps two or three sessions, tops. He was fully expecting Elaine to, in an artful way, tell him that he was a really bad guy, that he needed to adjust, to be a better person, and that he was just too sensitive.

ABUSE, HUH?

Emotional abuse? WTF? The idea that he was abused, aside from the treehouse, the drugging, and rape in Mumbai, was foreign to him. He believed in people. He believed in the goodness of humanity. He trusted Shilpa. He believed what she told him. He wasn't a psychologist. In his mind, he was the broken and damaged one. The defective piece. In his mind, he was the shameful one who escaped his pain with escorts and in massage parlors.

Psychological abuse. Huh? It hit him like a ton of bricks. The concept of an intentional pathological mindset of perpetuating emotional abuse to another, resulting in traumatic injury to the brain, including anxiety, chronic depression, and post-traumatic stress disorder.

Huh? He was beginning to awaken, awaken to the reality of his marriage, the reality of his life crossing paths with Shilpa fifteen years prior. The treehouse and the Mumbai club gave him shame; however, those events did not make him jumpy, jittery, anxious, fearful, and looking over his shoulder... but Shilpa did.

MOMENT OF CRYSTALLIZATION

At some point, a mental light switched on. Awareness. A blindfold was removed. A connection. An initial understanding. He began to realize that ADX Willow Tree wasn't just about the treehouse. He began to realize he was caught in a psychological web of deception and betrayal that was far more complex than anything he could fathom. His situational awareness changed. He could now see it. He could see the rabbit hole he had fallen into. He had no clue. Never had a clue. A maze. A web. A psychological Hell. Dumbfounded. How did he allow it? He was an independent mind, a thinker. He escaped Pestle Weed College and advocated for teachers who he felt were verbally abused.

How did he end up in the black hole?

All his life, he tended to avoid men. Sure, he had guy friends. But men in general. Sports. Those gang showers. He hated the demeaning gang showers in P.E. class. The idea of being forced to shower naked in front of other boys made him physically ill and sick to his stomach. Boy Scout camp. Jamboree. Gang showers.

He would shower late at night, in total darkness, with his little flashlight. No one was in the shower at that time. He was always more comfortable around women. Women were more compassionate, empathetic, and kind. Certainly, there were serial killers who were women, but generally speaking, women were even smarter than men. Subconsciously, he allowed himself to believe that women were safer than men. He never understood what kind of sign flashed on his forehead inviting abuse.

Women were safe. Nurturing. However, Shilpa wasn't a "traditional woman," whatever that meant. But emotional abuse? Targeted abuse? He realized that he had been so guarded against men that it left him vulnerable, vulnerable to a female predator.

Emotional abuse wasn't about one thing. An affair. A secret. A lie. Emotional abuse was about pathology, in which life was a game and the human mind was a rag doll to be toyed with for personal gain. Emotional abuse was about power and control over his emotions without him ever knowing. Emotional abuse was about the systematic disarmament of any mental defense mechanisms he had, should he choose to attempt to walk away. Emotional abuse was about living in a world that did not exist, a Truth to which his mind denied. Every word, every single conversation from day one.

Shilpa had not changed. He had changed. Shilpa had changed him. Shilpa had targeted him to control him. Emotional abuse was about breaking his mind.

TWENTY-ONE

DAY #26

His heart is heavy as he winds his way down Route 22, the Teton Pass Highway, into the valley and Jackson Hole, Wyoming. The Tetons hold a special place in his heart. He had visited once as a kid and the second time was on that horseback adventure with his mum and second father. This is his third visit. He enters town as a very fragile man, deeply conflicted about his choices and decisions. He is doubting himself every other moment, questioning everything.

He opens the door to his room at the Super 8, connects to the Wi-Fi, and opens his laptop. He reads an email from his father.

This is the only line he sees, "It's been over a week and I haven't heard anything from Shilpa," as all others are blurred out in his mind. Triggered.

His heart begins to beat rapidly. He starts to feel faint. He begins to feel nauseous. His mind races with so many thoughts.

Increasing panic. A nervous tick. He is frightened. He is afraid.

ABSORBING THE PAIN OF OTHERS

Suicide. The ultimate escape for a human being. The idea of being trapped. An escape from an individual's very own version of ADX Willow Tree. It pains him greatly. Life is a gift. Life has potential. Life has light. The idea that a person would suffer in silence to the point where a decision was made to trade in hope for an escape always shakes him to his core.

Bend, Oregon has shaken him. Rock bottom. No matter what has happened in his life, his mind always believes in tomorrow, in a new day, in hope. However, he knows that Shilpa is extremely impulsive. He remembers that nearly two decades earlier, when he tried to free himself from Shilpa and the relationship, she paced on the rooftop of an eight-story building in Mumbai, potentially jumping to end her life.

At that time, he had ended the relationship for the second time and was in Mumbai, visiting friends, Jaideep and Priya. Shilpa's inner radar had stalked him. She had shown up at the flat, creating a hostage situation. He hid in Jaideep's bedroom in the tiny Bandra flat while Shilpa waited in the hallway for hours and hours, pleading, crying, and getting angry.

Everyone's lives at that moment were turned upside down by the chaos. He refused to meet Shilpa. He didn't trust himself, his emotional self. Cue the manipulation. Shilpa began to tug at the heartstrings of Jaideep's wife, Priya. Woman to woman. To reel him back, just to talk. Shilpa understood that she possessed the kryptonite, an ability to leech onto his emotional fabric and take his power, all of his emotional energy. All she required was to get him, face-to-face.

Shilpa marched to the rooftop of the high-rise, knowing fully well that she had dropped hints of suicide before. Shilpa had said she was not able to live without him and that he was everything to her.

He began to worry, worry about Shilpa. He eventually caved and walked out on the rooftop where he saw a very shy, sheepish, and apologetic Shilpa.

Break-up attempt #2 aborted. He allowed Shilpa to contact him again. The slippery slope of the mind. He didn't want anyone to be hurt.

AT ODDS WITH HIS ATTORNEY

"Tell her to go ahead and do what she has to do!" boldly proclaimed his attorney.

He stared at his lawyer, dumbfounded. So cold. So emotionless. His attorney's advice regarding his concerns about Shilpa's potential suicidal nature was to just blow it off, to not give a shit. Huh?

He obviously wasn't qualified to be a lawyer due to the fact that he had a heart and soul. During his one-year separation period, within the 12,000 pages of Viber chat messages Shilpa had sent him, she had made several coded references to ending her life, to "proving" her love. Shilpa had even taunted him saying, "Don't worry. You won't be in any trouble." It was both a code and a taunt.

Living in India, every day there seemed to be an article in the newspaper about suicide. India wasn't gun-obsessed America. Jumping was common. Teens jumped off buildings due to poor exam results.

When he was traveling once to Delhi, his train was halted in a tiny village in Rajasthan. A crowd was gathered on the platform, a few cars behind his. A man. A farmer. A local. In two parts. Upper torso and lower. Sliced by the train wheel. Suicide. Gut-wrenching suicide. A split-second decision.

All night long, on the way to Delhi, all he could think about was that man, that farmer, who was no more. Why had that farmer lost hope?

It pained him greatly.

A HEAVY QUESTION

"Are you prepared for that? If Shilpa decides to end her life?"

No one had asked him such a question before. However, his friend and former Mumbai neighbor had. Directly. The same neighbor who had warned him against getting married to Shilpa. A seed was planted in his mind. Guilt for leaving. A sense of responsibility for Shilpa's well-being.

So consumed with worry, he had shared his fears with his counselor, Elaine. She was also concerned, from a distance, about Shilpa's ultimate mental health. Shilpa had hired her own competing counselor, to spin a narrative, and had had two sessions. Elaine suggested that he think about a few joint sessions with Shilpa and her therapist in order to diffuse the situation and inform the other psychologist. The goal was not couple's counseling to save a marriage. The goal was couple's counseling to ensure a life. He wasn't thrilled with the idea, but he agreed to follow though as he did not want Shilpa to harm herself.

Deer in the headlights. Shilpa's female counselor had an expression of utter shock and deep concern. His arrival at the session had turned things upside down. Shilpa had previously painted a rosy picture of marriage, that she had simply returned to India after his mom died to work. Shilpa claimed to have been abandoned and "thrown out into the streets." Shilpa claimed it was all a misunderstanding.

Shilpa's counselor could sense his authenticity and genuine fears. He trembled as he spoke. The tone of the meeting shifted abruptly to prioritizing Shilpa's welfare, emergency contact numbers, and an action plan should those thoughts arise in her.

Elaine had advised him to stay strong and to confront Shilpa in session with three of his concerns. Confronting Shilpa was something he sought to avoid at all costs. He wanted to avoid the fallout.

Concern #1: Threats of suicide. Concern #2: Who were the men on those suspicious calls for over a decade? Concern #3: Where exactly was Shilpa for one year after his mom passed? India was a large nation and Shilpa hated living for long periods in her family's small Mumbai flat. Where was Shilpa exactly?

Shilpa was unable to respond with anger and aggression since she had to maintain her façade in front of the counselor. The result was a full-blown panic attack. Anxiety of her own creation. Shilpa abruptly stood, walked out of the session, and quit counseling cold turkey. "This is not my culture! In India, I never heard of this. Why would I go and talk and talk and talk? What's the point? I don't have any problem!"

INSTRUCTIONS

He responded to his father's mail. He wrote, "This is very serious. Please go to my house tomorrow morning early and knock on the door. I am concerned for Shilpa's safety. She has threatened to kill herself in the past. If she does not answer, I need you to contact the police. If you do see her, please DO NOT tell her that I sent you."

He was trying to navigate No Contact and his trauma bond. He knew that he could not, in any way, let Shilpa know that he was worried. Otherwise, there would be emotional escalation designed to lure him back.

He understood that in an abusive relationship there never would be closure. A final conversation. A final letter. A friendship. Mutual respect. Abuse was a cycle that had to be broken. The energetic yin and yang. The hamster-wheel. Going full No Contact was a bloody psychological nightmare. His mind was used to the drama. His mind was used to being punched around like a rag doll. His mind was used to being owned by the Warden. Confronting a traumatic bond was war. An emotional war within, a war no one else could see. A war that only he could fight. No physical scars. No bruises. No police report. He was the man. He was supposed to be tough, not to have feelings. No Contact was his antibody. It was essential to repel the dark energies of Shilpa.

AN EMOTIONAL RIPTIDE

He parks his car at a vista point with the snow-capped Tetons in the distance. The parking lot is empty. The sky is cloudy. The highest peaks are, at times, hidden by the clouds. Guilt consumes him. The guilt of wanting to be free, of wanting to be happy. Tears begin to stream down his face as his mind goes into an unthinkable place of darkness.

He feels as if Shilpa has ended her life. He feels as though Shilpa's lifeless body is somewhere in the home, the middle-class American Dream. It is the box that he has worked so hard to check off the list, to follow the crowd, to make his mother proud, to be like everyone else, to be responsible, and to set aside his own pursuits. He wonders how she did it... He wonders if she had been in any pain. He wonders which room she is in. He wonders why it has to be this way. Why?

He blames himself. He feels as though he is selfish. His sense of shame is suffocating. He wishes that he had just gone back home to restart their life. Maybe his life wasn't so bad after all. His shame reaches a crescendo. His body becomes heavy with fatigue. A stress like no other.

He loathes himself for wanting to pursue happiness. He doesn't have a right to be happy. The majestic Tetons are a blur. He realizes he is doing exactly as he had feared. He stayed with Shilpa because he feared being abandoned and now, he was leaving. Shameful.

He drives back to the Super 8, unhappy with his existence. And then it is over. Two words. "She's fine!" his father writes the following morning. 18 hours of hell. Agony. Anxiety. Worry. Doubt. Fear. Grief. Pain. Nausea. Panic. Unable to soak in and absorb the beauty of Wyoming. Emotional abuse. A psychological web.

TWENTY-TWO

FINAL WEEKS OF 48 STATE JOURNEY

He feels as though he is on a backlot set at Universal Studios. At any moment, he may be caught up in a shoot-out with Wild Bill Hickok. 1876. No cars. No horses. No stagecoaches. No camels or cows. No monkeys. Only snowfall. Large phat flakes.

It's midnight in Deadwood, South Dakota. It's April, and there are six inches on the ground. A few saloon lights flicker. The neon glow of tiny casinos flashes. He loves the silence of snowfall. He loves how what normally would be background noise, becomes amplified.

He hears the sound of a saloon door swinging open. He hears the sound of laughter from a drunk couple, stumbling out into the snow. They were the only other people out.

Isolated sounds surrounded by silence. He is dressed in snow boots, jeans, his Henley, and a winter jacket. There is a childlike wonder, an innocence about snowfall. There is a purity that seems to cover the imperfections of life. After the emotional train wreck in Jackson Hole, he's happy to be a kid in the snow.

WHAT A FOOL!

It is as if the road signs of his 48-day journey are flashing, warning him of treachery. The South Dakota storm is vicious. Perhaps it is amplified because he is not local but a Southerner. He is appreciative to be in an SUV, with heating, as opposed to an actual stagecoach.

He realizes that Northern Plains Americans are indeed hearty souls. The winds whip out of Canada. Sheets of ice cover parts of the freeway. Trucks and cars are in ditches. In the median, spun out.

He finally reaches America's icebox, Minnesota. Exhausted. He longs for spring as he navigates the simple task of getting gas. The ice chunks on his car grew by the hour. Everything crunched.

The wind. The wind from the North Pole howls. Snow has blown into the credit card slot. He blows that out first. It is now eight degrees. The pump is frozen into the slot. He normally loves road trips, the longer the better. However, there is just something ominous about the entire day and it is more than just the weather. His soul has picked up on an uneasiness. He isn't fearful, just uneasy. It is that 6th sense thing he gets when it's too quiet...

And then he gets his answer. The other shoe has dropped. What commenced weeks earlier in Ocean Springs, Mississippi with divorce papers in the process to be served and his last communication with Shilpa prior to enforcing No Contact...

World War III. It is the launch of a war that he has dreaded. Cue the anxiety. Cue the rapid heartbeat. Cue the nervous ticks. Cue the overthinking mind. Cue the worst-case scenario mental replays.

What a fool he was, crying and worrying in Jackson Hole. What a fool he was, thinking that Shilpa had taken her life. What a fool he was for quietly hiring an attorney, in another adjacent town, thinking he could keep things discreet and avoid the grapevines of small-town gossip. What a fool he was for actually thinking he had rights, basic human rights, and the freedom to pursue a new direction in life. What a fool. A bloody fool.

Emotional Abuse whiplash. Advanced Placement. His mother's one and only divorce took six months and cost less than a thousand dollars. One lawyer. What a fool he was for thinking that perhaps he could follow a similar path. Nope. Not a chance.

Soon after checking into the Super 8 and thawing his body and mind out, he learns that Shilpa has retained Katherine Davis, an F5 tornado, the most ruthless divorce attorney in Culpeper County, and a woman with a reputation for cleaning house.

World War III.

SIMPLE LIVING, HIGHER THINKING. NO.

It should be simple. It could be simple. He isn't the first person to ever seek a divorce. He has not followed the cookie-cutter life plan approach in pursuit of the elusive American Dream. The assets are clear-cut. A house with a mortgage. One house. Two cars. A small savings account, viewable with a magnifying glass. One life insurance policy on his life. No children. No 401K. No IRA. No stock portfolio.

He has been living the tale of two economies, one foot in Indian rupees and one foot in US dollars. He prefers rupees since his life is much more economical and comes with lots of bells and whistles. His higher-thinking mind has accrued wealth in life experience, heart projects, and out-of-the-box visionary pursuits. However, according to the United States personal income tax bracket, he often lives in "poverty." The poverty line in America equates to a solid upper-middle-class life in India with a large flat, a car, a driver, a cook, a housekeeper, and lots of travel.

From the beginning, he wasn't interested in material items, only regaining control of his mind. He sought to avoid conflict. He is prepared to walk away from what minimal possessions he has acquired in an image-conscious glossy and flashy world.

No. No. No. Can't do that. "You've worked hard. You deserve something." He was told this over and over again by his attorney, his counselor, his energy healer, his family, and his second father. Everyone who cared about him said that he needed something and that he shouldn't just walk away empty-handed.

He relented, a little. His lawyer had drafted a basic settlement agreement proposal from the beginning. A 50/50 distribution of assets.

"Send me a list of everything you want. Material items. Furniture. We will include it in the draft," his attorney said.

His American house did have nice furniture in it but that does not matter to him. He submits a list of only two items to his lawyer. 1) A formal china set from his grandmother (Mum's side) and 2) A silver tea/snack tray that his mother had gifted on a wedding anniversary. Two items. He doesn't host dinner parties nor does he have English tea socials. However, both items are sentimental. They are reflections of two important women in his life, his mother and grandmother.

IDEOLOGY OF A COVER NARC

How dare he! How dare he walk away from me! He is nothing without me, the greatest human being that ever existed! How dare he choose to not devote his entire life to supporting the needs and whims of another human being? How dare he!

Assumptions, yes and no. "You don't have the guts to divorce me," proclaimed Shilpa, in the year following his mother's passing. "You know what I'll do!" Shilpa continued, in a low-key quiet taunt followed by a giggle. While he certainly does not live inside the mind of Shilpa, he understands the pathology, the way in which she views the world. Win. Win at all costs. He also understands that the greatest fear for any covert narcissist is getting caught in a world of their own deception.

HIS MIND

His mind is fragile. He is pursuing divorce as a shell of his former Self. His mind has been conditioned to anxiety, doubt, and irrational fear. His mind has been conditioned to cherry-pick only the happy moments, the good times. He is no longer the stubborn, independent, strong-minded idealist of his early 20s who was pursuing his creative dreams and social initiatives. He is now jumpy and easily rattled.

FLYING MONKEY

From the moment the divorce papers were served, Shilpa immediately began to implement her war plan. Enter the flying monkeys, personal henchmen/women who were recruited as heavy artillery to deploy abuse.

Truth twisting. Guilt-tripping. Gaslighting. Defamation. Slander. Libel. Across the community. Flying monkeys were the sideshow. It was an out-of-court, off-the-record shit show that was designed to unleash hatred, vitriol, and intensive personal attacks. Shilpa's initial strategy involved the "mental flipping" of several locals in Culpeper. It was a demand for loyalty at all costs and a complete disconnect from sane reality.

Grace was one such woman. She was a former family friend of his and his mother for twenty-five years. A churchy woman in her mid-60s. A churchy woman with a dark side. As a divorcee herself, Grace became filled with hatred and animosity toward him for being sinful. Grace, a woman who claimed to love Jesus Christ, bankrolled the F5 tornado Katherine to pursue war, not peace. Grace, a woman who claimed to live in the light of Jesus Christ, verbally berated and verbally assaulted his mother's very own pastor in a local Starbucks. She caused the mild-mannered pastor to flee and vow never to interact with anyone named Grace again!

AMERICAN BEAUTY

"There will be many chapters in your life. Don't get lost in the one you're in now. Smile. Good things are going to happen. Follow your heart. Breathe. Live in the present. Think outside the box. The best time to start was yesterday. The next best time is now." These were the words inside a framed picture he came across in Nappanee, Indiana. He had to buy it, these words that fit the moment.

He had no idea what his journey of 13,000 miles would bring him. As he wound his way back East and through New England, he chose to stay present, to stay in peace. He chose to find joy, beauty, and solace in the small towns, roadways, and images of his native America.

He was on a path to World War III, and there was nothing he could do to change that. He had taken the helm at the wheel of his own ship and was setting course in a new direction. He owned his decision. He knew that he had to keep moving forward no matter what. Quitting wasn't an option.

He never knew that Erie, PA had a peninsula in Presque Isle State Park. Brilliant. He had to visit the Norman Rockwell Museum in Rutland, Vermont. He imagined Rockwell painting his *EKTA* dancers in Ahmedabad, him and his pop stealing a road sign from Canada, his mother as superwoman, Christmas brunch with his second father, or just the INFJ cowboy in Mexican Hat eating a Gandhian steak. He set up his tripod and framed shots. Atlantic boulders and lighthouses in Maine. The Kennedy compound in Hyannis Port. Newport, Rhode Island was a new discovery, a true gem. Cliffside estates of very boujee American Titans of Industry. Quite the opposite of his $85--a-month Mumbai studio with a slab kitchen and squat toilet.

Perhaps his American/Indian dream was somewhere in between the bare minimum and over-opulence. Rich or poor, it did not matter. Authenticity did. Intention did. Life purpose did. Meaning did. Depth did.

A pit stop in Edison, New Jersey gave him some much-needed authenticity in the form of savory Indian food. He stuffed his face with butter chicken, jeera rice, and naan before heading across the street to the liquor store for bottles of Old Monk, his favorite Indian rum. Om Puri had poured him a glass of Old Monk. Perhaps he was in between addictions. He bought six bottles. He felt he deserved it. Alternative Therapy 101, which might come in handy, as he prepared to pursue the actual American dream, litigation.

Glory be to God.

SURPRISE PHONE CALL

He returns to Virginia but not home. He has no home. War has started. Shilpa has moved in with Grace to plot the battle. He pays the mortgage and the bills, but he could not live in the house. It isn't safe for his mind. The romanticism of a 48-day journey across America is over as he checks into a weekly motel. It is a decent small studio with random drug deals in the parking lot outside his window. There is a mix of good, hardworking American folk and shady ones. There is also the occasional rank smell of weed, his other nemesis. There are some fast-food eateries nearby. The buzz of intestate traffic whizzes by all night long. Thankfully, his credit cards still work. Charge it. Just swipe it. Reality hit hard.

He thrives at being a loner, but this is different. He is alone. He is isolated. Even the love of family and friends could not shake his profound sense of inner loneliness. He had no idea how truly fucked up his mind is. The corrosive damage of emotional abuse. He doesn't realize how far away from his goals and dreams he has drifted.

He thought he was in control of his own life. He thought wrong. He is a puppet on a complex web of strings. He is controlled, on every level, by Shilpa. He has cut the strings, but he doesn't know who he is.

He misses India terribly. His life. The people. The adventure. The meaning. The food. The chaos. Even the less-than-ideal toilets.

There is one conversation he needs to have but dreads. From the early days at Manav Sadhna, in Ahmedabad, and throughout the *EKTA* process, he has grown to admire Viren Joshi.

He was very stubborn, and in the early days, his philosophy and Viren's philosophy often clashed. But out of those differing viewpoints, a great deal of respect was born. He and Viren were on the same team, with the same mission; however, they just approached life differently at times.

He needs to have a conversation with Viren, to open up about his divorce, but he is afraid. He is afraid of being judged. He is afraid of disappointing Viren, of being a poor role model, and of letting down a culture. He is fearful that perhaps Viren might try to counsel him to stay married.

He picks up the phone and calls. He wishes he had a before and after photo of his face.

Two hours later, he is speechless. Two hours later, he is humbled. Two hours later, he is in tears. Viren had never sought to "interfere" in his life path, so Viren had always remained silent.

Viren shares with him, in great depth, feelings and viewpoints regarding Shilpa. Raw. Unfiltered. Truthful. Viren shares personal observations as well as those of Viren's elderly mother.

Viren says, "You took a wrong turn. Everyone in life takes a wrong turn. That's all. And now you just need to get back on track."

Viren assured him that once everyone at Gandhi Ashram and everyone across Ramapir No Tekro learns of his divorce, he would be fully supported. 100%. Viren closes by saying, "Whenever you need us, we are here for you. You come and stay here, as long as you need to. And don't worry, you will be safe and protected. Everyone loves you."

As he hangs up the phone, a tear rolls down his face. He remembers when he first arrived at Gandhi Ashram and stumbled across Manav Sadhna by accident. He remembers following his heart and leaving Mumbai and his fledgling movie project to work in the slums of Ahmedabad and to create *EKTA*.

It is the same Gandhi Ashram that had asked him to leave, eighteen years earlier. It is the same Gandhi Ashram where he had fought to prove his own worth, to carve out a little place for him. It is the same Gandhi Ashram that was offering him all the love and support in the world.

He is not Indian. He mangled Gujarati whenever he tried to speak. He is just a kid from Culpeper. But on the other side of the world, hundreds and hundreds of beautiful souls have his back. His soul is parched. His soul is running on empty. His soul has just received the nourishment of life, the right words at the right moment.

TWENTY-THREE

STANLEY TOOL KIT

He quickly learns that the American legal system was ill-equipped to tackle the ramifications of severe emotional abuse. It is quite the opposite in fact. It is a legal system designed to perpetuate abuse at every level.

To his mind, the system of fairness, equity, nobility, and the rule of "just" law are kind of like a Stanley Tool Kit. The kind one can easily pick up from Home Depot. Certainly, every American man and many women had Stanley tool kits in the garage or buried in a closet somewhere.

15,789 tools and gadgets. Organized. Snug into pockets. It is certainly one hell of an impressive tool kit. In reality, most things just required the Phillips or the Flathead, possibly a wrench. His mother's divorce utilized just the Phillips. A couple of months. No-Fault. Less than a thousand dollars in legal fees.

His world is not so comparable. The big caveat is simply that his own father is not a covert narcissist and was not hell-bent on destroying his mother's life. Fortunately for him, Shilpa is! One of his greatest fears is crossing Shilpa and by filing divorce papers, he has certainly stepped in a pile of camel dung.

A year-long legal assault followed in which all 15,789 Stanley legal tools were used to test his will and fortitude. For one year, Shilpa's legal team failed to respond or offer a counter to the initial settlement proposal.

Their goal was simple: Manipulate. Punish. Slander. Lie. Annihilate. Destroy. All legal. Justice!

FLIP THE SCRIPT

The trifecta of women — Shilpa, Grace, and Katherine — portray him as a stone-cold abusive man. He is the abuser. He is the swindler. He is the bad guy. He is the villain.

Shilpa is the angel. Helpless victim. Blindsided woman. Naïve. Innocent. A woman who was not familiar with American culture and customs. A woman disavowed and cut off from her family back in Mumbai.

He is portrayed as controlling. He hid the finances from her. Truth Alert Newsflash. Manipulation Meter Alert! He never allowed Shilpa to carry her own driver's license. Truth Alert Newsflash. Deception Meter Alert! Shilpa did all the work, she ran the business, but she was never paid a penny. Evil American exploitative family. Truth Alert Newsflash. Fake News!

He desperately needs backup from Frank Capra and Jimmy Stewart to reframe the narrative. For over ten years, he has worked tirelessly to genuinely build a small non-profit program and battle his own State

Department just to stay afloat and keep the lights on. He didn't receive hazard pay, government pensions, travel allowances, or per diems. His world is a real-life struggle and sweat equity. Yet, in his divorce, he is portrayed as a shady mob boss with a global operation and financial assets hidden all across the world. WTF?

FISHING TRIP

Shilpa, Grace, and Katherine ventured out into the deep blue seas of his life. They were in search of millions and billions, for money even he wasn't aware of. Tidal wave after tidal wave of Discovery projects with three-week deadlines. All year long. Normal requests and scratch-your-ass kinds of requests.

He was asked to produce all of his hidden bank accounts, offshore bank accounts, and bank accounts he used that were in other people's names. WTF?

He was asked to produce every personal and business bank record that existed and even the ones that did not exist. WTF?

He possessed a film degree from a very boujee Southern California college, not the School of Al Capone Center for International Studies. How to prove something that doesn't even exist?

CULPEPER COUNTY COURTHOUSE

"Your Honor, I use an Indian email service provider. Rediffmail Pro. Their system doesn't allow me to just push a button and download the emails in question. It is a manual process that by my estimate would take at least 45 hours and there are simply too many requests in the Discovery. Dozens upon dozens. I'm only one person. There are only so many hours in the day. I work full time just to fulfill the requirements of these requests."

Subpoenaed. He missed a deadline by five seconds and was served with a subpoena. His large-scale global operation had one staff in India. Mr. Negi. A man whom he had first met back in Pestle Weed College during his 42-day stint as an ESL teacher in the jungle. Mr. Negi worked in the administrative office at the boarding school and was the first Indian national to ever invite him home, to meet family, to share a meal. In Rishikesh. Mr. Negi had been his admin guy from the beginning. Honest. Trustworthy. Loyal. An asset for any enterprise, no matter the size and scope. He had been requested to provide three years' worth of communications between him and Mr. Negi. All emails. A form of gotcha justice.

Shilpa understood very well who Mr. Negi was and Mr. Negi's character. Negi was not a strange and nefarious figure. Covert narcissists often projected onto others aspects of the narc's own personality.

The courthouse exterior is historic and stately. It was constructed in 1874. There is a huge clock outside, high above. There is a courtyard next to it with a Confederate Statue set up in 1911. Inside are large arched windows and high vaulted ceilings. It is epic in size for a small town. One could play a football game or conduct a concert there. There is enough room on the bench to seat all 9 Supreme Court Justices.

The presiding judge sits about a quarter mile away, high up on the bench. As the defendant, he sits in the middle of the court, surrounded by a little white picket fence. A little box with a chair and a microphone. White Picket Fences were often part of the American dream. In mid-life, he has finally attained that elusive dream. In reality, he wonders why he has to obey the subpoena. Why should he follow the rule of law? Fair question. And then it hits him like a ton of bricks. He realizes he isn't the President of the United

States. Tweet. Tweet. Hashtag 45. He is but a mere simpleton — a regular bloke, middle class, hard-working, caught in the claws of justice.

The aging judge looks at him, a bit blank. He is speaking in English, though with a bit of a strong Indian-British-English hybrid accent. He realizes nobody understands what he's saying. Nobody in Culpeper has ever heard of Rediffmail Pro. Maybe he's making it up. Maybe he is playing a game. Maybe there really is a secret button for emails and he's hiding vast sums of wealth. Not only does he lose the court battle, but the judge orders him to also pay Shilpa's legal fees incurred by Katherine for the day in court. Lady justice! A beacon for all.

Forced by the judicial system and the Motion to Compel, he ended up logging 57 hours of manually printing emails and an ink/paper cost of $550. 57 hours of work. The typical American work week was 40 hours.

The Negi Emails were only one out of hundreds of Discovery requests. Just one. A full-time unpaid job. Forced by lawyers. Forced by the system. Forced to comply or face more legal harassment or jail time. The pure psychological impacts of the weight of a system leveled onto an already somewhat fragile and healing mind...

And all of it is perfectly legal. Perhaps this could be the draft notes for a thesis paper on institutional abuse. Ultimately, the fishing trip produced nothing. No nefarious operations. No code words. No mysterious third parties. No smoking guns. No revelations of Cayman Island account transfers. No international real estate portfolio. No private islands purchased. Only mundane and rather dull daily communications about exchange programs, applications, follow-ups, visa processing, and overall management. A massive deforestation project. A dolly cart piled high with emails.

YOUR MOTHER WOULD NEVER APPROVE!

According to Mark Twain, "If Christ were here now there is one thing he would not be – a Christian."

In his mind, Grace certainly illustrated those words. Grace, the God-fearing "Bible Thumper," made a conscious choice to wrap herself in hatred and vitriol directed at him. Grace, a divorcee, is certainly entitled to her opinion. She can choose to disagree with his choice, to not like him, and to even gossip about him among her local church folk all while projecting an image of serving the poor and caring for others.

As duplicitous in nature as Grace appears to him, the one thing she does not have any right to do was involve his mother. His mother is dead. With a squint of the eye and hatred on her face, Grace delivered those pointed words directly to his soul, "Your mother would never approve!"

It happened in slow motion. With a taunt. With a glare. With a self-righteous pious tone. Grace reminds him of everything he doesn't like about church. The people in it. Bloody hateful souls at times. Always judging. A sense of morality. Quite the opposite of the actual teachings of the Manger Boy. Point awarded to Mr. Twain.

He doesn't owe Grace any explanation for his right to exist as a human being and face the consequences of his own choices in life. But talking about his mama is a bridge too far. "How dare you? How dare you, Grace? You don't know my mama. She's right here with me, every step of the way."

HIS TURN

He has lost all sense of time and space. The world around him is a blur, a blur of Discovery projects and deadlines. A blur of paying his attorney again and again and again. Money goes but money sure doesn't come. He finally reaches the end of his legal homework and now it is his turn. The shoe is on the other foot. Now his attorney, the one who charges him for the oxygen to breathe in her office, wants to draw up Discovery requests for Shilpa.

Fun times. An eye for an eye stuff. Scorched earth policy. Simple living and higher thinking. He and his attorney collaborated to keep it simple, keep it brief, just one document and a few questions. A tiny fraction of what he had endured. Cue the laughter. Cue the laugh track.

Huh? The blowback from Shilpa's legal team is swift, aggressive, outlandish, and even comical. They genuinely seem offended that he has dared to ask any questions himself. In fact, a lawyer in Katherine's office responded by saying, "This case is not worth the trees we are killing." Translation. This MF is broke. This MF ain't got nothing but a mortgage, a car payment, and a college degree. The great irony is the fact that Shilpa's legal team seems to have forgotten how many trees he had killed printing emails. Shilpa's response to Discovery is classic Shilpa in the vein of those she admired, those like-minded folks. Tweet Tweet Hashtag 45. Deflect. Lie. Ignore. Lie. Manipulate. Lie. Omit. Lie. Deceive. Lie.

FACEBOOK DATA

By now, he understands psychologically that whatever Shilpa projected as true is basically not true. He is no detective, but he has acquired the skills needed to battle for his mental and emotional freedom. Shilpa's team has responded to the Facebook Data request. His lawyer is satisfied and marked it complete. However, he is not satisfied... at all.

His investigation reveals that each Facebook account has a series of subfolders, 28 folders to be exact, that track all aspects of a user's data. Shilpa's team has submitted 26 folders. He isn't a Harvard-trained legal scholar, and he had dropped out of precalculus in high school, but 28 minus 26 equaled 2. There are two folders missing. Further investigation reveals that one of the missing folders was for "Login Location History." Huh?

Interesting. Innocent omission? Careless clerical error? With a bunch as shady as Shilpa, Grace, and Katherine, he certainly doesn't think they have the combined net worth of innocence.

Shilpa's narrative, from day one, was quite clear. His mother passed. She did not abandon him but rather went to India to spend the year fully engrossed in work. Shilpa repeated that story over and over and over again. As they no longer had a permanent flat in India, Shilpa claimed to have lived in the tiny Mumbai apartment with her mum, brother, and two sisters. The same apartment she never actually liked.

To local Americans', it was a very believable story, which was why in the beginning, no one really doubted it. Of course, that's what Shilpa did. The truth was, while Shilpa spent a year in India, he continued to manage the business from Virginia. There were no new programs, no new business, and no new revenue streams. There was actually much less, very limited income.

Quite the contrary, Shilpa's behavior in the months following his mother's death was very peculiar. There were odd stories and out-of-character moments, even for Shilpa. Shilpa was indeed at her family's flat in Mumbai, but a year was a long time, and there were many gaps in her story.

Shilpa had a sudden interest in wanting to go on a "spiritual retreat." She wanted to be in silence for two weeks, with cell phones switched off.

It was strange indeed for a woman who lived for attention and phone calls. Perhaps she was grieving too. Perhaps not.

One of the biggest oddities in Shilpa's behavior was a sudden video call on Viber. It was made in the middle of the night in India time, around three in the morning. Shilpa held the phone out and spun it around to reveal the location behind her, showcasing a bedroom in her mother's flat in Mumbai. Shilpa rarely did video calls. Shilpa never spun the camera around. Odd behavior indeed.

And now, somehow, the "Login Location History" data file was omitted and never provided.

The devil really is in the details.

AN END IN SIGHT

A trial date has been set. Shilpa, Grace, and the legal team have zero interest in suggesting a settlement counteroffer. He learns that it would be held in the same courtroom, the one with the White Picket Fence. The stuff of dreams. Many years earlier, he had actually directed and produced a short film in the same courtroom.

Shilpa's goal is very clear. To fleece him. To defame him. To punish him. To spin a good tale to the judge of her own pain and suffering. Shed some tears. He is sure it would be Academy Award-level acting. Very believable. Other than that, it is a fairly amicable divorce proceeding.

Subpoenas have been issued to his father, his second father, and others. Shilpa is seeking property and inheritances from her soon-to-be ex-in-laws. Shilpa has convinced herself and her team that, somehow, he is a trust fund baby and is loaded down with untold fortunes left to him by his mother.

Another fabrication. Shilpa has a long list of witnesses, a few that even surprise him.

He is quite speechless when he learns that his mother, Jan, is listed as a witness for him on his side. He knows his mother would support him, but he isn't exactly sure how she was going to descend from Heaven. His own lawyer had made a mistake and not realized who Jan was since he and his mom had different surnames. His lawyer had a law degree. He had a film degree. Details do matter.

EQUITABLE DISTRIBUTION OF ASSETS

Shilpa's attorney, Katherine, has assembled a list of 80 exhibits for trial. One such exhibit is titled, "Equitable Distribution of Assets," and it is supposed to be a summation of what Shilpa and her legal team felt was "fair" to have a judge agree and sign off on.

The document has descriptions of items, including every single piece of furniture in the house, and a percentage listed in the far-right column. A classic list for the mind of a brilliant covert narcissist. "Mine. Mine. Mine. Mine. Mine. And Mine." 100%. 100% 100%. Nearly every item is listed at 100% except for two.

According to Shilpa's team, he is to be awarded 50% of the towels and 50% of the cutlery. Towels. Cutlery. For real? He is humbled. He wonders if he is truly worthy of a few spoons, forks, and knives. A few towels. An unbelievable honor.

Being the renowned international man that he is with high-end boujee taste and leading the CIA's social work division in the slums of India, he naturally is the proud owner of an exquisite collection of towels. 1,200 GSM woven with gold threads, gifted to him by the Sultan of Brunei. Not quite. It is more of a hodgepodge collection. There are some that match and some that don't. Designer brands from Kohl's and Target. Materialism. Money. Stuff. Shit. His door to freedom led to the linen closet.

TWENTY-FOUR

THE PRIOR YEAR

He knew that the greatest weakness and the only vulnerability in the mind of a narcissist was Truth. One would have to expose them, to puncture a hole in the complex projection, to puncture a hole in the false narrative which had been established. He knew that he was in a battle for control of his own mind. He would have one shot to free himself and reconnect with his life path.

He purchased a small recording device from a New York City vendor. It was a black USB drive, which served as a multi-directional, voice-activated, recording device.

One of the hallmarks of emotional abuse was extreme self-doubt, believing other narratives but not being in alignment with one's own inner intuition. Trying to make sense of the world was debilitating. It was not only the chaos in his mind but the whispers and unsolicited advice of outsiders that were crazy towns. Luckily, he only had to deal with a handful of flying monkeys and had limited contact; however, all of these outside voices fed into his jumbled-up mind. They created a fog, a blur, a haze between what he was being told as "real" and his actual inner perception of "real." He was a private person and did not feel the need to engage with everyone and present his case day by day in the court of public or flying monkey opinion.

He had been told that he was depressed and needed to be placed on psychiatric meds. He had been told to stop grieving his mother's loss. He had been told Shilpa loved him, cared for him, and was fighting to "save" the marriage. He had been told clearly and unequivocally that the only man Shilpa had ever been with was him. In a sense, he was publicly and privately shamed.

Confused, he held onto the USB device for several weeks. He was fearful of what Shilpa might do if she found out and riddled with a sense of deep guilt. Truthfully, he would make a lousy CIA or FBI Agent. It just wasn't his cup of tea. He hated the idea of living in a world where he believed everyone was out to get him, to make him a fool, to swindle him, to deceive him, and to betray him. Part of it was his own naiveté. Part of it was his longing, deep within his soul, for the innocence of humanity, the innocence of a whimsical child, the innocence of a world that did not see color, country, religion, or gender. Humanity.

He hated the idea of spying. He discussed his dilemma with his counselor. He wrestled with his own conscience. Did it really matter? Did he need to do this? What if he discovered that everyone was telling him the truth?

PLAN OF ACTION

He set forth on a two-month intel operation on Shilpa, all the while wrestling with his anxiety, jumpiness, and mental fog. The law required him and Shilpa to be legally separated for a full twelve months prior to filing, a year of documented separation. Shilpa was given the house to reside in while he continued to pay the bills, mow the grass, and do Shilpa's laundry.

Grace had taken Shilpa under her wing and vowed to fiercely protect her. Grace had also pushed Shilpa to get an actual job, which began as part-time. In classic Shilpa-style, she dutifully did whatever Grace opined, as she was using Grace while bitching to him about the job and the staff.

In short, he knew Shilpa's schedule. He positioned the USB recorder above the television in the den, behind a row of ornamental elephants. Each week, he would pick up the device, dump the data on his computer, recharge it, place it back where it was, and hope that Shilpa wouldn't accidentally discover it.

He collected hundreds and hundreds of hours — hours filled with lots of sounds and lots of background noise. For months, he screened and painstakingly listened to all of the clutter, taking notes, analyzing, and marking timestamps. Shilpa had the television on most of the time. He considered changing the location of the device, but his anxiousness stopped him.

THE REAL STORY: TRUTH

Even he was speechless... His soul and his intuition had been sending him signals, signals which he could never understand. Over time, a picture began to emerge of a masterful and seamless intricately woven deception. He was not a linguist. However, since he had lived in India for many years, he was able to recognize speech patterns by listening and observing Shilpa. He understood when the language was in Hindi and when it was in Marathi. He understood the tone, feeling, and mood of a conversation, even if it was not in English. He understood the speech patterns of Shilpa and how her linguistics changed based on whom she was speaking to.

Shilpa wasn't just fooling him, Shilpa had fooled his mother, his family, and everyone else. In fact, during one of his visits to the house to mow, Shilpa had made a particular comment about the President, Tweet-Tweet Hashtag 45, saying that the President was brilliant because the President had fooled so many. It was as if manipulation and deception were badges of honor for Shilpa. It seemed like a certain code language that she could sense, see, and appreciate — the idea of making fools out of others and exploiting vulnerabilities.

THE NARRATIVE

Shilpa had one story that she projected, and her story was very simple. His mother died and she left him to take care of business in India. She did not abandon him. She lived full-time with her mother and younger siblings in Mumbai. He was the only man Shilpa had ever been with. She loved him deeply. Everything was a big misunderstanding. She was not at fault. He was grieving the loss of his mother. He couldn't see clearly. His mind was messed up. Shilpa's narrative was laid out in the recordings, in the phone conversations with the wife of Pastor John, with Grace, and with a colleague from her new job. Shilpa even spoke kindly about him and said she was working hard to "save" their marriage. She expressed great confidence that he would move back in soon, any day in fact, and all would be back to normal. Shilpa was perfect and did nothing wrong.

ONLINE SEX CHATS

The audio recordings revealed online sex chats between Shilpa and a married man in Mumbai. The conversations were in Hindi, with a great deal of role-playing involved. The Hindi word for elder brother-in-law was "jeeju." Shilpa preferred to playfully refer to the man, on the other end of the video chat in Mumbai, as jeeju. It was apparent in the audio that Shilpa knew the man prior. It was not the same Dubai man from years earlier. The Dubai man spoke English and Arabic, not Hindi. Shilpa had a coarseness about her when she spoke Hindi. She spoke Hindi with a slang, a very brash street slang style. Shilpa often referred to the man's wife in a derogatory Hindi word. She would call the woman a "chuth," which was comparable to cunt in English. Her tone and playfulness revealed that Shilpa was thrilled with the idea of the man being an elder brother-in-law, a forbidden fruit. In reality, neither of Shilpa's two sisters were married or had boyfriends.

FAMILY IN MUMBAI

Shilpa created a very specific and emotionally dramatic storyline in Culpeper. Most locals in Culpeper had never traveled to India, nor were they fine-tuned with the cultural norms and customs of India. This allowed Shilpa to exploit the "American Heart." Shilpa claimed her family had disowned her, due to the divorce, which she claimed to be "forbidden" in India. Shilpa claimed her mother refused to talk to her, and she had zero ties to family in Mumbai. Cue the violins. Shilpa would never see her family again. Gut-wrenching.

Shilpa wove a tale of being victimized, of being thrown out by Indian culture, and of being helpless in America. A tall tale of victimhood, being abandoned by an American husband, and thrown out like garbage. Shilpa was a masterful storyteller with rich and nuanced detail and complex storylines.

However, Shilpa's story was bogus. It was a con job, playing on the heartstrings of others. In reality and on audio, Shilpa was in regular communication with her mom and family in Mumbai. She was speaking fully in Marathi, with a bit of English. In fact, he learned that Shilpa's younger brother, the one she was closest to, was actually in America. The brother was in New Jersey, working in Wildwood. Shilpa carefully guided her brother on the ins and outs of American culture and gave pointers. Shilpa was unable to have her brother travel to Virginia to "support her," simply because it ran against the storyline she had set in Culpeper.

LONG TERM-BOYFRIEND

The most painful revelation in the audio was the discovery that Shilpa had a long-term boyfriend. The boyfriend was a doctor, a man who did not speak Hindi, a man who seemed to live outside of Mumbai, but close by in Maharashtra. Shilpa often walked and paced when she talked. In the recordings, she would drift in and out of range. What struck him the most was the tone of Shilpa's voice and the short phrases and short sentences used. Shilpa was using the exact vocabulary and sentence structure in English as the conversations she had had with him 18 years earlier when he was living in his tiny studio flat in Mumbai, dreaming of making a little movie. Shilpa was speaking to this unknown man in the exact way that she spoke to him all those years ago. Rhythm. Tone. Cadence. It was painful, not because he was in love with Shilpa, but because of the depth of the betrayal. He had believed Shilpa. His mind, his mind never had a clue.

Since the phone was not tapped, only a mumbled and muffled male voice could be heard at times; however, Shilpa's voice was very clear, very audible. Shilpa knew the layout of the hospital this man worked at. She knew this man's schedule. Shilpa knew what the man's home looked like. Shilpa knew what this man's bedroom looked like. Shilpa knew what kind of deodorant this man used. She knew this man's exact routine. Shilpa commented on how the guy ate, chewed his food, and drank water. Shilpa knew every subtle detail about the doctor. He sensed that the doctor was a foreigner, not Indian. But he was unable to discern the exact ethnicity or country of origin.

In one conversation, Shilpa said, "...*When you be with a person for such a long time, you know everything about them.*" Shilpa giggled and laughed and teased the man when the man mispronounced Hindi words. Shilpa and her long-term boyfriend spoke 2-3 times daily. To account for the fact that Shilpa had started working, she projected a story to the doctor that she was taking local college classes and even talked about some of those courses, courses that were entirely fabricated. It took mad skills to tell that many lies and keep that many stories straight. He got the strong sense that the mysterious doctor in India truly was being played and had no idea that Shilpa was married or that he even existed.

MIND-BLOWING

Cold. Brutal. Calculating. Dishonest. Manipulative. Deceptive.

Where to begin? Shilpa, the "innocent victim," the religious woman, the caring and loving wife who was fighting to "save" the marriage was living in multiple realities, projecting multiple stories.

The truth was Shilpa was fighting to hang on to her lifestyle. She wanted to keep him in his place, serving the Queen. Shilpa's anxiety was that of her own making, a fear of getting caught in the web. The human mind was a game to Shilpa. People were objects. The goal was to manipulate everyone, all the time, for personal gain, for influence, for a sense of power, and for fun. Tweet. Tweet.

It was all beginning to make sense to him. He understood why Shilpa so gleefully described the actions of a US President hell-bent on subverting the pillars of democracy, pitting Americans against each other. Shilpa admired dishonesty and deception. It was all a game. Shilpa subconsciously understood the weaknesses and vulnerabilities of a human being and she exploited them.

Shilpa had fooled him. She had fooled his mother. She had fooled his second father. She had fooled his father. She had fooled everyone. And the Oscar, the Golden Globe, the BAFTA, goes to...

MOMENT OF CRYSTALLIZATION

His mind was finally beginning to connect the dots. The hazy confusion of fog that left him in perpetual states of confusion and uncertainty was lifting. However, the psychological damage was done. He realized that the life he had been living, the business he had worked hard to build, and the "good times" he shared with Shilpa were all a fraud. Nothing was real. None of it.

His relationship and marriage to Shilpa was a reflection of his self-worth. Discovering the level of the betrayal and discovering the brutal fact that he was targeted from day one was debilitating to his sense of self. He thought Shilpa cared about him. He made the choice to walk into the courthouse in

Bandra, India and step into a nightmare. He had absolutely no idea that he had not been in control of his thoughts and feelings, that he was trauma-bonded, taken hostage. He was unsure of himself and if he could ever trust his own judgment.

NUCLEAR BOMB

He had held onto the audio for a year. Ten days before the trial was set to commence in the historic Culpeper Courthouse, a single audio clip and a 12-page translation were submitted to Katherine Davis.

Game changer. He had listened to his gut. He had anticipated the psychological fight of his life. He had discussed the legality of the audio recordings with his attorney, who had selected this audio out of a sampling of others. He had picked out the audio clip, on a hunch, and had it translated a year earlier through connections in India. However, to be valid in the Commonwealth of Virginia, he was required to have a court certified and approved audio transcription/translation. He followed up on his own and sourced an accredited translation company in Northern Virginia. The second Hindi translation cost him $1,200.

The first draft of the translation came back to him with a G-rated Disney dialogue. He discovered that entire words and sentences had been omitted by the Hindi transcriber in America. WTF?

Something was off and made no sense. Either his source in India had given him the wrong translation or he paid $1,200 for the wrong one. In his mind, he knew the words and the tone. He sensed the vibe of the conversation, and it turned out to be exactly as he thought. His sense of observation, mental filtering system, and intuition had allowed him to pick out a particular conversation out of thousands of hours of audio, junk, and day-to-day noise. It was a smoking gun in a different language.

The Virginia translation company was completely flabbergasted to learn that their own Hindi-approved transcriber had fucked up! His life was on the line. This wasn't a Pixar script. He realized that the accredited translator was most likely quite conservative and accustomed to legal and corporate documents. The idea of translating Hindi slang and trash talk littered throughout with "chuth" and "chutiya"; cunt, fucker, cunt-licker, motherfucker and asshole, most likely caught the translator off guard. Once again, he was doing all the work. Then again, it was his life he was trying to save. The company was embarrassed and very apologetic; yet, they did not waive any of the $1200. Capitalism.

The audio translation dropped on a Friday. By Monday morning, Katherine, Shilpa, and Grace were on their heels, ready to make a deal. He had popped the narcissistic balloon, the projection of victimization, the Big Lie that Shilpa's marriage was "rigged and stolen."

On October 31st, hours before the planned November 1st public trial, Warden Shilpa signed the settlement agreement. The thought of audio revelations in court proved to be a devastating blow. Shilpa was caught in her own web on Halloween.

Checkmate.

TWENTY-FIVE

THE DAY AFTER

The sound of running water. A red-tailed hawk soars above. A quaint valley nestled up along the Blue Ridge Mountains, just down from Skyline Drive. A crisp late fall day. The leaves, orange and burgundy, are past peak and many have blown off the trees. Serenity. A tiny one-room wooden church built in the 1800s sits up on a hill. He sits alone, next to a swift-moving stream. That sound of running water.

He's dressed in his usual jeans and a black fleece. Freedom came with a price. He has broken out of ADX Willow Tree and is in a state of shock. He feels lighter, but his immune system is wrecked. His sense of being is wrecked. His basic human dignity has been thrashed. Not only was he raped in the heart of Mumbai, he was raped by the judicial system. The stress. The anxiety. The abuse. The criminalization of divorce. $25K in legal fees.

To many, $25K was just a drop in the bucket, but to him, $25K was enough to wipe him out. A more realistic figure for the financial impact was closer to $55K. He had lived on the run, off-grid, bouncing around weekly hotels, remote mountain cabin rentals, and the couches of friends.

The sound of running water. It soothed his mind. It nourished his soul. His anxiousness of fear had been replaced by an anxiousness of the unknown. All he had wanted was to have ownership of his mind, his story, his narrative, his voice, and his body. He hasn't prepared for the day after...

ONE-OF-A-KIND DESK

He has been granted ownership of his home. It is a gift that came with a cash-out refinance, a much higher mortgage payment, as well as full ownership of all the business debt. Shilpa receives cash, all the furniture, and a three-year lump sum alimony. Several days have been scheduled for Shilpa to bring a team and remove the furniture. Shilpa doesn't disappoint, even removing 78 screws for specialty shelving units from a closet that had been installed by his mom and second father, especially for Shilpa with love. Yep, Shilpa used a Phillips head to remove 78 screws from one closet and leave the holes. Mine. Mine. Mine.

The moving team even left an overflowing toilet bowl that ran water unattended for nearly twenty-four hours. He has not lived in the house in two years. Since he is still enforcing No Contact, his father is the one given the keys to the house in order to allow Shilpa and the movers inside. New locks have been installed.

When he first purchased the house, his life had him living six months in India and six months in America. His new house in 2010 was empty, of course, but not for long. His mother and second father had surprised him on his return from India with a six-foot one-of-a-kind real wood antique desk for his home office. A desk that was filled with character and was off the beaten path, like him. He loved it!

The desk had been the perfect place to think, to work, and to write. His mother was dead. His relationship with his biological father had been strained and non-existent for a year due to the fact that his father actively promoted Shilpa's projection as opposed to understanding the needs of a son.

The desk, a special gift, the collateral damage, turned out to be a gift with supernatural powers. Special indeed. He speaks to his father on the first night of furniture collection as his father wandered through the house.

"What about the desk? Is it gone?" he inquires.

"Yes. There is no desk in here." "Why?" His father senses a bit of sadness in his voice.

"Nothing. Mom gave it to me and it meant a lot," he says somberly.

"Why didn't you ask for it?" his father replies.

"Wasn't worth paying lawyers more money to argue about it. It's just material."

A week later, Shilpa has just left the house with the movers. His father calls him and is livid. "Goddamn bitch took it all! She took the sofa and the bed too! She told me last week she had decided to leave the sofa and the bed for you. To have something."

While he is used to hearing his father angry, it is the first time that anger is directed at Shilpa. A 180.

"Let it go. It doesn't matter," he says.

"But she lied to me! I'm so goddamn pissed right now. That fucking bitch!"

He tries to calm his father down. "I told you she wouldn't leave anything. It's nothing new. It's the way she is. Very petty."

The sofa and the bed are just the opening act. It is the desk, the antique desk, that strikes his heart and soul.

What his biological father says next absolutely blows him away. "I asked Shilpa last week if I could buy the desk back from her. I told her I wanted to give it to you for Christmas."

"Really?"

"She told me she'd think about it. Tonight, I asked her about the desk and she directly said no. Said she won't sell it to me because she knows I want to give it to you. I got angry and said things. Shilpa started yelling. Goddamn that bitch! I'm done. I'll never speak to her again!" his father ranted.

His eyes well up with tears as he listens to his father.

His father has reached a breaking point. His father has come full circle. Shilpa had used his father, just as she had used everyone in her orbit, to serve her needs. And then she burned the bridge in a callous fashion.

He is crying because his entire life, his father had always operated in a world that was solely about his father. His mother had been in charge of caretaking and nourishing his childhood. With his father, he felt a conditional love, one where he had to prove himself, prove his value in an award or a merit badge. He was an only child; yet, he longed for the attention of his father, the understanding of his father.

He loves the old desk and is sorry that it is gone. However, the actions of his own father are unexpected and priceless. His father had attempted to get the desk back for him for Christmas. It is a gesture that spoke volumes, a gesture of kindness, and a gesture of love.

It touches his soul.

THE CHINA SET AND THE SILVER TEA TRAY

The only material items requested in the initial settlement offer are two items of sentimental value. He is an INFJ hermit, not exactly one to host evening masala chai with friends or host dinner parties in order to use his grandma's china.

Both items were stored high up in a cabinet in the kitchen. Both items were taken and swindled by Shilpa the moment the divorce papers were served. Shilpa had kidnapped the china and the tea set, most likely hiding them out at Grace's house, her self-righteous Bible-inspired friend.

Emotional abuse is petty. Emotional abuse is about power. Emotional abuse is about control, emotional control.

Shilpa swiped the two items because it was in her DNA. Berating, abusing, manipulating, and lying were just what she did. These were things she excelled at. Valedictorian-level abuse. Therefore, it came as no surprise that the china set and silver tea tray became part of a whirlwind last-minute pre-Halloween negotiation between lawyers. Shilpa invoked the name of her ex-mother-in-law, his mom, the woman with the PhD in kindness, the mom who would be aghast to learn how her son had been treated for decades. Shilpa wove a tale that his deceased mother had gifted it to her and that it meant so much.

In the end, he let the silver tea tray go too. He was allowed to keep the china.

BEETHOVEN

His white Land Rover enters his neighborhood. It's been a couple of months since Halloween. It's the dead of winter, the start of a New Year as

Beethoven's "Coriolan Overture" underscores him. Will he, or won't he?

His car pulls into the driveway. The suspense builds in his mind. His heart begins to beat faster. Beethoven's orchestra builds. He wonders. It's the million-dollar question. It's the hanging Chad. It's the *Dallas* who shot J.R. cliffhanger!

He walks into the garage and is about to enter the house. He takes a deep breath and opens the door. He moves toward the kitchen and the small marble-top island. Beethoven reaches a crescendo. He places his right hand on the drawer and opens it. He lets out a huge sigh of relief. Fifty percent of the cutlery. Still there. He hasn't counted, but it looks like 50%! Of course, the nice heavy solid, more expensive cutlery is gone. The 50% that remains is the starter cutlery, the kiddish, cheapish, tiny-sized cutlery.

The chords of Beethoven soar to new heights of suspense. He turns around. His eyes are locked on the cupboard. He rushes to open it. Plates. Dishes. 50%. He breathes another sigh of relief. Exactly 50% remain. Such a gift. Such a joy. The simplicity of material wealth. Curious, he inspects further. He laughs when he notices the sets of plates and dishes have been divided, meaning that a set of four red plates, red bowls, and red cups are now a set of two. Rather than taking 50% of the dishes by keeping actual sets intact, Shilpa chose to split them down the middle creating a mismatched hodgepodge of dishes.

He then races upstairs to check out the linen closet...

THE SAFEWAY APRON

Confirmation. Clarity. A message from his mom. A clue from God.

Aside from the piles of discarded clothes, the house is nearly empty. He learns that the local Episcopal pastor in town will perform an official house blessing ceremony, among other things, to ward off evil spirits. He booked a house blessing. A detox.

Soon after, he discovers something that Shilpa has forgotten. In a closet, buried in a stacked plastic storage device, he comes across a black Safeway apron. Attached to it is Shilpa's name tag. His mother had worked as a pharmacy tech at Safeway. His mother had gotten Shilpa a part-time job at Safeway over the holidays when he and Shilpa were in town for a couple of months. His mother's goal had been to boost Shilpa's confidence and independence.

As he opens the apron, out falls a pregnancy test. He is wide-eyed and confused. He lived in a sexless marriage, hence there was never a need for any such test. He's actually never held one before. He looks at it. Negative. He digs deeper in the drawer and finds the box. His keen mind digs a bit further to reveal the manufacturing date and expiration window.

2016. *Hmmm.* The foreign doctor. The missing Facebook login location data file. The audio tapes.

Closure.

GOD KNOCKS, AGAIN

He receives compassion and an apology from a most unlikely source, the Law Offices of Katherine Davis.

Huh? He is signing a document and picking up the china. *Fortunately,* Grace arrives at the same time to pay a check. At first, he thought it was a cruel set-up since seeing Grace triggered him and made him physically ill. It was a coincidence and Grace had no official appointment.

It is God's timing. The staff of the law office rushes him to a back conference room and sits him down. They can see and sense he is emotionally triggered. A flood of emotions. The Hell he has been through. He is in the Lion's Den. He sits, holding his chest, breathing heavily.

"We had no idea, Brad. We don't always get to choose our clients," opines an administrative assistant.

"We're paid to do a job and that's what we did. But it's over now. You never have to see Grace or Shilpa again," says a lead attorney.

He turns toward both women. "It's what she did to me."

With compassion, the assistant says, "You're exactly right. It's what she did to you. You stay here as long as needed. Take your time. Let me get you some water."

To him, it is an acknowledgment, a validation in his mind that he has not experienced a "normal" divorce. There are no kids. There is no fortune.

Shilpa and Grace utilized the legal system to perpetuate monumental abuse.

NO WAY, GOD! NO WAY

Immediately after his surprise law office episode, he drives over to Gold's Gym for a workout. He is already dressed and had planned to go. He sits at a leg press machine as a figure in the far corner catches his eye. He squints his eyes to reconfirm. His face turns to shock as he looks up toward the ceiling in disbelief.

"God is that who... No way..." he says as a man walks by, a man that he recognizes. He shakes his head. He is speechless. It has been 33 years. It has been 33 years since he has seen the husband-and-wife construction team that had worked on his childhood home.

A flood of memories overwhelms him. The Willow Tree. The nail-gun. *Da Swoosh. Da Swoosh. Da Swoosh. Da Swoosh. Da Swoosh.* Their names are Norman and Ana. They had absolutely no idea. They had no idea that they were his lifeline, down below, on the other side of the treehouse walls. Norman and Ana are such kind and loving souls, a great team. He has so many images flashing through his mind. Fear and silence and shame have stolen his voice.

He has just signed the final document at Katherine's office. He has paid the final alimony check to be released from a nightmare, to be free from a wrong turn in life. He has not seen them since he was a child. Nobody knows about ADX Willow Tree. Nobody knows about his secret, except Adam, who is dead. Nobody knows about his pain. Only God knows.

He makes his way across the gym to speak to Ana. It is another puzzle piece in his life path. He learns that Ana is not aware of his mom's passing. He learns that it is their first day at Gold's Gym. Are you kidding? Ana and Norman have just joined at that very moment. At that exact moment in time, decades later, his path is intersecting with theirs. A feeling of inner comfort winds its way through his body.

He has a sense of knowing. He knows that his mother is indeed up in Heaven sitting in the control room with God. She is watching the moment that her son finally understands that it wasn't his fault.

The anxious little boy who always ran — ran from God, ran from religion, ran from sermons, and ran from himself — received a gift that day, a gift from his mom. It was a seed, a seed planted in his mind, in his heart, and in his soul. It was the seed of faith.

He can no longer look away. He feels it within every fiber of his being. He is birthing his own revelation of Self. He doesn't have the answer or know how the journey will unfold, but he knows that his message, the message he has always been searching for, is tied to his trauma, to his set of life experiences.

TWENTY-SIX

SERENDIPITY

Her dark eyes are very soulful. Her cheekbones are very distinctive, like that of a runway model. Physically, she is stunning. However, it is her light that captivates him, placing him in a bit of a trance. It is a light that pours out from her being in all directions, a light that fills the room. She possesses an infectious spirit.

She is Latina with family roots in El Salvador. Her name is Isabella, and she is his hairstylist. He knows very little about Isabella aside from his keen observations in the high-end local salon that she manages. Isabella is very tight-lipped and private in regard to her personal life. She is always focused on others. He is just a client who sits in a chair once a month. All he really knows about this light is that she is about ten years younger and has two small kids. He isn't the only one in awe of Isabella's glow, everyone is. He observes the other clients in the salon. It's the most boujee in Culpeper, a place where doctors and lawyers and principals and people with status and degrees seem to congregate. Female clients, old and young, linger well after their haircut. Isabella has an aura around her, a glow that everyone wants to absorb before venturing back into their own lives and worlds. She seems to bring out the best in everyone. He isn't there for just a haircut; he wants to be in the presence of that Isabella vibe.

SHARED GRIEF

His first haircut was shortly before his mom passed. He learned through loss that oftentimes, most people didn't really know what to say or they would say rather silly things, such as "time heals."

The physical relationship with a lost loved one changes, but time doesn't heal. In fact, at a family gathering following his mother's Celebration of Life event, a distant cousin shared with him a story about how her mom was on a train and didn't answer the phone. His distant cousin told him she had been so worried something happened to her mother. It probably wasn't the best story to share with someone whose mother had actually just died.

His mother's death, the loss of his North Star, was a catalyst for Isabella to crack the door open just a bit and share a story of her own devastating loss. Isabella had an older sister and a younger sister. Isabella's only brother had gone with friends to spend a day at a lake and never returned. Isabella was in middle school at the time and described the moment a police officer arrived at their home with William's backpack, but not William. William had drowned. Her mother held onto the backpack with all the items inside.

Life moved on, but time didn't really heal.

THE AMISH

Eventually, he learns the names of Isabella's children — a little girl named Ana and a little boy named Cody. He has begun to sense that behind all the light that Isabella projected into the world, there is a much deeper story, a story of great struggle and hardship. It is just a sense, an intuitive feeling. Just as he was inspired to create *EKTA*, his Gandhi-King show, another moment of inspiration comes over him.

He doesn't know Cody and Ana, but he wants to do something small for them through Isabella. The idea is actually a reflection of his current state in life. He is at his own crossroads.

He has chased dreams in India for decades — to prove himself, to make his mother proud — but life didn't work out that way. His mother's loss had shaken his soul and caused him to reflect on all the little things in life he had missed out on — the little moments, the fabric of life — all while pursuing big-picture goals. His mom was always focused on local small acts of kindness and compassion — the little things, moments that actually made a difference in people's lives.

ADX Willow Tree was also a motivation for him, a big one. Rather than waste money in some seedy massage parlor trying to feel loved, why not invest a little something into the lives of two little kids? Part of him feels it is a selfish act, not a selfless one. He ponders and overthinks the idea before mentioning it to Isabella at his next haircut. The part he doesn't tell Isabella is that, in a roundabout way, his act of kindness is a Hail Mary pass to heal his own pain.

He is an Elite Member of the IHG hotel group. Lancaster, Pennsylvania, the land of the Amish is only a few hours away. As a child, he had always loved the short visits to Amish Land. As an adult, he is a firm believer in out-of-the-box life experiences for everyone. No tricks. No gimmicks. No conditions. No creepy vibes.

It is just an offer for Isabella to take the kids to Lancaster for a small vacation. He would use some hotel points for Holiday Inn and pay for a night. He isn't going or planning to be anywhere near Pennsylvania. It is just for the kids to see something outside of Culpeper.

Isabella is speechless. She accepts the offer. During the Easter school holiday, Isabella, along with Cody, Ana, and Isabella's mom, all pile into her blue Jeep and head to Lancaster. Horse and buggy rides. Turkey Hill ice cream factory. Shopping. Isabella shares a few pictures with him, pictures that touch his heart profoundly. He is able to put a face to a name when he sees the kids' pictures for the first time. Ana and Cody appear to have as much light as their mom.

A YEAR LATER

A double-lane road arches high, crossing a narrow body of water. Houses, with long wooden planks, line the waterway. A boat passes beneath the bridge. The sun is high. The topography is flat. Puffy white, almost tropical cumulus clouds dot the brilliantly blue sky. A blue Jeep Liberty appears and drives up onto the bridge.

Isabella is at the wheel. He rides shotgun. Little Ana and Cody are in the backseat with Zoey, a 12-year-old partially blind chihuahua. Isabella slows the Jeep. She presses the button to lower all four windows. Salty, humid, warm air spills into the vehicle. Isabella appears to melt into a state of trance.

Directly ahead of them is the Atlantic Ocean. Oak Island is a barrier island just south of Wilmington, North Carolina. Isabella abruptly stops the car in the middle of the road at the top of the bridge. She looks toward the waterway and then at him. His eyes and Isabella's eyes engage in a whimsical blend of chemistry and comfort. Without even thinking, their hands interlock and they smile at one another. He can feel Isabella's experience without her saying a word, but he asks anyway.

"What do you think?"

"It's perfect. Looks like a dream," she says.

The Jeep is parked in a large public lot. The back hatch is open. There is so much gear it looks as if they have moved to North Carolina. An overloaded large red beach wagon is on the ground. Coolers. Food. Chairs. Towels. Toys. Umbrella. Shoes. Little wave runners.

He is organized and he is a packer, but Isabella is giving him a run for his money. He's not sure about the actual weight limit of the wagon since he never reads instructions.

"I think it's stuffed!" he says.

He then watches as Isabella finds a way to cram and pile more items into the wagon.

Isabella turns to him. "I think we're good now."

He smiles and reaches down to give the wagon a tug. Hmmmm. It doesn't move. He hasn't been to Gold's Gym for a minute and guesses the wagon is 350 pounds. It seems like they have already outgrown that size.

He waits along with Little Ana and Zoey as Isabella struggles to rub sunscreen on Cody's back. Cody squirms and squirms. Thirty minutes after arriving in the parking lot, the crew of four, plus the partially blind dog, march out, single file, like an army unit.

He stands, already sweating, at the edge of a broken and weathered boardwalk. It is a walkway in need of Botox. It is low tide. The beach is wide. Along the beach are little clusters of families with plenty of space in between. He much prefers the space rather than the elbow-to-elbow action of urban or European beaches.

With Isabella, he is a puppy. He follows and listens to Isabella like a puppy. It's those cheekbones and soulful eyes.

"Picked out a spot yet?" he asks.

Isabella has drifted into her beach coma again, absorbing every second of the present moment. She points right. "How about over there? Looks perfect."

"Yep," he replies, the tone of a teenager.

However, the location Isabella chooses appears to be about 2.5 miles down the beach. Between the wetter and compacted sand are many yards of thick, soft, and deep dry sand. He has 350 pounds of beach gear. The sagging, pitiful red wagon with wheels that are not 4-wheel drive!

Anticipating diminished lung capacity, he quickly grabs his asthma inhaler and takes a couple of puffs to provide him a boost. He closes his eyes and tries to channel his inner Dwayne Johnson, his inner Sylvester Stallone. As a little kid, he loved *Rambo*. He bought the Rambo dress-up kit with the headband, the plastic gun, the plastic knife, the most epic and coolest crooked smile in the world.

As he contemplates and overthinks, Isabella, the kids, and Zoey are long gone. One of the pitfalls of being an INFJ is the fact that his mind never stops thinking. There are dozens and dozens of thoughts and scenarios. He looks down and flexes his muscles one time, then he grabs the handle of the wagon and reaches deep inside his soul to effortlessly appear to glide across the sandy landscape, making everyone else feel as though he has superhuman powers.

MISSION TO CONTROL: BASE CAMP HAPPINESS

He is taking a break. He sits in a beach chair and has both feet buried in the sand. He holds a plastic cup with some sort of happy juice.

Isabella has more extroverted leanings which seems to balance his more introverted ones. Isabella is his personal beach bartender and whatever she hands him, he drinks. He is a puppy dog after all. He rarely drinks since he is a part-time Gandhian. He isn't opposed to drinking, but he only preferred to do so with a close friend, not at a bar or club. In fact, some of the tremendous weight in the red wagon is from the beach bar he lugged out.

Picture Perfect. A mirage or a dream? The frame in front of him is completely clear. The silhouettes of Isabella, Cody, and Ana are visible as they stand along the edge of the water.

He is not looking for love. He was a man locked away in ADX Willow Tree. Love and fairytales are for the movies and other people, not him. If God were to step into his mind and create the perfect woman for him, she'd be perfectly imperfect in every way that suited him and his vibe. That perfect woman would be Isabella.

An accident. A coincidence. Synchronicity. Divine Plan. Whatever label it has doesn't matter because he is on cloud nine. His life has intersected with Isabella's at just the right moment in time. He sips on his happy juice and momentarily drifts into lust for Isabella. He has a type and she is it. Those curves and contours. That bathing suit she is wearing. All of Isabella is delicious.

Physical attributes aside, what drew him to Isabella like a magnet were her mad mom skills. Isabella is a dope mama. The world is filled with moms, many good, a few great. Isabella is a great mom, the top 1%. She is fully immersed, genuine, and authentic. She is the safe zone, a mom who gives all of herself to her children.

He knows what a great mom looks like. He got to experience one for forty years.

The more he learns about Isabella, the more he cannot ignore the role that Divinity had played in the orchestra of life. Isabella was born a city girl in Northern Virginia, outside of Washington. During high school, Isabella's family moved to northern Culpeper County and a rural boondock hamlet named Jeffersonton.

His mother had grown up on that dairy and chicken farm in Jeffersonton. Isabella's favorite flower was the sunflower. His mother's favorite flower was the sunflower. Isabella's favorite type of pizza was Hawaiian — the kind with pineapple and ham, the kind most do not prefer. His mother's favorite pizza was Hawaiian. Isabella has a favorite pastime, antiquing. Isabella and the kids love to search for treasures in antique stores, another of his mother's favorite hobbies.

For him, these aspects of Isabella's character feel like a sign — a sign that both God and his mom approve, that it is okay to be happy.

Cody is seven. Handsome and 110% high octane. Cody is the exact opposite of what he was like as a child. Cody has a sensitive interior but an exterior of a lion. Cody enjoys collecting. Cody has rock and gem collections and coin collections.

Cody is highly imaginative and can pull entire comic book stories out of thin air and with immense detail. Cody hates to wear shoes. Cody can be extremely loud without any concept that anyone else in the world is around. Cody is very emotional. Cody can explain, in minute detail, about every aspect of geology; yet, Cody is unable to focus at a table. It is difficult for Cody to complete a basic homework assignment without twisting and turning and doing everything else under the sun except focus. It is an element of behavior that seems to be a little off, beyond just an age thing or a kid thing.

Cody is extremely protective of Isabella and always requires her attention. Cody is unable to sit and play alone in his room or be alone. Cody is a sweet child with a quick temper and an inner emotional instability.

Little Ana is four years old. Ana is a beautiful child, a miniature version of Isabella. Ana looks like a doll in a Toys-R-Us that has come to life. Ana has lots of thick and very curly black hair. She has rosy cheeks.

What stands out the most about Ana is her spirit. According to his observations and Google Medical Degree, he has determined that Ana had an undiagnosed form of CAS, Childhood Apraxia of Speech.

He knows from Isabella that Ana's brain has experienced trauma before her birth. Isabella would not specify the exact details. He knows that Ana is at high risk for seizures. Ana's brain struggles to develop plans for speech movement. For her age, development-wise, she is behind. Ana's brain has difficulty directing and coordinating movements. It has difficulty telling the speech muscles how to move the lips, the jaw, and the tongue in such a way as to accurately articulate sounds and words spoken at normal speeds and rhythms.

At four, Ana has a very limited vocabulary. What Ana cannot express in words, she excels at in spirit, in energy, in presence, and in expressiveness. Little Ana even seems to have a highly developed intuition. It is almost like a spiritual gift of sensing and knowing things.

He takes another sip of the cocktail as Isabella, Cody, and Ana arrive holding shells they have just collected. Ana runs up to him, throws a feather on his stomach, and darts off.

He looks at Isabella. They are both speechless.

"How does she know?" he inquires.

"Must have heard us talking."

Little Ana is a four-year-old Buddha with a soul beyond her years. Ana understands that he has been collecting feathers ever since his mom died. Ana has never seen him pick up a feather, but Ana knows and brought one to him.

He is in awe of Little Ana's spirit.

A BEAUTIFUL FAMILY

Smithfield's Chicken 'N Bar-B-Q has one of the best Carolina minced barbeque sandwiches. It is piled high and topped with coleslaw, and there is no need for any sauce. He sits at a corner table with Isabella and the kids. The kids are silent. This is a rarity, and it means the food is a hit. A family next to them has stood and is preparing to leave as the husband speaks to Isabella. The husband hands him a business card for a mountain camp with family-owned cabins in West Virginia.

"If y'all ever make it over the mountains, give us a call."

He looks at the card and is surprised to see the location: Grafton, West Virginia. Another coincidence?   The small town of Grafton had a special importance to the lives of his mother and second father. It was a place they visited each year. Out of the 19,500 incorporated towns in the United States, he receives an invitation to Grafton. He wonders if he has become a spiritual overthinker. Perhaps a CINO in transition?

The man looks back and says, "Y'all have a beautiful family. God Bless."

He has no idea if Isabella is paying attention to the comment or what her thoughts are. However, in his mind, he silently answers, *"Yes, I really do."*

It is as if God, the Universe, or just plain luck has sent him a magic flying carpet that fills his life with a loving, off-the-wall, crazy, high-octane customized family.

He is in love with all of it.

TURTLE-GATE

The Fort Fisher Aquarium is packed with families on summer vacation. Ana is making herself known to everyone, not only at the marine museum but across the State of North Carolina.

"Noooooooooooooooooooooooo! Noooooooooooooooooooooo! Noooooooooo-oooooooo!" she screams.

Ana loves turtles. Ana is obsessed with turtles. Ana wants to take a turtle that she has picked out home, back to the hotel. Ana is not realizing that it's not a pet store. Little Ana screams, shrieks, and cries as she stands next to the live turtle exhibit.

Isabella tries to console Ana. He never knew that little rosy-cheeked sweet-face Ana, such a tiny little human, could reach the decibel level which she projected.

Ana has a marching band inside of her being. He has zero prior knowledge and no experience when it comes to dealing with a child, especially a young girl who is "his" child, but technically is not "his" child. He is living in a gray area, and Ana is on fire with walls up. He finds himself to be utterly useless, helpless, paralyzed, and a bit embarrassed at the fact that he's useless. He feels the intensity of the judging. The glances. The eye rolls. The stares. Lots of side eyes. Ever since his first-class train ride in India, he could smell attitude.

He is a parenting failure. He can't explain to everyone in the marine museum his relationship with Ana. He also can't argue his defense as to why he is standing around like a moron and not engaging and consoling "his" child.

Ana's emotion pierces his heart. He feels as if he will do anything to make little Ana's pain go away, her sadness. He had stolen the blue road sign in Canada. He contemplates stealing the turtle if everyone would stop staring at him. He could just steal it and take it to the hotel. Surely the Aquarium can manage with one less turtle. It's only petty theft!

DRIP SAND CASTLE

The day is slightly overcast, and he's back at Base Camp Happiness with his family at the beach. The umbrella flaps in the wind. The chairs are out and empty. Huddled nearby is Zoey, the surveillance unit for Mission Control. Even Zoey has a war story. He always hated the idea of a chihuahua, even though he was a dog lover, but he adores Zoey. Zoey doesn't yap in a high-pitched yelp all day long. Zoey is a one-of-a-kind little dog with an epic personality. He knows why. Zoey's mama is Isabella, and Isabella lights up the world and every creature in it.

Down by the sea, a massive construction project is in full swing. A towering castle is being built with the traditional "drip sand" method, a method perfected over generations. Isabella serves as site manager, doing some of the heavy lifting and also laying out the architectural blueprint.

Cody works very intently as the Director of Creativity, building a large tower. Cody reaches his hand into the bucket that has just the right mix of water and sand. Cody grabs a fist full of sand and lets it drip from his palm along the southeast tower that is a good two feet off the ground.

Little Ana is the Director of Digging. Ana twists and turns her head, living in her own little world. She is digging in a random pattern, one scoop here and one scoop there.

He works opposite Cody on the southwest tower and has been hired as a day laborer. He is a failed Hollywood Intern, "Man Without a Face." He is a failed Bollywood film producer. He has pursued and failed at many things in life, but he can build a drip sand castle. He is fortunate to be hired as a day laborer, paid in happy juice mixed by Isabella and the warmth of smiles from his kids. Everyone is quiet, focused. Only the wind and the ebb and flow of nature can be heard.

Drip sand castles remind him of his childhood. He and his mother would make them. Isabella and Cody are experts. His work on the castle is a bit slower than the others, mainly because he loses himself in the moment. He fills his hand with sand, looks over to Cody, then turns to watch Ana dig. All the while, half of his sand has already oozed out of his fingers.

He's mesmerized. He thinks this is how people live in the movies, a real-life romantic comedy. He glances over to Isabella with her hair blowing in the wind, wearing a sexy one-piece. She is a beach bunny, a beach model.

He wonders what he did in life to be so lucky. He got an instant family, the perfect package. All those failures don't really seem to matter. He doesn't want this moment to end. His mind takes a series of mental snapshots. Isabella, Cody, and Ana have changed his world.

Cody's imagination begins to take over. "Quick. Get in your tower, Brad. I think we're about to be attacked!"

He looks over to Cody and doesn't skip a beat. "Hold on. I just got in. What can you see?"

"They're coming for us, Brad. Hundreds of them. Looks like they have crossbows!"

"My side is clear. Wait. Wait. I see something. Oh, my god! Must be a thousand!"

Cody momentarily snaps out of his mind and looks over to Brad.

Cody smiles and realizes they are both the same age; one big kid and one small kid.

"Don't worry. I have a super blaster!" Cody says.

"A super blaster? You got an extra one?" he inquires.

Huh? "There's only one super blaster! It takes lots of training to operate."

Bredbhai proclaims, "I've got super mental powers. I'll send a wave of mind energy to wipe them out."

Cody looks at him. Eye rolls. Head shake. "That's not gonna work, not with these people. They're from Nabulus! They don't think like we do. I found an extra blaster. Come to your tower window. I'll throw it across!"

He nods. No matter how many trips around the actual world he has taken, Cody is in control of this operation. He's just along for the journey. He and Cody have really bonded on this day as if it's just the two of them on the beach. Out of nowhere, a rogue wave comes, destroying half of the castle and filling every crevice with water.

In a split second, his fairytale castle crumbles.

TWENTY-SEVEN

A NEW NORMAL: PART I

Isabella's fingertips gently caress the back of his neck, then the side of his neck, just below his ear. His eyes drift open and shut. He appears to be in a trance, completely relaxed. No anxiety. No worries.

The living room is still. They are bathed in the glow of the television set. The volume is loud. The credits of the latest animated film roll. A clock on the wall reads midnight. There is a small dining table against the wall with two chairs and a bench. Some toys litter the floor. It is a tiny place, but it is a warm place.

He and Isabella are next to one another on the L-shaped faux leather sofa. A huge ottoman takes up much of the floor. Cody and Ana are zonked out. Both kids are lying across the sofa covered in blankets, bathed in the colorful light of Poppy and Branch.

Isabella's left foot rubs against his ankle. His black Henley is unbuttoned. Isabella's hand caresses his chest. Natural. Organic. Subconscious affection. Both he and Isabella are also half asleep as DreamWorks' *Trolls* ends. He has found his happy place at the Elm Street Cinema.

Touch, the idea of affection, is something new and revolutionary for him. Touch isn't lust. The idea of touch is deeply personal to him. All his life, he craved to be touched — to feel a sense of affection from a partner, a companion, someone that wanted him.

When Isabella first began to touch him, he felt awkward and deep down, undeserving. His mind questioned it. Why? Why was Isabella touching him? He wasn't in some dark alley paying a stranger to touch him and provide the illusion of feeling loved. It wasn't transactional. It wasn't mechanical. It wasn't on the clock. It wasn't void of any emotion.

Isabella wasn't just physically touching him; she was touching his soul. Life in ADX Willow Tree, since childhood, had messed his mind up. He didn't know normal. He doubted whether or not he was worthy of normal.

However, around Isabella, he certainly feels like a happy little troll.

How does Isabella know? They never talk about it, so how does she know? It was all in his head, in his mind, in his past. Isabella is drawn to him, and Isabella knows what his soul requires. Everything about Isabella's touch is dreamlike, natural, organic, and romantic. Isabella has no idea that she had begun to demolish one of his most rigid internal belief systems.

In his world, in his life, there are two train tracks. Love is on one. Intimacy and sex are on another track. They are not connected and have never crossed paths. His introduction to anything sexual was in the treehouse as a young boy. It was not love. Being drugged and raped as an adult in Mumbai was not love.

He is a master at detachment and dissociation. His ADX Willow Tree orthodox beliefs allowed him to have love for a partner without a need for intimacy. He understands that it is a messed-up philosophy, but he accepted it as his normal.

It was a belief system that allowed him to contribute, to serve, and be a caretaker in his marriage without ever questioning why his spouse never wanted to touch him.

Not only is Isabella breaking a wall, but her actions are also triggering him. At times, being touched is frightening. His romance with Isabella is the very first time he is able to merge both train tracks into the same soul — love and intimacy. It is groundbreaking and earth-shattering internally.

A NEW NORMAL: PART II

Children were never part of his life equation. He never imagined having a child nor did he want to have a child of his own. His reasoning was simple: the Willow Tree. He had the best mom in the entire world; yet, she wasn't able to protect him from darkness. He loved his mom and knew that as long as she was alive, she would never know about the treehouse. He didn't want to hurt his mother because he knew that she would internalize his pain and blame herself for missing something.

He understands his psychological battles, his walls, and his life at ADX Willow Tree which is why he could not imagine any child, let alone his own, suffering from trauma. It is a difficult balance to allow one's child to live, grow, and experience life while at the same time offering 24-hour unconditional love and protection from evil. It is a job he feels unqualified for.

He loves kids and the idea of childhood. He is an architect of ideas and programs for kids and youth. *EKTA*. Boy Scout Troop Mark Twain. International Exchange Programs. He loves to imitate the quirks and mannerisms of youth, to joke with kids, to make them smile, and to create vehicles for transformation and learning; however, there is a limit, a line in the sand, and a certain emotional wall. There was a disconnect between him and the idea of being a dad.

And then God sends him Cody and Ana. Two little hell raisers, two little rug rats who were sent by slingshot into his life at a time when he least expected.

Life has provided him an opportunity to experience childhood all over again through the eyes of Cody and Ana. It is his second chance. The Nerf Doomlands 2169 Vagabond Blaster has blown up a belief that he could or would never be a father.

PAPA BREDHBAI

Ana is a complete mess. Her long curly hair looks as if she has placed her finger in a light socket. Birds should be building a nest in her head. Ana is in the middle of an Olympic gymnastics performance for everyone. She stands up on the back of the L-shaped couch. Ana readies herself for her move as a thick strand of hair falls down in front of her eyes. She reaches her little arm up, and with tremendous force, brushes the strand of hair back while exhaling at the same time. One of Ana's front teeth is missing. It is a tooth she had knocked out some days earlier. Ana places both hands in the air and proceeds to jump, flip over, and roll off the other end of the sofa. He sits on the sofa. Isabella and Cody are nearby. He holds up his hands, all ten fingers. He gives Ana a perfect 10 and knows she is on her way to striking Olympic gold in a few years' time.

Ana rushes over to the sofa and jumps on his lap! She has more energy than the Tasmanian Devil. His nickname for Ana is "The Cranium Cracker." Due to her partial disability, depth perceptions are sometimes impaired. And so, like a wild bison in Yellowstone, Little Ana rams a headbutt.

Bam! Bam! Ana's head comes crashing into his, creating a cranium shockwave that really hurts. No personal space. No boundaries. Face to face. Eye to eye. Little Ana, wide-eyed with a face that stretches and contorts endless expressive emotion, is locked in a duel.

Due to that disability, Ana is unable to speak full words or construct sentences; yet, she begins to speak to him with great power and eloquence in a new language, one that they have created together.

"Ka. Bo. La. Ning. Da!" shouts Ana.

Cody and Isabella watch as he, without skipping a beat, responds to Ana. "Bing. Kaaaa. Ku!"

Ana takes a deep breath and softens her reply. "Chi. Sa. Bu. Kaaaaaaa."

He grits his teeth together and is eyeball to eyeball with this little spitfire galactic force. "Keeeeeee. Ka. Moo. Na. Pikaaaa. Zalu. Kimbatu."

Cody begins to laugh and looks at Isabella. "What are they saying? What are they talking about?"

Isabella laughs as she watches her little daughter and Bredbhai communicate in a human language only they understand.

Being rammed in the head continuously by a small child was not a part of his life resume, but life in India had provided him with a human language skill set. Certainly, words, sentence structure, and grammar are part of every civilized society. Language allows depth, meaning, and insight into the mind. However, he would argue that in the emotional fabric of humanity, non-verbal communication is important and transformative. Human energy. Human emotions. There is a life force within every human soul, regardless of race, class, ethnicity, gender, country, religion, or alphabet.

Little Ana calls him "Bad." Ana has captivated his mind. Ana has become his little buddy. Ana has stolen his heart.

Cody is always a bit more guarded. Cody is quite protective of Isabella and is somewhat fearful of opening up fully to Bredbhai as Ana had done. He senses that Cody is out of alignment, afraid to let his guard down or has a fear. However, there are breakthroughs over time, some of which had to do with fart machines...

He has purchased the loudest one from Target. He and Cody often blasted each other. Cody doesn't need a fart machine since Cody proudly lets them rip. Cody even has a special jump and a half-squat that is done prior to each explosive blast.

Cody is always the entertainer. Cody loves to wear a favorite wizard robe and loves to create comfortable relaxation zones around the sofa with lots of pillows and layers of blankets, all for movie nights at the Elm Street Cinema Hall.

There is also Sleepy Time Tea. Cody would always take charge, assigning seats and zones with Cody always getting prime real estate snuggled up next to Isabella. However, Cody does "allow" him to be close to Isabella. He and Isabella, despite their chemistry and attraction, always prioritized the kids and always respected the children first. In front of and around the children, it was always about family time and family moments.

Cody is a master dessert maker. Cody calls them "fancy desserts," which often include ice cream, milk, crushed cookie crumbs, and some kind of syrup. He and Cody would bond over a mutual love for reruns of *Everybody Loves Raymond*. Cody has a particular fondness for Frank Barone, played by the late Peter Boyle. When a line delivered by Frank hits Cody's funny bone, Cody would replay the scene over and over and over, dozens of times. They would both laugh. However, he was in his forties, not ten, so by the 18th time of replaying the scene, he was worn out.

At times, he and Isabella would be required to dig out one of the five remotes from a peanut and candy-filled crack in the sofa to push mute when *Raymond* veered into adult content. He and Isabella are always on the same page. Protective, like hawks. He adores Isabella's mothering skills.

He rarely watches movies primarily because he lived and worked immersed in India. He would see a block of movies on long 24-hour journeys back and forth from India in his prior life.

However, this all changed with Cody, Ana, and Isabella. *Trolls. Spirit. Despicable Me. Sing. Boss Baby. The Polar Express. The Secret Life of Pets. Minions. Beauty & The Beast. Aladdin. The Incredibles. Shrek. Shrek 2. Shrek 3. Shrek 15. Shrek 21.* He loves them all.

Isabella is an amazing chef. She might have a roast in the oven or some homemade meatloaf. Isabella might have her amazing chili topped with grated cheese.

Isabella is a red wine drinker. He and Isabella share lots of red wine together, more often than not in a romantic boujee kiddie cup, sippy cup, plastic cup, or whatever is washed.

The little condo on Elm is a happy place, a dream. He, Isabella, Cody, and Ana rip and run up and down the stairs playing hide-and-seek. They scare each other and are fully immersed in the innocence of childhood. He and Cody build forts together. Ana runs up to him with her Halloween candy and repeats the words, "Nick or Neat."

He buys Cody a rock tumbler so that Cody can spin and polish gemstones. He buys Cody a bigger bicycle for Cody's birthday, and they take turns riding around the parking lot. He purchases little placemats for kids that are maps of America. Cody often points to a state and asks him how it is there since Cody knows that he has been to all fifty.

He and Isabella swing the kids, one by one, in a blanket and toss them safely onto the sofa. Cody has grown comfortable with him. Cody even jumps on his back and asks to be picked up and swung by the legs while laughing all the time.

He is a part of Isabella's larger family. He is welcomed into Isabella's world by her mom, her sisters, their families, and the nieces and nephews. He is a part of family cookouts and gatherings, which with a Latin family, tends to be very often, very loud, and last for days. Isabella's world has accepted him, just as he is.

At Christmas time, he brings bags and bags full of gifts for his children. His new addiction is watching Ana and Cody's faces light up each time they open a gift.

The kids don't sleep in their room. Cody and Ana always snuggle up to Mama Bear in the small double bed. There are six arms and six legs poetically interconnected in various directions and at various angles, a Rockwell painting titled "Unconditional Love."

THE REAL BOSS

Cody often asks, "Brad are you coming over tonight? Come. Come over! For a little bit."

However, Cody always keeps a watchful eye on Mama Bear, making sure that any private moments are limited. After all, Cody has exclusivity.

"Mom!" Cody shouts.

Silence.

"Mom. Mom. Mom." Cody is upstairs, well out of sight in Isabella's room, and is supposed to be asleep.

Downstairs, in the yellow glow of a light above the stove, he and Isabella are making out, just like teenagers. He had planned to leave twenty minutes earlier, but those lips which Isabella had in her possession held him back. He and Isabella are all over each other, very handsy, very passionate. Magnetic. Fluttering heartbeats.

"Coming. Just a second, Cody," Isabella responds.

In Cody's world, that is the wrong answer! Cody climbs out of bed and walks to the top of the stairs. Cody is still out of sight from the kitchen but is getting closer.

Cody gets anxious. "Mom. It's late! When are you coming?"

He and Isabella head toward the door. The bottom of the stairs, the front door, and the narrow hallway all converge at the same place. By this point, Cody is halfway down the stairs. Cody is the man of the house at eight.

"Good night, Brad. Drive home safe," Cody says.

LITTLE ANA'S MAGIC

At times, it would be just him, Isabella, and Ana. Cody would be hunting or fishing with Cody's biological father.

Cody likes to roam and be outdoors. Ana prefers her mom at all times. Both Ana and Cody have the same biological father; however, it does not seem like the kid's dad has much involvement or interest at all. He doesn't really ask many questions. He has never seen or met Cody and Ana's actual father.

In general, it seems like the kids spend, at most, two weekends a month with their dad. However, even those are often cut short since their dad changes plans abruptly, cuts it short, or cancels the entire weekend, on average one hundred percent of the time.

Each time, Isabella drops the kids off and picks them up. He's never seen the guy, ever. And quite honestly, he is too immersed in the tiny moments and details of reliving his childhood again and the fun he's having being Bredbhai, Baldano, Brad, and Bad to Cody and Ana to wonder about their father.

Ana walks around the living room carrying her pride and joy, an old doll that used to be Isabella's. It now has a missing leg and arm. Ana walks up to him with the limbless doll.

He looks at Ana. "Oh, wow. Is that your baby?"

Ana cannot pronounce the word "baby," so instead Ana shouts, "Beebe!"

"What's your baby's name?" he asks.

In true epic Hollywood melodrama, Ana closes one eye and looks up toward the ceiling, as if she is thinking. Ana then lowers her head and looks at him.

"Beebe!" she says.

He laughs. "I see. So, your baby's name is *Beebe*?" as he imitates Ana.

He arrives at Elm Street one winter day wearing lip balm. He removes and hangs up his jacket and then takes a seat on the sofa. Isabella brings him a cup of red wine and sits down.

Ana rushes up to him with a paper towel and climbs up on his lap. As he is talking to Isabella, Ana begins to scrub his lips. Ana uses the paper towel like sandpaper. Ana never ceases to amaze him.

He and Isabella are in awe of seeing how Ana's mind works. It's a moment of revelation for him.   Children really do pay attention to every detail, every word, every action, every sound, every tone, every moment — everything that an adult does. He is a guy. His lips are not supposed to be shiny. Maybe Ana thinks he made a mess just like she does...

Little Ana started a special program before kindergarten with a speech pathologist. Ana is not feeling well, so she stays home from school. He is sitting on the couch with Isabella when Ana approaches with her blanket. Ana crawls up and lays her head onto her mother's legs. Ana then rests both her tiny legs across his legs. Ana has made a little nest. She is curled up under a blanket between him and Isabella.

Priceless. Humbled. Honored. No words can describe moments such as these, moments where his heart swells with emotion. Nothing in the world could have prepared him for what it feels like to watch a little girl's face light up every single time he walks through the front door. He learns that whenever there is a knock at the door, Ana is only concerned if it is two people: her grandmother or "Bad." Every. Single. Time. It does not matter what Ana is doing. It does not matter where Ana's mind is. As soon as Little Ana sees his face in the doorway, she beams as if she were Queen Poppy in *Trolls*.

Nothing in the material world, nothing in the physical world, absolutely nothing is more powerful to him than experiencing unconditional love from that little girl, his Little Ana.

TWENTY-EIGHT

VALENTINE'S DAY –
7:30 A.M.

He drives into the parking lot of the condo complex on Elm Street. Isabella hates living at the condo due to a few shady neighbors; however, it's a restart, a safe zone, and a roof over the head for her and the kids.

The condo is meant to be a transition from Isabella's old life to a new one. Isabella works extremely hard and earns very well; yet, raising two children by herself is expensive.

His heart had led him to Isabella, Cody, and Ana. He doesn't require a cliffside mansion in Malibu. He had slept on cardboard in the back of a truck in India and lived in concrete flats with squat toilets. It suits him just fine.

He wants to arrive before the kids go to school. He is there for Cody and Ana. A dozen Ecuadorian red roses are scheduled to be delivered to Isabella at work later in the day. He has prepared two Valentine's Day goodie bags for his kids. Along with a ton of each of their favorite candies, there is a toy.

For Cody, it's a robot that climbs up the wall. For Ana, it's a horse from her favorite movie *Spirit*. He is addicted to watching the children open gifts, and he can't wait for any opportunity to get them a gift.

The entire process is exciting for him — the idea, the shopping, the planning, the preparation, the anticipation, and the delivery. With bags in hand, he eagerly knocks. The door opens, and Isabella is surprised. It's a routine morning, and he normally never just shows up unannounced. He holds up the bags.

"Just want to surprise them before school!"

Isabella smiles and her eyes widen. "Go on upstairs. They're still in bed. Just waking." He is only planning to be a few minutes. It's a cold winter morning, and he is wearing his bulky black Columbia ski jacket, jeans, a USC "Country Club" cap, and his shades. He makes his way up the stairs and into the bedroom.

Cody's eyes are still closed. Ana sees him enter. A big smile comes across her face as she quickly and sheepishly flips over and buries her head in the pillow, always the little actress. He places the bags on the bed.

"Happy Valentine's Day, guys! Look what I found."

Little Ana melts. It doesn't matter if it is a $1 box of candy or an expensive $100 toy. Ana is always immensely grateful. He has never seen any child in the world get so excited. Ana's face beams! Her eyes get so wide. Her mouth opens all the way. There is so much expression, so much emotion, and so much feeling that radiates out that it is as if her soul is speaking. It is captivating.

He and Ana have a super special bond. He thinks that this is what the phrase, "daddy's little girl" means. Ana pulls out the candy. With each box, she grins for twenty seconds of unfiltered joy. She is a little light force.

Cody is older and increasingly more guarded with feelings. He sees a glimmer in Cody's eyes, the feeling of accepting love, but Cody quickly tries to hide that expression.

Isabella enters the room and looks surprised. Isabella has placed large chocolate hearts next to Cody's and Ana's pillows for them to wake up to.

"I thought it was Valentine's Day? Looks more like Christmas!" Isabella says.

Ana hands him her *Spirit* horse and wants him to open it. Ana, with her bird's nest hair, follows him downstairs to the kitchen. He pulls out the scissors and cuts open the box along with the 500 little zip ties that bolt the toy to the box. He finally frees the horse, allowing circulation back to its legs so it can gallop again. Ana is off the charts excited and runs back upstairs.

He follows her upstairs, for just another minute, to say goodbye and wish Ana and Cody a great day ahead.

Isabella is in mom mode. She is working through a mental checklist of morning rituals and rushes back downstairs.

STORM CLOUDS - 7:45 AM

In the blink of an eye, the world changes. The sound of terror ripples like shockwaves, shaking the entire foundation of the heart space on Elm Street. A loud pounding is heard downstairs at the front door. Not a knock. Not a banging sound. It is a pure wrecking ball. The repetitive motion of a fist banging and punching the door.

"Open the fucking door, Isabella! Open the fucking door now! Open the fucking door!" calls out a male voice.

The shockwaves strike his heart. He sees a look of fear on Cody and Ana's faces. He stands with the kids just outside the bedroom door.

"Oh, God!" Isabella says out loud from downstairs.

The tone in Isabella's voice is unforgettable. It is a tone he's never heard from her before, a tone of anxiousness and trepidation.

"Open the fucking door! Right now!'

It sounds like a bull barging through a gate. He continues to stand with his kids, unsure of how to react. He hears a push at the door. He can't see it, but he thinks maybe Isabella cracked open the door.

Whatever transpired, a rabid bull is now inside condo #133.

"Where the fuck is he? Where the fuck is he, Isabella?"

Isabella's voice, monotone, repeats the same thing, "James. James. James. James. James."

The bull is loud and rambunctious. The bull screams, "Where the fuck is he?"

Upstairs, he understands that "he" was the "he." He understands that he is the target of the raging bull. His heart beats faster. He chooses to stay next to his children. He sees their sweet faces are now filled with stress, worry, and fear.

He has experience with trauma, lots of trauma, but somehow this moment feels different. It's very dark. The energy of the moment is suffocatingly tense. It is new for him. Part of him feels confused and unsure. He has absorbed the fear in Isabella's voice, the faces of his kids, and his internal guidance. It doesn't feel good at all. It feels crushing, heavy, and dangerous. It is an awful feeling.

He moves to the right, takes a couple of steps down the stairs, and then it happens. The raging bull appears at the bottom of the stairs and stops. James Thomas Jenkins, the biological father of Cody and Ana, has entered the building and is bringing darkness on Valentine's Day. James locks eyes with him, just as a heat-seeking missile locks in on its target.

James runs up the stairs. A scruffy White guy who appears unkempt, unwell, unhinged, and stands about the same height as he.

DEMONS ARE REAL

In his mind, James Thomas Jenkins appears to him as a living and breathing manifestation of Satan. At this moment, everything that radiates out of the inner being of James Jenkins is dark.

"Stay away from these fucking kids!" James screams.

He responds with silence and observation.

James is not angry. The idea of anger is an insult. He is not witnessing anger. He is witnessing something much deeper, much more evil, and much more sinister. Squinted Eyes. Hatred. Vitriol. A trembling face. Convulsions. James is a man filled with inner rage. James is a *Nightmare on Elm Street*. Code Red. Mayday. Code Red.

He feels a rare moment of alignment — a moment in which all of his red flags, radar systems, and internal intuitive guidance is reading and processing not only the rage of James Jenkins, but also the energy, the soul, and the spirit of such a truly dark force. At this moment, it is as if James' body has been possessed by evil. It is a lot to process. He is frozen, literally frozen, in the moment.

"Stay away from these fucking kids!" Lucifer repeats over and over. Each time, seething, boiling, and trembling with rage.

It's as if James is striking him with words, piercing the innocent bubble of love he has for Cody and Ana, a love that has been welcomed by Isabella.

Utter shock. Disbelief. How did the innocence of Valentine's Day end up as a bird's eye view into Hell?

Cody and Ana stand frozen just a few feet away at the top of the stairs. When he last saw Isabella, she was downstairs at the bottom of the steps. His eyes are locked with the demon.

His mind is T.D. Jakes with a sermon. His mind is Maya Angelou with a pen. His mind is Michael Jordan with a basketball. His mind is Elliott Erwitt with a camera. His mind is Max Park with a Rubik's Cube. He doesn't possess a degree in psychology, but he has lived through enough abuse and trauma in his life, has studied the mind for years, and has unlocked his own door to ADX Willow Tree.

In real time, he is connecting the dots. He is connecting the dots to questions he never asked to situations and behaviors he has observed with his kids to emotional challenges the children face and to Ana's physical brain trauma before birth. His mind is the sharpest it has ever been.

He realizes that James Thomas Jenkins is not just some deadbeat father who doesn't give a shit about Cody and Ana. James is a stone-cold, flip-the-switch abuser. He sees it. He feels it. The hatred is petrifying. All he thinks about are Cody, Ana, and their extreme emotional sensitivities. He can only imagine what they are sensing and feeling.

He understands that, at this moment, he is the trigger for James. His plan of action is simple: de-escalate. It's very much like the moment when one has to choose the right wire to cut in order to diffuse the bomb and shut off the countdown clock. Therefore, he chooses not to engage verbally with James. Instead, he plans to slowly head down the stairs and exit the condo. With each second that passes, he can feel a sense of James Jenkins ticking away, almost as if on the verge of an explosion. He feels as if James is ripping him apart mentally. The hatred is thicker than molasses.

TOO LATE

James grabs his black Columbia jacket with both hands and tightens the grip. It's a fleeting instant, but in his mind, it plays out in slow motion. With as much force as a jet engine, James shoves his back against the wall and violently shoves him down the staircase. He tries to regain balance but gravity takes over.

He tumbles. *Bam. Bam. Bam. Bam. Bam.*

His legs get twisted. He lands at the bottom of the staircase. His head crashes into the wall. He falls onto a basket of shoes. His neck and back are in pain. He is bewildered. He is dazed. He is in shock. He hates conflict. He's never been violently attacked before.

The bubble has just popped. Elm Street. Cody. Ana. Isabella. His happy little family has a secret in the closet, a devil in the closet. James lunges down the stairs and hovers over him like a wolverine. He manages to stand up. To his right, he sees Isabella standing, silent. At the top of the stairs, he sees Cody's face. Cody's eyes are wider than he has ever seen them. Cody's mouth is wide open. Cody appears terrified. He is unable to see Little Ana's face since James "Anti-Christ" Jenkins is in the way.

James is stuck to him like superglue. "Stay away from these fucking kids! Or I'll knock your fucking teeth out!

He slowly exits the front door, walking backward. There are a couple of steps outside the door leading down to the sidewalk. He navigates them backwards.

James is stuck to him at every step.

He utters his very first words to Lucifer. "Relax. Just relax."

James instantly bristles. "You want me to fucking relax? Fucking relax? If I ever catch you around here again, I'm gonna knock your fucking teeth out! Stay away from these fucking kids!"

At this point, many of the neighbors, neighbors that he knows and is friendly with, are watching from their doorways. He makes his way to the car, gets in, and slowly drives away. An EF-8 tornado has just plowed through Elm Street. A Category 7 Hurricane. A tsunami has just crushed the drip sand castle.

It feels like when the bomb goes off in the movie and the heartbeats of humanity are silenced. The only sounds that remain are car alarms, ringing cell phones, and circuit boxes exploding. It feels as if, in a fleeting second, Hell has scorched the earth and destroyed a land that has been flowing with love, life, innocence, compassion, freedom, milk, and honey.

ORIGIN OF LUCIFER

He doesn't know much about James Thomas "Lucifer" Jenkins. He only knows bits and pieces. He has never met James. He never really asked and wasn't really told much.

Mr. Jenkins is local, a few years older than him, and from the same high school. Everyone is supposed to know everyone in a small town, but he doesn't know James and has spent decades out of the country traveling back and forth to India. James is a part-time charter fisherman, a part-time "Woodchuck", and a full-time son of a bitch.

Lucifer Jenkins hails from a large Catholic family, the kind with nieces and nephews named after Biblical characters. James is supposedly a man of the Lord. Faith. Family. Guns. Lucifer wheeled around in a jacked-up burgundy monster truck, a twenty-year-old Ford. James put the monster in monster truck.

His prior relationship with James Thomas Jenkins simply did not exist. Nada. Zilch. Nothing. It was an out-of-sight, out-of- mind relationship.

FACT PATTERNS

Regarding the kids, there was no marriage, no divorce, nor any structured custody agreement. It is a gray world, a gray zone. He has hung out with Isabella, Cody, and Ana for nearly two years. He has spent many nights at Elm Street, is part of Isabella's family, and joins in on holidays and family functions. During that entire time, not once did James Thomas Jenkins show up at Elm Street. Nada. Zilch. Nothing.

Cody and Ana would spend one weekend or half a weekend a month with Mr. Jenkins. Isabella struggled to obtain any sort of regular child support payment. James paid whatever he felt, whenever he felt. Mr. Jenkins refused to assist or buy medical insurance for the children or assist with medical bills.

James Thomas made lots of promises to the kids but never followed through on any of them. James had promised Cody a trip to Disneyland. Cody got excited, only to not go.

Isabella has, from the beginning, defined herself as a single mom with two children, and she very much appears to fit that description.

RED FLAGS OVERLOOKED

While Cody and Ana spent very little time with their biological father, the returns home to Elm Street were anything but normal. Both children were emotionally on edge, extremely sensitive, and extra clingy to Isabella. It might take the kids twenty-four hours to acclimate back into the comfort of Isabella's little condo.

Isabella had mentioned to him once that James made Cody and Ana take off the clothes James had purchased for them because those clothes could not be worn in Isabella's house. Cruel. Twisted.

Over time, he heard whispers from Isabella's friends and family, whispers about James Thomas Jenkins. It seemed that no one in Isabella's family liked James. In fact, it wasn't that they did not like James, it is that they detested him. The idea of James invoked a very strong negative reaction from the adults in Isabella's life.

He heard vaguely about a weed habit, a womanizing habit, and multiple Facebook accounts. He had also heard about late-night cocaine deliveries. Lucifer Jenkins certainly did not seem to be competing for Father of the Year but, once again, he never saw the man. Ever. He never paid any attention to James Thomas Jenkins for two reasons: one, the information he heard was hearsay and did not impact life with Isabella and the kids, and two, Isabella always placed a "positive spin" on any negative comments about James from others. Even when Isabella briefly mentioned being "pushed to the ground" at James' house, the story was told in such a way, minimized in such a way, that it didn't seem like a big deal. Isabella brushed everything off.

Isabella is masterful at shining her light, shining her smile, and projecting others in the best possible light. He is dating Isabella, so if she wasn't worried about James Jenkins, then why would he be worried?

In no way, shape, or form could he have ever imagined that Isabella's inner light would have been entangled with such immense darkness. It is a mind-blowing reality to confront.

BOMBSHELL DISCOVERY

A few months prior to Valentine's Day, he learned the reason why he should have asked questions. His heart had already been tattooed with Cody, Ana, and Isabella when he serendipitously discovered the reason James Thomas Jenkins was never around.

James' driver's license had been suspended for three years following an arrest on a third DUI charge and a verbal altercation with Sheriff deputies. Huh? James had only recently gotten driving privileges reinstated.

Isabella had informed James that she had a boyfriend. Lucifer's reaction to Isabella's news initially was not one of anger but of control, manipulation, and deception. Lucifer's reaction was to imitate the role of an actual father and to suddenly take an interest in the lives of Cody and Ana. Lucifer's response was to project to Isabella, Cody, and Ana that Lucifer was a changed man.

However, on Valentine's Day, the mask slipped and the real James popped out, the spirit just below the surface. Violence, Control, and Fear were the true trademarks of Lucifer.

Valentine's Day is a game changer. It is the moment he meets the real James Thomas Jenkins, not Isabella's projected version.

Happy Valentine's Day.

TWENTY-NINE

MOMENTS LATER

He sits inside his car in his garage in a state of shock and confusion. His body feels empty and hollow. Only his mind is working, trying to make sense of the cliff he has just been thrown from.

What the hell happened? Did he do something wrong? Maybe he's a coward. Maybe he should have stayed. He is well versed in emotional violence but not physical violence. It's a lot to process.

The bubble of innocence he is living with respect to Isabella, Cody, and Ana no longer exists. His experience with decades of emotional abuse has damaged his mind, and it is still in a state of healing. It has impacted his ability to think clearly, to see past projections, to trust his reality, to doubt his reality, and to always blame himself.

His mind replays the attack over and over. Those eyes. The eyes of a demon. Witnessing a monster in full-blown rage is unforgettable.

Cody's face is branded into his memory, a face of pure terror and fear. His children. What kind of person are they dealing with? He can only think about Cody and Ana, the emotional trauma of such a violent moment of pure insanity.

ONE TRUTH – TWO REALITIES

"I just wanted to apologize," Isabella says in a quiet, calm, withdrawn, and remorseful tone.

He has cautiously decided to drive back to Elm Street to make sure everyone is okay when Isabella calls.

He is a bit curt, unintentionally. "Apologize? Isabella. Why are you apologizing? You didn't do anything."

Isabella's mind begins to immediately rationalize events, and she blames herself. "I should have never left Cody's backpack at James' house. It's all my fault. I forgot."

He listens to Isabella, but he does not recognize her. He has always admired Isabella's fierce independence, business acumen, strong intuition, epic mom skills, compassion for others, and spirit that beamed like a light.

The Isabella he is speaking to on the phone is a dim reflection of that light. It is jarring to hear Isabella in this tone.

"Maybe James thought you spent the night."

"So? What if I had spent the night?" he responds.

Silence.

He switches gears. "How are Cody and Ana?"

"We made it to school on time. Cody says he's worried now."

"Worried about what?"

"Cody said now he'll get in trouble with his dad for the candy and gifts," Isabella responds.

WTF? Huh? Cody's his buddy. He's given numerous gifts to Cody, too many to count. He quickly realizes that he and Isabella are suddenly living on two different sides of a giant wall.

Isabella's response to the violence has been to rush the kids to school as if it were a normal day. Perhaps it is normal for Isabella, but violence is not normal for him. It is also odd that despite being overly compassionate, Isabella doesn't ask him if he is okay or injured. Isabella projects zero compassion toward him. Isabella's mind refuses to acknowledge the truth as an automatic defense mechanism. Instead, deflection.

"Now I've got a big hole in my wall!"

His heart begins to sink. "What? Did James punch the wall?"

Isabella calmly replies, "No. There's a big hole in the wall at the bottom of the steps where you tripped."

What? You have got to be kidding. Huh? At this very moment, he is emotionally blindsided. On one hand, he is fighting to hold on to his reality, his sense of self. On the other hand, he is listening to the woman he loves rewrite history, rewrite the script, all while omitting his personal truth.

His reality, the reality of being violently assaulted, hasn't just been minimized, it's been erased by Isabella. For the first time ever in their relationship, he raises his voice on the phone. "Tripped? Tripped! Isabella, I didn't trip. I was thrown down the stairs as the kids watched."

Isabella has no response. There is only pin-drop silence.

I'M NOT AS TOUGH AS YOU THINK

His heart believes Isabella knows what happened. His mind is witnessing her subconscious defensive mechanism to minimize, deflect, rewrite history, and project a watered-down version of Lucifer Jenkins.

He has always been in awe of Isabella's strength of character; however, there were a couple of moments when Isabella remarked, "I'm not as tough as you think."

His car is parked in the nearby movie theater parking lot as he begins to realize that Valentine's Day has given him a front-row seat, a glimpse into Isabella's own version of ADX Willow Tree. It is an internal prison in which she is still very much trapped.

The very idea that Isabella, Cody, and Ana have normalized the unhinged freak show insanity of James Thomas Jenkins' explosive rage is frightening. The roots of Cody's fear and Cody's recent and sudden emotional distancing now make sense.

"Cody needs to see how his dad really is," Isabella's own sister commented once to Isabella.

Today, he has seen the true nature of James Jenkins and he is not at all impressed. He understands that Cody and Isabella have both been conditioned to prioritize James' point of view and needs rather than their own. He understands the goal is to not make "Dad" mad, not trigger "Dad," no matter what.

He is speechless and dumbfounded at how casually Isabella seems to disregard the reality of their shared history, intimacy, closeness, family moments, and bonds with the kids.

"Isabella, I was attacked. I've never been attacked before. I should have called the police. I had no idea what to do. I was worried about you all. I knew he wanted me gone so I left to diffuse the situation," he says.

Isabella remains emotionally withdrawn. Quietly, she says, "Do whatever you feel you have to do."

He sits in the car, staring out the window.

Out of nowhere, Isabella simply says, "They need their father. They need him."

There is an inner sadness behind Isabella's tone. She speaks almost in a rehearsed manner.

"Did I ever say that? That the kids didn't need their father. I never said that. What just happened this morning? In that condo. No child deserves that! No one."

He and Isabella continue on different wavelengths.

"I'm their advocate. I do whatever Cody and Ana want," Isabella replies.

It is a disjointed conversation. It is as if he is a mirror and Isabella is talking to herself, repeating a belief system.

He says, "Isabella, you are the adult. Being their advocate means fighting for them, to protect them from trauma. You have to see it."

INTERNAL EARTHQUAKE

As soon as he returns home that morning, he opens his computer to memorialize his truth, his reality, and his experience in great detail. He has had no further contact with Isabella that day and assumed the dozen red roses had arrived at the salon.

The next morning, he visits the local police station to speak with an officer in an attempt to make sense of what happened and to see if he was overreacting.

The officer articulates the meaning of assault and battery as well as his rights. Should he choose to press charges via the local county magistrate, they would need to find probable cause before issuing an arrest warrant. He learns that should he press charges, he would be represented by the Commonwealth Attorney's office.

It is an overwhelming reality to wrestle with. It is a crossroads moment for him. On a personal level, he never had the courage to stand up for himself and had always minimized trauma in the same way Isabella has. On the other hand, it is as if Lucifer Jenkins is the manifestation of a perfect storm — a storm that triggers him, triggers his fear of not being able to protect his children from danger, from harm.

CONTEMPLATION

Isabella has ghosted him. After their last conversation, he knows that Isabella is not as strong as he thought; she was right about that.

Isabella's emotional abandonment of him is collateral damage. He needs to make a decision and wants to gain some perspective. He reaches out to Elaine, his long-term counselor, who is familiar with his transition out of ADX Willow Tree. Elaine suggested he press charges, that accountability is needed. She also says that perhaps by pressing charges, a boundary would be set and Isabella might be able to build on it and begin to psychologically free herself to really protect the kids.

His ex-Marine second father says the behavior of James Jenkins is completely unacceptable and that there should be accountability; otherwise, James will not stop.

He also reaches out to his energy healer, Stephanie, who is keenly aware of narcissistic injury and psychology. Stephanie reminds him that James is well aware of his presence in the lives of Isabella, Cody, and Ana for several months prior to the attack. There was no sudden surprise on Valentine's Day nor was there a misunderstanding of who he was or what he was doing in the condo that morning. There was no threat.

"Are you going to talk with Isabella about this?" Stephanie directly asks.

"I was thinking about it. I worry about their safety. But Stephanie, I never asked to be put in this situation. It's not fair."

Her response surprises him. "Don't. Don't speak to Isabella. Because you might doubt yourself." Stephanie is beginning to sense that his mind may be wavering.

He thinks back to his last conversation with Isabella. "I did mention on the phone that I could go to the police. And Isabella did tell me to do what I had to do. That was a talk, but following through is different. It's scary."

THE NIGHTMARE ON ELM STREET

What would Gandhi do, turn the other cheek or prosecute? What would Jesus do, empower a bully or make a phone call to God? What would Dr. King do, give a soaring speech on the cruelty of domestic violence against children or pursue justice?

His gut told him he has to. His three trusted inner circle advisors have all confirmed that he should.

In reality, he is scared. He loathes conflict. He doesn't think much of lawyers and his experience with the legal system in America left him unimpressed. This isn't a psychological study at Stanford, it's real life. Lives are involved, kids are involved, and relationships are involved. No matter which angles he looks from, all of it is messy.

One act of violence on Valentine's Day uprooted everything; however, it is clear to him that he needs to be a voice for Cody and Little Ana, children of abuse.

THIRTY

VERB. NOUN. ADJECTIVE.

"Anger. You can't say rage. You have to say anger," the Commonwealth Attorney explains.

Do what? He is seated in a small conference room across from the seasoned Commonwealth Attorney, a female attorney assigned to his case, and the head of Victim Witness. It is a bit of an unusual meeting to have for a misdemeanor case, but he is an INFJ and that means leaving no stone unturned.

Everyone appears to believe him and even tells him that he is exhibiting post-traumatic behaviors, responses, and actions that they are accustomed to witnessing based on decades of experience in domestic violence cases. He is still visibly shaken and wants to know each and every detail of the process.

He wants to know what he could anticipate and how he could best prepare himself to calm his constant state of anxiety and dread for an upcoming trial that had been scheduled for mid-April.

He is being told he could not use the word "rage," but he has no idea why. He has not experienced anger. He would get angry at times in his life. All humans get angry, especially religious folk.

Why is the judicial system editing his vocabulary? Why is the judicial system watering down his truth, his reality? Adjectives for Rage included; Sheer Impassioned, Primal, Terrifying Murderous, Savage, Mindless, Raw, and Frightening. These words certainly described the face of Lucifer Jenkins on Valentine's Day, not merely anger.

Ultimately, the judge would decide if he is to be believed or not. However, the idea that an American trial, one that is to be held in the English Language, would forbid him from using English words makes no sense. He feels as if the system is attempting to rewrite or manipulate his reality, his freedom of expression, and his truth.

VICTIM IMPACT STATEMENT

The opportunity to compose his thoughts and feelings into a carefully crafted impact statement is the only thing he feels in control of. It is the only part of the trial he is at ease with, and he has already begun to draft his statement.

"That's not allowed," opined the Victim Witness Director.

He has hit his second brick wall. First, American justice is editing his English and now he learns the "land of the free" is an illusion. His case does not qualify for a Victim Impact Statement, as those are reserved for certain felonies like murder. He gets the feeling that in the court system, his case is essentially on the same level as a parking ticket, an expired inspection sticker, or driving 35 MPH in a 25 MPH zone.

The limits being placed on him by the "system" are profound. The entire process is messy. He hasn't asked the police officer more questions because he has no frame of reference since he isn't used to physical violence.

Had he known that his basic human rights would be curtailed in a court of law, then he might have reevaluated his decision to press charges.

It becomes clear to him why so many people just let things slide, remain silent, and enable abusive behavior to continue. Rather than making him feel more secure, hitting both legal brick walls made him more anxious and eager to put the entire event in his rearview mirror.

Just a Day in the Life, a Day in the Life of Bullshit.

A PSYCHOLOGICAL KNOT

Life is about choices and the consequences of those choices. His decision to press charges against James Thomas Jenkins is well-meaning, well-thought-out, and in consultation with others. It is not an emotional reaction, a made-up accusation, or low vibrational revenge.

If it had only been about him, he could have said "fuck the drama" and walked away. His North Star in all of it is Cody and Ana, two little children he so very much loved.

Isabella always had this light-hearted saying: "Nobody messes with my kids, my money, or my man!"

Being completely ghosted by Isabella for weeks took his breath away, pulled the rug from under him, and was something he had never anticipated. They were good. They never fought. Isabella brought him into her world, allowing him to foster solid relationships with Cody and Ana. It had not been an illusion. It was very much a reality.

However, since Valentine's Day, there has been total silence. Since Valentine's Day, Lucifer Jenkins' monster truck has been parked at the little condo on Elm Street night and day.

Ironically, the condo is only half a mile down from the Courthouse and situated along one of the primary North-South routes through the town of Culpeper. It is a road that he had always traveled his entire life but now it is one that he avoids.

He has so many questions in his mind. He understands if Isabella is angry with him for pressing charges. However, he wishes she would tell him, yell at him, text him, write him, or tell him to "fuck off." Silence is dangerous as silence allows his mind to make assumptions and draw conclusions.

For nearly two years, he had been in and out of that condo, spending many nights there. Since he was attacked, James Thomas Jenkins has not left. James Thomas is not paying the rent, not paying jack shit in child support, nor doing much of anything to contribute to society in general.

Isabella is a strong-minded, independent, and fierce woman. She is a great mother. In no way did James Thomas Jenkins match the light of Isabella. James and Isabella were completely opposite energetic beings.

Why would Isabella allow such a violent human being into her home? Was he supposed to pretend he wasn't assaulted? Were Cody and Ana supposed to be subjected to domestic abuse?

To him, it feels like a hostage situation. He feels that it is a manifestation of Lucifer Jenkins' guilt and psychological pathology to control, influence, manipulate, and witness tamper.

Lucifer Jenkins has the advantage of biology, and the right of influence as the "father." Lucifer Jenkins also has ample time to sow seeds of doubt into the minds of Cody and Isabella about what really happened.

WALKING THERAPY

Progressive Deep House. Prince. Tibetan Singing Bowls. Ice Cube. Irish Tenor Ronan Tynan. Gujarati Bhajans. Pearl Jam. "Mujhe Le Chalo Madina." Mary J. Blige. Adele. U2. The Cranberries. Bollywood.

He walks and walks and walks. He walks more than *Forrest Gump*. He walks to calm his anxiety. He walks to second-guess himself, beat himself up, and blame himself.

He walks to blow off steam from the feeling of being drop-kicked by Isabella. Without any communication to explain anything, it is as if he is sidelined from the relationship and abandoned as if he never existed. It is confusing and perplexing.

His mind interprets Isabella's actions, or lack thereof, as anger toward him. He cannot stop by the condo because of James. He no longer feels as if it's appropriate to schedule a haircut. Isabella doesn't call, text, or email him. All he can do is respect Isabella's decision and let her have her space. Perhaps it is Isabella's version of closure for what they had together. All he can do is focus on his trial date and put an end to the nightmare. All he can do is think about Cody and Little Ana.

THE KNOCK

During a visit to the condo early in the relationship, Isabella had gone to run an errand with the kids. He sat in the living room, watching cartoons when he suddenly heard a sound. It was a sound that he had not heard in a long time. It had a rhythm to it. It was a knock, but it was no ordinary knock.

DA. DA. DA. DA. DA. EXHALE. DA. DA.

The knock had startled him. It was the exact same knock signature that his mom had. It was his mother's secret code. He was hearing the same knock, but his mother had died. The door opened, and Cody and Ana came rushing in.

"Who knocked?"

Cody looked over at him. "I did. It's my mom's secret knock!"

DADDY'S GIRL

"Ana, hold his hand."

Ana, without hesitation, lifted her left arm and locked her tiny hand with his. Ana trusted him. Ana felt safe with him. Ana was comfortable with him.

He, Isabella, Cody, Ana, and many of Isabella's family members were walking down a long gravel driveway in a rainy mist. They were all leaving a baby shower gathering.

Isabella was busy nourishing an emotional wound from Cody's sensitivity when she asked Ana to hold his hand. The driveway was wet, muddy, and dark. He was honored and humbled to hold Little Ana's hand. She was a tiny little human being whose spirit was a force of nature.

It was a priceless memory.

SUBPOENA

To subpoena or not?

It is the question he has been presented with. Everyone, including the

Commonwealth Attorney, his trial lawyer, the Victim Witness Director, his counselor, and his energy healer, told him that he needs to allow them to subpoena Isabella for trial.

He is told that had there been a police report filed on Valentine's Day, Isabella would have absolutely been subpoenaed. However, since he had driven home, had not called 911, and had pressed charges through the local Magistrate, the ball was in his court.

His legal team would require a green light from him on the subpoena. Doo- Doo. Dung. Poop. Feces. Shit. Excrement. None of this is in the Assault & Battery Response Training Manual.

He is living in a messy nightmare haunted by a Valentine's Day that never ends. It is a battle between his mind and heart, a tug-of-war. While he seeks justice and accountability and respects the advice from everyone, ultimately, his heart prevails. There would be no subpoena. No. Nope. Never. Nada. This is his fight. He never asked to be attacked by the Devil. Isabella is not speaking to him, and the last thing he would ever want to do is hurt or traumatize Isabella in any way.

He informs his team of his decision. Somehow, he is just used to doing his own thing, following his own drumbeat, and wandering down a lane all by himself. The road less traveled seems to have his name on it. After all, he is the one who has to sleep at night; therefore, he wants to be at peace with his mind, to be comfortable, and not second-guess his decision.

Instead, he chooses to simply text Isabella and inform her that there would be no subpoena. He sends a second text which includes the name and contact of his trial attorney along with the message: "If at any time, you feel in your heart and in your conscious, that you wish to lend your voice to this matter, please feel free to contact my lawyer."

2.14.19 FEAR - CLASS 1 FELONY

In a healthy, happy, and normal world, he would have simply driven home on Valentine's Day with the images of Cody's and Ana's happy faces lingering in his mind. However, his life took a detour into darkness. As he relives the moment, he imagines the classification of a new felony in the Commonwealth of Virginia — a Class 1 Felony, the crime of violence being fear.

He wonders how many women, men, and children there are across America and across the globe that lived in utter and debilitating fear, trapped in their own version of ADX Willow Tree.

Fear of retribution. Fear of losing a child. Fear of being raped. Fear of being killed. Fear of saying no. Fear of preferring to paint the room blue as opposed to white. Fear of another eggshell. Fear of the justice system. Fear of not being believed. Fear of the police. Fear of wearing the wrong skin color. Fear of choosing to end a relationship. Fear of those demonic eyes. Fear of the darkness. Fear of failure. Fear of not being good enough. Fear of a new chapter. Fear.

Fear is the greatest unclassified felony in the world. Trauma and triggers are unequivocally linked to living in a state of fear. His mind creates the legal statute in honor of the date on which his own trauma and triggers collided, Valentine's Day.

On that day, he had been planning a family trip and worked up an XL sheet plan. The idea was for him, Isabella, Cody, and Ana to fly out west to Denver to visit Rocky Mountain National Park, then head over to Arches National Park to collect some rocks for Cody's geology collection, then watch Little Ana run across Sand Dunes National Park. He so much wanted to experience his kids' first plane ride. Those moments were his new dreams, before Valentine's Day.

THIRTY-ONE

ALONE ON THE MOUNTAIN

"100% beyond a reasonable doubt. It's an extremely high burden of proof. There is no police report. There have been no subpoenas. No witnesses were called. It's just he said versus he said. The case could go either way, but it's going to be really tough to get a conviction," opines his attorney.

It is a sobering pep talk. Truth and justice seem to be a crumbling mirage. He just wants it to be over. The reality of all the chips stacking against him is like quicksand to his mind. He has disagreed with a comment made by the Head of the Victim Witness.

"James is not a very smart guy. Throwing you down the steps wasn't smart," says the Head of the Victim Witness.

Everyone, including Isabella's friends and family, views James as "not too smart."

He had never commented, but after interacting with James and observing him, he disagreed. What he saw behind James' exterior façade was a manipulative, sophisticated, and deceptive human being.

Psychological violence leaves no marks. No black eyes. No books were thrown at him. No bruises. He simply "tripped down the steps." His mind was confused. What happened really didn't happen.

Psychological violence made it very easy to muddy the water. How could he prove 100% beyond a reasonable doubt if rays of self-doubt crept into his own mind?

Emotional Abuse 101.

GUT PUNCH

"We had a chance to speak to Isabella. And we are going to step back from the case, due to ethics rules. The trial is still set for Monday, but you will be on your own, to present your case."

His heart sinks. He is hallowed inside. Time seems to have frozen. Even his own attorney is walking away, abandoning him.

"It's not that we don't believe you, it's just that we have to follow ethics rules. This may be better for you, as you will be free to do your thing, whatever the judge will allow," his attorney explained.

He feels gutted. He was hoping the call from his lawyer would have been a confidence booster, a last-minute rally to calm his nerves. Does his own lawyer not believe him? Does his own lawyer think he has an ulterior motive? There is numbness throughout his body. The pursuit of justice sucks.

The conversation that morning centers around a discrepancy about Isabella's exact location. His last known situational awareness of Isabella placed her at the bottom of the stairs. Cody and Ana were a few steps up, almost eye level to his left. Did Isabella witness the attack or not?

His own lawyer confuses him as he relives the moment. Isabella was present in the house. She was aware of James Jenkins' state of mind, and she had been desperately seeking to calm James down.

It was a tiny condo. It wasn't a 25,000-square-foot cliffside mansion in Malibu where Isabella was a half mile away doing yoga. Whether Isabella had directly witnessed the physical assault or not, certainly the circumstances and the environment mattered. One minute, there was happiness, joy, and Valentine's goodie bags. The next minute, a raging lunatic was barging in, bringing darkness and violence. As a result, he ended up twisted at the bottom of the staircase, leaving a hole in the wall. Nothing about Valentine's Day morning was normal from any angle.

He hangs up the phone. His mind is a mess. He wonders what had really transpired on that phone call with his attorney. Was it Isabella or was it someone else? He wonders if Isabella has turned against him. He wonders if Isabella truly believed he had "tripped" and told that to the lawyer. He wonders if it was more sinister.

He understands the deceptive nature of narcissists and the fact that Lucifer Jenkins has seemingly moved into Elm Street. Narcs are highly skilled at collecting intel. Did James read his text message to Isabella with attorney details? Was Isabella coerced into making a phone call to say nothing happened? Did someone pose as Isabella on the phone?

It is easy to get lost in all the rabbit hole theories. Perhaps, it is very simple and not sinister at all. Perhaps Isabella, feeling some guilt, has made a phone call in good faith. Maybe, due to past traumas, her mind has selective memory, and is conditioned to keep good memories and bury the negative ones.

Perhaps the Commonwealth Attorney's office really does have his back. Maybe they are turning him loose on the justice system to give him a better shot. His mind and heart are in another tug-of-war.

His heart is filled with compassion for Isabella and how she had seemingly taken a wrong turn in life, just like he had, and wound up tangled in darkness.

His mind feels the opposite as a sense of betrayal begins to creep in, a sense that perhaps Isabella might even show up in court to speak out against him.

GUIDED BY TRUTH

He could not wallow in self-pity or conspiracy theories. It is Friday, and he has a case to prepare. He knows what happened, and God knows what happened. It isn't about winning; it is about truth and accountability. It is about the faces of his two kids, traumatized by fear. It is about the Class 1 Felony of Fear. He has forgotten that he possesses an Associate Degree in Criminal Justice from the School of Jack McCoy. Time to dust it off.

He makes a late-night run to Walmart at 1 a.m. for more printer paper and ink. On his way home from Walmart in those wee hours, he decides to take the route that goes right by the little condo on Elm, the road he has been avoiding.

As he passes Isabella's condo, his heart sinks again. In the darkness of the dimly lit parking lot, there is the big red monster truck. James Thomas Jenkins is parked at the front door, mere hours before the trial.

He looks over at his Walmart supplies and shakes his head. He asks himself, "Why am I even doing this? Why bother? What's the point?"

MONDAY MORNING

The early morning rays of sun filter into the den. He sits on the floor in front of a large coffee table. On the table is a lamp, his damn Buddha statue, his small Jesus wooden crucifixion cross from Serbia, his money plant gifted from Isabella, a framed childhood picture with his mother, and a small jar of holy water given to him by the local Episcopal priest at the house blessing ceremony performed when he moved back into the home with his 50% of the cutlery and towels.

He bows his head in prayer. "Dear God, you know my intention. You know what is in my heart. You know my Truth. You know what happened on the staircase. Please be with me today. Please be with me in court today. I am at your mercy. If it is your will for me to prevail today, for there to be a conviction despite all odds, I accept that. If it is your will for me not to prevail today, for there to be no conviction, I accept that as well. Please send love and light to Isabella, Cody, and Little Ana. Amen."

CULPEPER COUNTY COURTHOUSE

"You an attorney?" inquires a local Sheriff's deputy.

He is standing near the magnetometer for security screening. He wonders if the Deputy can hear his heart pounding or feel his anxiety. He hides it well as he gives a smile and confidently replies, "Today I am!"

He's dressed in the same black suit in which he buried his mother in. He's a man who has traveled to all 50 American States and 30 Nations.

However, on this day, life has brought him back to his roots to represent himself, to stand up for the little boy in the treehouse who was silenced. It's April 15th and on the docket is the case of Bredbhai vs. Lucifer.

He enters the General District Court and takes a seat in the back row. The GD is a smorgasbord of misdemeanor cases, so it is not exactly riveting television. It surprises him that there aren't carnival tickets being sold and vendors selling deep-fried snacks. He sees lots of lawyers milling about, with group huddles and sidebar whispers.

There is a shift in energy as Lucifer enters the room alone and takes a seat. While he's against classism, sexism, and racism, he immediately realizes that he and James are dressed for two different events. James, whom he knows has driven to court straight down the road from Isabella's condo, has a rodeo vibe going. Mr. Jenkins sports dark blue jeans, a fancy buckle, boots, and a tucked-in flannel shirt. He catches a whiff of attitude and arrogance. It is the cologne that Lucifer wears.

His early morning prayer has helped settle his mind and prepare him for anything. He realizes that God has placed him at this moment for a reason, even if it is one he doesn't fully understand. He feels a sense of gratitude for all of the things that did not happen. He's thankful that he did not receive a subdural hematoma from the impact of his head hitting against the wall. He's thankful that his spinal cord is intact and that he escaped Valentine's Day with minor bruising and joint pain. He's thankful that he is navigating his own ship, free from the rules of law school. He's thankful to have met Cody and Little Ana, two sweet souls who crumbled a wall of his at ADX Willow Tree. He has much to be thankful for, no matter which way the day unfolds.

Judge Theresa Carter has recently been sworn into the 16th Judicial Circuit Court. Judge Carter has made history as both the first Black and the first woman to preside over the 16th Circuit.

He knows he is living in a nation that progresses and backslides, a nation of breakthroughs and setbacks, and a nation that is always evolving. In a courthouse built in 1870, in a town surveyed by George Washington — a town at the heart of the Civil War, with a Confederate Statue in the courtyard — seeing Judge Carter on the bench is a reminder of progressive democracy.

"Do you have an attorney?" Judge Carter asks James.

"No."

The Judge stares at James. "You were supposed to retain an attorney. It's been nearly two months!"

"I ain't had time. Been working."

He continues to sit in the back of the court and shakes his head. In his mind, he says to himself, *that MF starts off with a lie.*

He is witnessing James Thomas Jenkins' game plan unfolding. He has researched James' previous DUI cases, ones in which a defense lawyer was present. In those prior cases, James' lawyers always used delay tactics. They were able to get a continuance with trial dates getting pushed and pushed and pushed.

James Thomas Jenkins is no dummy. James knows how the court works. James thinks all that has to be done is play dumb and get a continuance. In essence, there are no witnesses present. It is a he said, he said trial. Delaying the trial can introduce doubt, fuzzy memories, and the kind of justice which favors an abuser.

His female prosecutor, the woman who was representing his case up until he was dropped on Friday, approaches the bench to formally recuse herself, but not withdraw the case.

Cue Joseph Bologne, Chevalier de Saint-Georges, AKA 'Black Mozart.'

Judge Carter is a bit perplexed, but she has a decision to make. "If the State is not going to be involved, then I'm going to have to take any potential jail time off the table. But we will proceed."

Game time. There will be a trial after all.

Lucifer is stunned, rattled, and knocked off course.

A WEIGHT REMOVED

With the possibility of jail time off the table, he feels much lighter and freer. It's a twist he hasn't expected, but it is one he welcomes. The idea of jail time has been a barrier for him in this particular case. While the maximum is a year, the reality is that a conviction might result in a few days, weeks, or a month in jail, and then what?

He's in court to defend himself. He's in court for his kids. He's in court for the record, to set a boundary. James has had months to demonstrate a sliver of compassion, regret, remorse, or empathy. James has had months to offer an apology, to own up to what transpired, to seek forgiveness, and to allow him the opportunity to see Cody and Ana again.

However, that never happened. James has chosen to walk a different path. James decided to take away his children, to deceive, to manipulate, and to double down on a projection. Mr. Jenkins chooses to take the hard route by going toe to toe in court with a Boss Baby, a Weed Free Gangsta, and an INFJ armed with facts who is represented under the legal counsel of God.

Good luck.

THE TRIAL

He stands a few feet from James. Both men are sworn in and promise to tell the truth. He opens his leather briefcase and takes out his labeled case files.

James stands empty-handed.

He's prepared to argue his case in the Supreme Court if required. As an INFJ, he prefers to articulate his thoughts in writing and has prepared a 7-page double-spaced opening statement. No backstory. No interpretation. No marketing. Just the facts.

Judge Carter has the discretion as to whether she will allow him to read a prepared statement.

"I will allow it. But I must tell you, if you start to wander into unrelated events, or thoughts, or feelings, I'm gonna have to stop you. Only the facts," she warns.

"Yes, Your Honor. I understand. Thank you." Before he commences, he has a question. "Your Honor. Am I allowed to use profanity in court? As it relates to the statements made by Mr. Jenkins."

The judge nods with a slight grin.

His Plaintiff's List of Exhibits includes twenty-one items to be utilized as supporting evidence as well as intellectual intimidation.

1. Assault & Battery – My Truth
2. Medical Bill – Virginia Orthopedic
3. Medical Bills – CVS Pharmacy
4. Elaine- Counselor Receipt
5. Elaine – Bio Summary

6. Stephanie – Counselor Receipt
7. Stephanie – Bio Summary
8. Photo – Valentine's Day gifts
9. Photo – Valentine's Day gift bags packed
10. Target receipt – February 13 (Toys)
11. Dollar General receipt – Feb 13 (Candy/Snacks)
12. Total Itemized Expenses – Summary XL
13. Photo – Brad, Isabella, Cody, Ana at Baltimore Orioles baseball game
14. Photos – Christmas gifts for Cody, Ana
15. Photo – Cody opening Christmas gift
16. Photo – Ana with a gift from Brad
17. Photos – Personalized tree ornament gifts in taekwondo
18. Photos – Cody opening USA coin collector gift set
19. Photos – Various trips and events with Cody and Ana
20. Photos – Cody and Ana at his parents' home with their dog, Bree
21. Closing Statement

"Never happened. I never touched him!"

James keeps it simple. James doubles and triples down on the Big Lie. James doesn't deny being present at Elm on February 14th.

"He could have bumped his knee playing tennis," James says, offering the Judge a possible reason for his knee and joint pain.

He hasn't played tennis in three decades and yet James has profiled him as a yuppie, one of them boujee folks. He understands James' psychological profile and senses the discomfort James must feel from being in court. James is unable to shout and scream and rant and do all the things that demons do behind closed doors, around loved ones. He understands that James is like a pressure cooker of emotional instability, and he knows that what he is about to do next will rattle James psychologically.

He tests his theory during the trial as he holds up an 8 by 10 glossy printed picture of beautiful Little Ana. He knows very well that a photo of Ana as evidence of a child witness is totally inadmissible; however, it's about the psychology, the reaction. He wants to observe both James as well as Judge Carter. He's not Yale-trained. He's cashing in on his Cali film degree.

Judge Carter motions for him to put down the photo; however, he has added a layer of realism and planted an image inside Judge Carter's mind of the little girl he is in court fighting for.

James is another story, a bit zesty. James is absolutely pissed seeing him hold up a photo of Ana. James, agitated, spins around in court like a rodeo ballerina. Hashtag twirl.

At one point, the Judge asks him if he would like to ask James any questions. He turns to look at James. "Why on earth did you throw me down the stairs? Why do it?"

Crickets. Cue the awkward silence. James looks at him like he's just spoken in Gujarati.

In the last paragraph of his closing, he says "We are here today in court because of due process. The greatness of our nation and our legal system is that James Thomas Jenkins is granted due process and rightly so. The irony, however, is that violence has no due process. An assault on me is an assault on my freedom, my civil liberties, my mental health, my friendships, and my ability to live and function as a human being, in this same great nation, the United States of America."

18.2-57. ASSAULT & BATTERY (VIRGINIA)

VERDICT: GUILTY AS CHARGED

FINE: $642; NO CONTACT: 2 Years; DNA COLLECTION

He is overwhelmed with emotions as Judge Carter reads the guilty verdict. He has proven his case, 100% beyond any reasonable doubt. Everyone had turned their backs on him. It is a hollow victory but an important one. He stood up for accountability. He believed in himself and let God in. His eyes begin to water up a bit as he absorbs the moment.

Mr. Jenkins is not a happy camper. James stands in disbelief, acting victimized. The summons for DNA collection is a flash point, a trigger. The mask James wore begins to slip as James speaks very sternly toward Judge Carter.

James, in a very aggressive tone, said, "That's not fair! That's not fair! That's not fair!"

In an instant, the "mild-mannered hard-working" Lucifer Jenkins becomes disrespectful, impulsive, hostile, and aggressive. Flip the switch. It is a revelation into the true nature of James Thomas Jenkins, the darkness under the surface.

Judge Carter says to James, "When he asked you a question, you didn't bother to even answer."

For the first time, there is a mark of accountability for the criminal actions of Lucifer Jenkins.

THIRTY-TWO

IMPLOSION

It's 3 a.m. as he tosses and turns in his bed. The bedroom is dark and the ceiling fan spins. His head moves back and forth. He mumbles. He is restless. His mind is lucid as he is in the middle of a dream.

At first, it was a nightmare. His nightmare has him driving along a desolate forest in the dark when suddenly, he is surrounded by the innocence of many deer. Deer surround his car as an uneasiness engulfs his body. The deer suddenly morph into evil spirits with piercing eyes and contorted faces. They seek to run him off the road. Terrifying.

His body gets tangled up in the bedcovers. Still unawake, he throws them off. A sense of calm overtakes him as his nightmare transitions into a dream. He stands in front of Little Ana, and he sees a beaming source of light energy radiating around her. Little Ana reaches her hand out to him. There is a tear in her eye as he is unable to reach her.

Da. Da. Da. Da. Da. Da. Da.

All the sirens in his house begin to wail. A battery has gone out of one smoke detector. Which one? He jumps out of bed and into the noise. He is disoriented and agitated as he tries to make sense of which alarm is going off and which battery needs to be replaced. He manages to bring peace and calm to the house. While many in the flock have a "come to Jesus moment," not him. Nope.

HIS SPIRITUAL DUMP

Dear God,

Fuck off!

You could have taken me out in Bend. Why not, huh?

I'm tired, God. I'm tired.

I'm trying. I'm trying to do right. I'm trying to move forward. I'm trying to do good. For what?

My whole life is a fucking red flag. I've got red flags coming out of my ass.

Who can I trust?

Don't tell me that Jesus never just said, "fuck this."

"Fuck this desert. Fuck all these people and their problems. Fuck this cross." I know it's there, God. It just never got translated! They left that part out. Canceled. Scrubbed. King James' clean version.

* * *

I never wanted any kids, God! Never! You know that!

And then You gave me two. You did. You. You. You.

And then You ripped them out of my chest!

Why?

Justice is empty.

I wanted to watch Cody and Ana grow up.

To be there for them, to protect them, to love them.

To make goofy faces.

To run around with that fart machine.

To help them with their homework.

To watch them open presents.

Why?

I don't want a cliffside mansion in Malibu, God.

I just want my kids back!

Why?

This is on, You, God. It's on, You! Own this!

You tell that little girl that I didn't walk away. Never.

You let Little Ana know I didn't abandon her. I did everything in my power!

* * *

It's over, isn't it?

Some fucking life lesson that I'm supposed to learn.

I know the lesson.

Never have any fucking kids! That's the lesson.

Because it's impossible to protect them from evil.

Good night.

Amen.

THIRTY-THREE

THREE MONTHS LATER

Ground launch sequencer is a go for auto sequence start (T-31 seconds). Activate launch pad sound suppression system (T-16 seconds). Activate main engine hydrogen burn-off system (T-10 seconds). Main engine start (T-6.6 seconds).

It's 17:25, which in "American" is 5:25 p.m. A slender jet black Royal Jordanian aircraft lifts off the tarmac of Queen Alia International Airport, in Amman, Jordan. On board, in seat 15, sits "The Man Without a Face," from the rural hinterlands of Virginia. He looks out the window at the brown barren desert landscape.

Part of him is running. Part of him is seeking. Without his kids, he doesn't want anything to do with his native place, Culpeper. He has dusted off his suitcase, cashed in some United Air Miles, and chalked out the mother of all slingshots — an around-the-world two-month odyssey to find himself, to nurture himself, and to seek personal atonement for losing it in a profanity-laced prayer to God.

Hong Kong. Hanoi. Da Nang. Siem Reap. Chiang Mai. Krabi. Bangalore. Ahmedabad. Dubai. And a grand finale to Jerusalem and Bethlehem.

Throughout his life, he sought to prove himself — prove his worth, prove his value, prove that he was deserving of love. It is in his blood; it is part of his DNA. He hopes that by traversing the heartland of the Holy Land, he might somehow be forgiven for his blasphemous prayer. He didn't mean those words. He was grieving the loss of possibility and holding on to hope.

The very idea that he changed planes in Amman and is flying into Tel Aviv should have been enough to resurrect his mom, to send the little PhD of kindness down from Heaven for a bit to witness a true miracle. Her little Christian rebel is headed where? It is a jaw-dropping thought really.

He is a full-blooded CINO. He is in possession of a few unopened Bibles. His first Bible was presented to him by the Culpeper Methodist Church on September 11, 1983, and it was engraved with his full name, middle included. His second Bible, a smaller black one with a zipper case, was actually his mom's. Her name was engraved on it. It's as if he and his mother were branded. His third Bible was a doozy, a piece of history, a kind of *Jumanji* Bible. It was the family heirloom, printed in 1823 in Philadelphia. It was passed around through the generations, and it had landed in the house of a rebel with a Buddha statue.

Flying into Tel Aviv was never on his bucket list, his back-pocket list, his little black book, or anywhere in his mind. Of course, flying to India at sixteen was never on his list either and he knows how that turned out. As he sits on the plane, he thinks *"the Devil made him do it."* God's honest truth.

He met Lucifer on the staircase and never knew Satan drove a jacked-up Ford F350. No matter where he was in the world, that face haunted him. That face of rage. He held it together in court, made it through the trial, and secured a conviction, but his heart had been broken into a million little fragments. He is the definition of an empty vessel. Landing at the bottom of a staircase had knocked the hope out of him.

In many ways, he is seeking an antidote to hatred, to evil, and to the darkness that had visited him on the staircase at Elm Street.

He is not a Born-Again. He has never left. He never could remember any movie dialogue, much less any scripture. His Bible is not the King James version. His Bible is not the New Living translation. His Bible is not the Latin Vulgate translation. Nope.

He is a newbie, a Divinity Intern. His approach to the Divine has to intersect with his inner being in a way that makes sense to him.

CliffsNotes. CliffsNotes was his high school friend. It guided him through the great literary classics of the world. His Bible is the CliffsNotes version. It is fairly straightforward, just a page.

AMOR. PREM. HUBUN. AHAVA. LOVE, translated into all of the 7,100 languages of the world.

He stands opposite the Immigration Officer at Ben Gurion Airport, unaware if the officer knows his true identity.

CIA PROJECT NAME: "ENERGY 101"

CODE NAME: LOVE-75

NATIONALITY: AMERICAN

RELIGION: C.I.N.O. (CHRISTIAN IN NAME ONLY)

FIRST NAME: BRAD

ALIASES USED: BREDBHAI, BRAUD, BRAYED, BRED-BABA, BRED-JI

SURNAME: BALDWIN

ALIASES USED: BALDINI, BWALDO, VLADVIN, BALDANO

BIRTHPLACE: C-TOWN, NORTH SIDE (CULPEPER, VIRGINIA)

POLITICS: INDEPENDENT

LANGUAGES SPOKEN: ENGLISH (BARELY)

LANGUAGE RATING: C- (POOR GRAMMAR, POOR SPELLING)

EDUCATION:

- CULPEPER COUNTY HIGH SCHOOL – 1993
- GEORGE MASON UNIVERSITY — 1995
- UNIVERSITY OF SOUTHERN CALIFORNIA — 1997

TRAINING:

- SABARMATI ASHRAM, AHMEDABAD INDIA
- RAMAPIR NO TERKO (HARIJAN-UNTOUCHABLES)

WEAPONS EXPERT:

- CROWN CHAKRA: Understanding, Enlightenment
- THROAT CHAKRA: Communication, Healing, Creativity
- HEART CHAKRA: Love, Hope, Compassion, Empathy

Fortunately, he passes through immigration, receives his arrival visa, and is free to pursue his mission. In reality, he is a blank slate. He only has eight days and the hours, minutes, and seconds that make up eight days. His personal mission is very clear. He wants to feel the energy of the land and immerse himself in the world. He wants to get a better sense of perspectives and points of view — to listen, to observe, to feel. He has no agenda. He has zero expectations. His life in India had taught him that nothing is black and white and humanity is filled with shades of gray and a great deal of nuance.

Throughout his life, any awareness and background noise connected with the Holy Lands was negative — strife, conflict, violence, empty rhetoric from American politicians seeking votes, Camp David handshakes, and failed peace agreements. It seems that religion has a price and that price is violence. Not exactly the award-winning images for an eco-friendly travel brochure to Judea... A 7-Day All Inclusive Tour to Israel with a 24/7 potential for conflict or a 7-Day All Inclusive Tour to the Amalfi Coast and Tuscany with the possibility of ingesting too much wine.

His plan for eight days was simple. He has shortlisted a few Christian historical sites to show God he really is serious. However, the heart of his visit is about understanding. His basecamp is to be divided: four nights in Jerusalem and four nights in Bethlehem. In Jerusalem, he has booked an Airbnb in the home of a middle-class Jewish family. In Bethlehem, he has booked an Airbnb in the apartment of a Palestinian family. He has never met a Palestinian. He has never lived with a Jewish family. He has no idea what to expect. His visit is intended to provide him with an authentic and meaningful experience, one in which he is greatly looking forward to.

TIMING?

I never meant to hurt you.

Just two days prior, he suddenly received a one-line email from Isabella. He had not heard from Isabella in five months and had not seen her since he was assaulted on Valentine's Day. Isabella had no idea where he was, that he had been traveling the world, that he was at the Holiday Inn in Dubai, or that he was just hours away from flying to Israel.

Five months of silence had been broken with a line. There was a backstory. On his final night in Ahmedabad, he was part of an *EKTA* reunion and was thrilled to reconnect with his fourteen brothers and sisters. The young teen cast of *EKTA* were now adults with spouses and children of their own. It was heartwarming to meet their children.

Bharat had gifted him a personalized Rubik's Cube which was filled with images from the tour in 2002. It was the most creative and most meaningful gift, one that touched his heart. Meeting the children of *EKTA* made him long for Cody and Ana. He left the dinner party and headed straight to the airport for a middle-of-the-night flight to Dubai.

He was exhausted and emotionally drained when he checked into the Holiday Inn at 4 a.m. He held the *EKTA* Rubik Cube. Triggered. He missed his kids profoundly. He missed Isabella deeply. After a long time, his soul cried out. He cried himself to sleep. One of those transformative cries.

When he woke up, Isabella's email was in his box. Was it random? The timing. Was it just a coincidence? He had no idea what it meant, but his first reaction was to exhale. He felt a sense of relief. It was an immediate sense that maybe Isabella did not hate him after all. He and Isabella exchanged a few emails, and he told her where he was and where he was headed. He learned that before Isabella sent the email, she had gone to his house and knocked on the door to find him. When he didn't answer, she emailed him. Timing.

CARTOGRAPHY 101

He is the son of a geography teacher. He grew up surrounded by maps and *National Geographics*. He has a keen sense of direction and can navigate the globe. However, he has absolutely no idea what or where the border is between Israel and the West Bank. He has no idea that Bethlehem is actually in the West Bank, that word in the news. Bethlehem is in Palestine. Just the mere mention that he is going into the West Bank created fear in the minds of a few local Culpeperites who know he is traveling.

The beauty of news media is that it creates carefully drawn mental maps of what is safe and what is not safe. The U.S. Department of State advertises in their two cents with color-coded travel advisories for nations, but seems to not classify gun-slinging American towns and cities with any advisories.

The images are real. The violence is real. All of it is interwoven to create a narrative in the minds of many Americans that Israel is safe and the West Bank is not. Period. For Christ's sake, he is just going to the birthplace of Jesus. He isn't going to have dinner with Kim Jong Un or plot to hijack American democracy with Tweet Tweet Hashtag 45. Jesus!

WHAT AN ARRIVAL!

"Get in. Quick! Quick!" shouts a mid-60s Jewish cabbie.

He has just arrived in Jerusalem by train and maneuvered his way through five thousand people and into the only tiny elevator at the station. He is soaking in the spiritual air — taking his time, getting oriented.

"Get in! Quick!" The taxi whizzes through the well-paved streets as a cool night breeze blows through the window. "All I can do is drive you to the border. That's it. I'll drop you and you walk across!" The cabbie has an anxious vibe. With his personality type, he easily absorbs the emotions of others. He picks up on the anxiousness and as a result, his heart beats a bit faster.

"What am I supposed to do exactly? What's it like on the other side?" he asks.

The cabbie glances back at him and shakes his head, "I don't know. I've never been! We're not allowed to go there. Jews are not allowed!"

He realizes that perhaps he should have done a bit more research and a little more homework. The closer they get to the West Bank, the more anxious the cabbie gets. His enthusiasm and excitement to loiter around the birthplace of Jesus is beginning to turn to anxiousness and second-guessing.

He isn't Ben Wedeman. He isn't Clarissa Ward. He isn't Richard Engel. He doesn't speak 23 languages. He didn't pack a helmet or flak jacket. He doesn't have press credentials. All he has are an American blue book, a Virginia driver's license, and a Gujarat State driver's license. He wonders if he should have booked a meditation retreat in Bali instead.

It is July. In February, he was attacked by Lucifer Jenkins. He isn't looking for trouble. He only played *Rambo* as a kid, but he didn't really have the physique or the skill set. Gandhi Ashram in Ahmedabad isn't this stressful. For a moment, he considers pulling the plug, letting Jesus know he is sorry, and turning the cab around.

He is a low-tech, low-app, and low-gadget guy. He has his iPhone, but he only uses Wi-Fi wherever he stays. No SIM cards. No roaming plans. No GPS navigation. Only the brain that God gave him and his intuition.

He uses his MacBook to check emails and manage what was left of his business. However, when he is out, he is freewheeling and off-grid, Gen X style. His philosophy is basic: He is either glued to his electronic devices or he is glued to experiencing the actual moment. Imagine that.

He grew up in an era where one talked as long as the phone cord could stretch. He grew up sitting shotgun on family road trips and flipping through large Rand McNally Road Maps of America. He is also a bit digitally challenged. A one-finger texter. Middle. Index, rather.

His Palestinian Airbnb host had instructed him to call once he reached the border wall, in order to be picked up. Living in India for decades, he had learned that time was relative. In India, nothing was ever on time; yet, 1.3 billion people somehow managed. Therefore, he had given his host an ETA.

He stands at the Border Wall as the Jewish cabbie speeds off into the night. There is a dim streetlight. There are no guards. No one is around. He has no idea where he is and has no phone service. He feels a bit Amish as he looks up at the towering wall. He doesn't see any ladders. He finds an entryway and walks inside, rolling his four-wheeled black suitcase.

He thinks, *Here I come, Jesus. Protect me!* He walks along the concrete corridor. Since the cabbie had driven away with all the anxiety, he actually feels quite relaxed now, more curious. And just like that, voilà... He has entered another world. Within a matter of yards, he has traveled from first-world infrastructure to the developing world.

It hits him. He feels like he is back in India, at sixteen, for the very first time — minus the shouting autorickshaw fan club. He sees at least ten cabs. Palestinian drivers are hanging out, chatting in Arabic. It is quiet. Bethlehem is a small town of about 28,000. It is sort of a Judean Culpeper.

He reaches into his pocket to take out a piece of paper with his chicken scratch scribble. On the piece of paper is the address of his Airbnb and the contact number for his host, Ameen. He is not in a hurry. Jesus died over two thousand years ago. The Collette tour bus isn't waiting. He figures he will find his apartment at some point before morning. He randomly picks a cabbie and voilà, the cabbie knows Ameen. He loves small towns. People know each other, gossip about each other, and get on each other's nerves. *It's a Wonderful Life – West Bank Sequel.*

After 43 years, Bredbhai, Bred Baba, Bredji has just touched down.

Dope.

THIRTY-FOUR

WEST BANK

It is early morning as he stands on the large balcony of his apartment. Thousands of electrical wires hang outside. The road below him is very steep. For some reason, he has pictured Bethlehem as this dusty little desert town, a flat little town. Unless it's the wrong one since there are a dozen Bethlehem's in America. Maybe Jesus was born in North Carolina?

The little town of Bethlehem is perched at an elevation of 2,500 feet and is built across the arid rocks of the Judean Mountains. The entire town is like Lombard Street in San Francisco, complete with hairpin turns, blind spots, and steep roads. The sound seems to be magnified on the street below as the roar of diesel delivery trucks make their way up the steep road, the sound waves bouncing back and forth between the concrete apartments. The sky is blue. The rays of sunlight are intense.

Across the street, he sees a Palestinian woman hanging clothes out to dry on the roof. He feels quite at home as if he is sitting in one of his flats in India. His apartment block has few lights at night and no lights in the hallways outside. He has learned that the apartment he is staying in is Ameen's former home and Ameen and family have recently moved to a new house. Ameen's uncle runs a small mom-and-pop grocery store just down below the building. Many of Ameen's relatives live in other flats in the building. He is only a five-minute walk — a very steep, asthma-inducing walk — to the Church of the Nativity and Manger Square, the birthplace of the Original Gangsta.

The previous night, upon arrival, Ameen's warmth and hospitality was infectious. Long flight. Immigration. Trains. Taxi. Border Wall. If he thought resting and unwinding was on his agenda, he was wrong.

Seconds after he dropped his bags in the apartment, Ameen whisked him away in a tiny white Fiat through the late-night streets of Bethlehem. He felt as if he were in a video game or a Jason Bourne flick as Ameen zipped through the streets — up and down and around tight corners.

They picked up Ameen's oldest child. Ameen's daughter, dressed casually in jeans, was in her final year of high school. An absolutely universal fear shared by all high school students was final exams and college admissions, which she was preparing for.

Ameen was the epitome of the Energizer Bunny, a man full of spirit and hustle. Ameen's day job was connected to the local police department. Ameen had visited the United States once, to Washington D.C. and Northern Virginia, for a police and security-related conference.

The Airbnb was a side gig and Ameen's attempt to bring in more tourism to Palestine in order to promote economic development. He, Ameen, and Ameen's daughter stopped to pick up chicken shawarmas — to die for delicious stuffed wraps. The windows were rolled down as the little car zipped through the streets of Bethlehem. His shawarma was still in its bag. He waited patiently, as customary with his British ancestry etiquette, thinking he would eat once he returned back to the flat. It was dark, and he was on a roller coaster.

Not Ameen. Ameen unwrapped the shawarma. Ameen had one hand on the wheel and one hand on the sandwich, all while navigating the turns with a single finger.

NO ROADMAPS

Healing has no roadmaps. There are millions of self-help books, blogs, and news articles, but healing has no map. Healing is a day-by-day, single-step, individual process, as unique as each human being. Healing is a flood of emotions followed by intense calmness. Healing is about new discoveries. Healing is an opportunity to rebuild the Self by holding on to the good stuff and letting go of the bad stuff — the addictions, the ADX belief systems.

Healing happens at different paces. Healing does not fit in a neatly wrapped box. Healing is messy. Healing has unexpected random moments of epiphany. There is no right way or wrong way to heal. Healing has no awards, trophies, or certificates. Healing is free of expectations. Healing isn't some boujee catchphrases or hour-long therapy sessions. Healing isn't some "woke" agenda. Healing isn't masculine or feminine. Healing isn't a weakness. Healing has no tax bracket. Healing is about personal growth, discovering the authenticity within, finding purpose, and finding joy.

THE MANGER MYTH

He makes his way up the hill, inhaler in hand, to the Church of the Nativity. He thinks back to the little Bible School Trailer that was parked a few times a year outside his public school. He thought about the entire Christmas season. In his mind, he assumed Jesus was born in a manger, a Biblical Motel 6, surrounded by Joseph, Mary, the Wise Men, and some animals on a dusty road in a flat desert with a few palm trees. He soon learned that was fake news. Finding out the Truth was a revelation. A cave? Do what? Underground? Huh? Even as a CINO, he never heard about a cave. Perhaps the myth started when the world was flat... If the world was flat, then that meant Bethlehem was flat and the Biblical Motel 6 was flat.

He wonders what other realities he may discover, those that differ from the Bible Trailer. He has never seen a Bhagavad Gita Trailer parked outside any school in India. He has also never seen a Pali Canon Trailer parked outside any Thai schools.

The Basilica itself is a mesmerizingly ornate structure. It was first built in the year 326, at a time when Native Americans dwelled in the land that would eventually become the United States, before the Christian invasion. He learns that the Church of the Nativity is run by three factions of Christians: the Greek Orthodox Church, the Armenian Apostolic Church, and the Roman Catholic Church. Every day, 365 days a year, a small but steady flow of tour buses enter Manger Square. It is a pit stop for spiritual pilgrims to stand in a long queue before heading down a few steps and touching the ground where baby Jesus first tooted. It seems that many religious tours, however, do not include Bethlehem as it is in the West Bank and deemed "unsafe."

Every day. Every single day. He learns that every day, Greek, Armenian, and Roman Catholic teams have their specific prayer ceremonies at the pious site, in the cave. Everyone has their prerogative, but he doesn't vibe well with orthodox dogma in general. He prefers to be in a congregation of one, just himself, without all the politics and rituals. He learns that the cave in which Jesus was born was the site of regular disputes among theological branches. Their squabbles and entanglements would hold up the line of visitors who had come from all parts of the world. Each denomination has their way of doing things — their ritual, their interpretation, and their timetable.

He wonders if it was really necessary to dot the i's and cross the t's every day of the year. He wonders what Jesus might think. He wonders what Jesus might whisper to the line of tourists who are waiting patiently while *rare* daily rituals are undertaken.

The Church of the Nativity is guarded by Palestinian Police. They are often amused, bewildered, and at times, irritated by the inter-family conflicts between Church parties. Ironically, Muslim police officers have side gigs as peacekeepers and diplomats.

In his divorce, he was portrayed as a mob boss. He knows that Christianity has many denominations, but he wonders how these three — Greek, Armenian, and Catholic — managed the local power play in the streets of Bethlehem. What about the Methodists? What about the Southern Baptists? What about the Presbyterians? What about the Pentecostals? Is there a democratic process? Are there elections? Are there term limits on occupation? He imagines Jesus sitting in the last pew, undercover, dressed as Santa, observing the flock.

What would Jesus think?

HOLY PLACE SIN

Tiny lies are known as "white lies." He doesn't know what tiny sins are called. Technically, he doesn't know if "cutting in line" is even considered a sin. After dealing with lust, cutting in line seems more like commandment number 555. Life in India had taught him quite well how to cut in line. After all, he is Christian, which means all he needs to do is ask for forgiveness on Sunday morning and all would be fine.

Ameen knows as many people in Bethlehem as his mom did in Culpeper. Ameen is indeed connected, which means Ameen is connected to the local police guards at the Church. Translation: He gets to cut corners by entering the cave of Jesus through the exit door, an exit door heavily guarded by Palestinian police.

He has learned the art of dipping in and out of places by using shortcuts and bypassing lines during his nearly two decades in Gujarat and Mumbai. In and out. Don't draw attention to oneself. Don't stick out. Look natural.

He realizes at that moment that perhaps he could have been a legit CIA operative, as opposed to a rogue humanitarian with a film degree from Cali. He stands near the exit of the cave. Waiting. Yes, he finds himself, even with his newfound connections, waiting. Waiting for who? The Armenians! Armenia is a nation that is 138th in size on a list of 195 countries. Patience is a virtue. Eventually, the Armenian Orthodox clergy wraps up the daily ritual. He makes his way down and hands his SLR to Ameen. He places his hand near the engraved star which marks the site of the birthplace. He prays. It isn't exactly a Kodak moment. It isn't exactly a quiet Zen space to go deep. However, he is grateful that the Armenians have allowed entry.

COEXISTING

He noticed a large mosque, the Mosque of Omar, located opposite the Church of the Nativity on the other side of Manger Square.

"I'd like to meet with the Imam. Can you arrange something?" he asked Ameen.

He wanted to take a moment during his time in the West Bank to engage in an unofficial, unsponsored, off-the-beaten-path, and non-political moment of Human Diplomacy. He has learned that the little town of Bethlehem is 90% Arab and 10% Christian. He finds it to be insanely symbolic that two faiths, two paths, Christianity and Islam, which account for four billion, half the world's population, share space around Manager Square.

In large cities in the United States, it is certainly much easier to find a melting pot of avenues to worship. However, in rural America, the idea of building a mosque next to a church would send shockwaves and fear down the spines of the local Republican County officials and right-wing pundits.

Invasions. Invaders. Others. Sharia Law. Conspiracies. Translation. White People Overload Syndrome. Conditional-based democracy. Conditional-based separation of church and state. Conditional-based rules and laws. Conditional-based equality.

Bethlehem was not the first time he had seen a Church and a Mosque side by side. India had a small Christian population, mainly in the South, across Karnataka, Kerala, and Tamil Nadu. Traveling through rural India, he always noticed a tiny cross peeping out from a palm tree and a short bit down the road was a small mosque. Two lanes. Different belief systems. Coexisting in a primarily Hindu nation.

Orthodoxy is a challenge to him, a challenge to his inner being. Christian.

Jew. Muslim. Hindu. With respect to regular Church folk, it often seems to him that there is a difference between being inspired by the Word and being suffocated by the Word. It isn't a scientific study, just a feeling. He has a sense that the tighter the Word, the more judgmental, less inclusive, less compassionate, less tolerant, less understanding, and less loving one could be. He understands that even a CINO would most likely not walk into a mosque or a synagogue or a temple for one simple reason: it's a different lane. Part of it is the human psychology of identity and a fear of loss, a fear of somehow losing one's identity by stepping into another world.

He is the odd man out. He was the last kid selected for dodgeball in P.E. class. He has a different philosophy. He follows the CliffsNotes Bible which allows him the opportunity to step into a mosque or other place of worship without losing his identity. He isn't lost. He isn't experimenting. He isn't transitioning. He isn't an atheist or a scientist. He has no secret agenda. He does not hand out Bibles. He does not preach conversions. He does not have to have any ulterior motivations, only the essence of love. He can still be a Christian and do things differently. He can believe in Christianity and still be free to interpret his life and his world in a way that allows him the freedom to step into the Mosque of Omar, have a quiet moment of prayer, and proceed to have coffee with the Imam and somehow not lose any part of himself in the process.

Ameen has scheduled the meeting one evening after prayers and takes him to the Imam. His personal mission is to connect as human beings. He wants to have an organic chat, to hopefully find humor and share a laugh, but primarily, to plant the seed in the mind of the Imam that Americans are not all politicians, war hawks, and extremists. Most Americans are just regular hard-working people with a hint of self-righteousness shaped by their social media and cable news echo chambers. He has no idea what to expect. Ameen is on hand to translate the conversation. What was supposed to be a simple meet and greet with no official agenda turns into a 90-minute Coffee Summit.

Unfiltered. Unscripted. Human to Human.

ANOTHER WALL

He sits in a rickety chair. It is flipped around. He has both arms placed on the back of the chair. He is casually dressed and wearing his specs. It is nighttime. Behind him stands the 30-foot Border Wall, littered with artistic graffiti. Wires run across the top of the wall. The little town of Bethlehem is actually in a box. Across the street is a gas station. The desolate side street runs parallel to the wall.

Outside the entrance of the gas station, Ameen sits with the owner and one of the owner's friends, a Jordanian. They are having a few snacks. On this night, Ameen brought him here to experience the wall and for his photo shoot. Ameen, always gregarious, has struck up a conversation with the gas station owner. The station owner has invited both him and Ameen to join them. It's the kind of openness and generosity he has experienced for decades in India. A random invitation to sit down, eat something, drink something, and share a moment in time.

There is no hurry. He has no place to be. There is no 25-stop per-day tour schedule. He has never known about the wall. He lived with tall walls much of his life, but he has never sat next to such a tall wall. He's quite embarrassed that his Gujarati, Hindi, and Arabic are not too good. The wall is like a lure that pulls him back and forth. He spends a little time sitting with the fellas before drifting over to walk along the wall. He sits for a bit, then drifts back over for a few snacks. It is a cycle that repeats for hours on this night.

He walks to the spot where Pope Francis prayed a few years earlier. He can tell the walls are not Biblical in nature, as they appeared to be just slabs of concrete without much character. The initial idea of building a barrier happened in 1992, the year he first visited India.

He knows a thing or two about walls. Forty years at ADX Willow Tree, a life sentence for which he got reduced to time served. He walks along the wall in silence, just thinking. He knows that the Republicans are the party of walls, mostly talk and little action. He wonders how a fifty-foot-high concrete slab across Texas would prevent 35,000-foot illegal immigration in the form of valid visa overstays.

In India, all bungalows and many apartment buildings have compound walls, a clear separation of space and property. In India, curb appeal is compound wall appeal. He wonders what the intention really is, beyond just "security." He is curious as to why the Israeli government chose to exclude Bethlehem as a place of cultural significance for Jewish folk.

He wonders if the West Bank Wall is really a Trauma Wall. He believes that with an ADX Willow Tree mindset, it is very easy to build walls and block out all the light. He wonders if the construction of the wall is more than a response to Hitler and twisted evil and is instead a subconscious psychological response to centuries of running, centuries of actual and feared persecution.

Did the wall resolve things? He is curious to know the correlation between the Palestinians and World War II. He understands that it is easy to label others, to find faults in others, and to blame others for all the ills in the world. It is much harder to look into the mirror and shine a light on the broken parts, the fears, and the insecurities in order to heal. Or course, what did he really know? He was just a CINO, a Divinity Intern, who was allergic to hatred, in all forms.

He wrote screenplays, unproduced movie scripts that collected dust on his bookshelf. He wrote essays and letters and term papers. He wrote opening and closing statements for court appearances. However, the only book he had ever written clocked in at a whopping six pages. It was written in the 9th grade and entered into the Virginia State Reading Association Young Authors Contest. He drafted the story and printed it out on his dot matrix printer from his Tandy. He bound the book and designed the front and back covers. The name of his little book was FREEDOM AT LAST, a story regarding reunited families during the fall of the Berlin Wall in Germany.

The front book cover was a collage of magazine cut-outs. Smiling faces. Champagne bottles. Allied Checkpoint Charlie. People standing on top of the wall. People climbing up and over the wall, a shorter wall than Bethlehem. The front cover was in color. The back of his book was a more formal arrangement of black and white images. A title Wall of Shame 1961-1989. Barbed Wire. Shadows. Tunnels. Soldiers. Children playing near the wall. The Wall of Bethlehem had come to represent so much to him, the inner and outer walls of humanity. Cycles of trauma. Life lessons. Personal growth. The meaning of freedom. The price of freedom.

Nuts. Seeds. Dates. Juice. Fruits. The sounds of laughter. Bits of English. Bits of Arabic. A lighthearted conversation. Peaceful energy. Bohemian vibes.

He enjoys his time with Ameen, the station owner, and the Jordanian. Colorful graffiti art looks back at them. He really does feel like he is back in India, sitting on a cot in a small village in Kutch, just hanging out. He is beyond comfortable.

He thinks about the Jewish cabbie that had dropped him off days earlier on the other side of the wall. The trepidation in the voice. The anxiousness. The drop and run. He doesn't know how long the cabbie lived in Israel, but it is hard to fathom the idea that the cabbie has no idea what really exists on the other side of the wall. That is a trauma in itself.

He isn't naïve to think that such a complex tapestry of layered history among Jews, Christians, and Arabs is as simple as a CliffsNotes interpretation; however, his CliffsNotes articulation is aspirational and for him, there is nothing wrong with a little hope. He is not sitting in the projected image of the West Bank of Palestine. He is not sitting in a risk mitigation meeting with a travel operator. He is not sitting in a terrorism training camp. He's simply at ease, chewing on a date, smiling, and engaging in the human language.

ELEPHANT IN THE ROOM

He wanders the streets and lanes of Bethlehem with thoughts of the elephant in the room, the elephant in his life. Not the Republicans, Lucifer Jenkins. He is relieved that Isabella had reached out to him, but he is unsure of the road ahead, of what kind of life awaited him when he returned to Virginia. He is no longer living in Isabella's projection. He is now living in his reality. It isn't about letting go and moving on past Valentine's Day, it is about boundaries, about health, and about psychology.

During his pre-trial research, he reviewed a series of domestic violence links on the Los Angeles Police Department website. He read the exact words that Isabella had robotically said to him out of nowhere after he was violently assaulted. "They need their father" was a common response for women traumatized by violence.

Growing up, his father got angry and had a temper, but that anger was never directed toward him or his mother. The fear of living in violence is heartbreaking to think about. The untold trauma in the minds of Little Ana and Cody is heartbreaking. The basic fact that Isabella was unable to acknowledge his Truth, acknowledge his reality, and acknowledge the fact that he was attacked and instead pivoted to an almost rehearsed talking point indicated to him very clearly that he and Isabella were on two sides of a Trauma Wall.

Isabella had been living a false sense of freedom with James' mobility curtailed by a DUI conviction. Now that James had wheels and the freedom to stalk, harass, intimidate, and manipulate, how would Isabella handle that reality? Was Isabella strong enough to enforce boundaries? Could Isabella 'see' her reality?

His heart is flooded with love for Isabella and the idea of a continued romance, but his mind is much more cautious. He isn't going back to prison. Would he get to see Cody and Ana again? Past images flood his mind; the kids riding in the back of his Land Rover, jet skis at Oak Island, and Little Ana's expression the first time she saw him. Isabella had trusted him with her precious cargo, as he often watched them for a few hours when she had to work late. An honor for him and a monumental responsibility.

Would there be established boundaries with James? Would Isabella be emotionally available to him?

It is a future only time would tell and only God knows.

WHERE IS THE FLOCK?

He sits in Manger Square, sipping on Arabic coffee with cardamom, just opposite the Palestinian Peace Center in between the Mosque of Omar and the Church of the Nativity. He's an observer of life. Eventually, a small tourist bus arrives and a group of tourists exits and stand in line, waiting for the Armenians, the Greeks, or the Catholics to finish their rituals.

Other than that, Bethlehem is quiet. It's the middle of summer in the Northern Hemisphere. He can't help but wonder where everyone is. There were 2.3 billion Christians in the world. Where is everybody? This is the epicenter of the Christian world, the birthplace of the Carpenter.

All across the world, people uttered the name of Jesus. He heard the televangelists. He read the bumper stickers. The yard signs, Jesus Loves. He has walked by the Chipotle or the Starbucks in Culpeper and heard men and women, huddled in small groups or counseling sessions, speak the name of Jesus. Every small church in every corner of Timbuktu America had a mission fund, a mission charity, or an undercover Bible crusade promoting the Word in China.

Jesus is a slogan. Jesus is a meme. Jesus forgives all sins and all crimes. Jesus even forgave politicians and attorneys. And yet there is only a trickle of the faithful pilgrims on a short stop. Pilgrims without time to engage with the people of Bethlehem — the locals, the school students, the refugee camps, the business owners, the local leaders, the clergy, and the imams.

He certainly does not expect Walt Disney to have a Biblical Theme Park on the West Bank. He certainly does not expect the Naked Cowboy to relocate from Times Square to Manger Square. He certainly does not expect Manger Square to look or smell like Hollywood Boulevard or have a Walk of Stars for all the personalities mentioned in the Bible.

He realizes, at forty-three, that he is a bit late to the game. His spiritual awakening has been dormant and stunted his entire life. He had witnessed hundreds of thousands of Hindus flock to holy sites and temples. He had flown on airplanes, out of Ahmedabad, filled with Muslims on their way to the annual Hajj Pilgrimage. He had known of a few of his exchange students who had traveled to Hajj.

The juxtaposition of those life experiences hit him like a ton of bricks. The weather is nice. The Arabs are friendly, the coffee is good, and the history is Divine. The only thing missing are the sheep, and not just at Christmas.

BOLLYWOOD STYLE

He walks into a large and loud male-only reception hall. He didn't really pack anything formal since he did not anticipate a wedding invite. He wears a nice pair of jeans and a button-up shirt. He finds himself in a very usual territory, the only White Dude in a room full of a hundred Palestinian men, young and old.

Ameen's cousin is getting married and Ameen has invited him. No formal guest invitation required. No hyperventilating wedding planner. The music is dope. A young baby-faced DJ plays a mix of traditional folk, Arab dance, and pop. He sits at a long table next to Ameen and is greeted with handshake after handshake by the Gen Z's, the Millennials, and Gen Xers. He is greeted by long lingering stares from the elders in attendance, the Boomers, men from villages, and men wearing Bedouin Shemaghs and Arab Keffiyehs, traditional styles of headdress.

Ameen has given him a brief pregame rundown. The main event and wedding venue are next door. The elderly members of the large extended family are more conservative, meaning that there is a separation in event space for men and women. It is a formality and out of respect for the elders.

However, a few hours later, once the older folks went to sleep, he and Ameen would head into the main wedding hall, which was coed. The DJ in the first hall cranks up the dance music and suddenly, a group of men and young boys begin traditional and contemporary dances. Ameen's youngest son, a child that could have been on the cover of *Gap Kids*, is huddled with a group of cousins. They are all dancing. Ameen is in the middle of it all. He is invited many times to dance, but he is allergic to dancing. It is the whole self-conscious thing. He parties in his mind, lets loose in his soul, but his anxiety holds him back from wowing the Arabs with his White guy dance skills.

The main wedding hall is set up like a Bollywood film set. There is a huge stage, colorful lights, a bold set design, and an actual television-style camera on a boom crane that zigged and zagged over tables and across the stage. Arab vocals. Dance. Trance. Large round tables with formal table clothes and place settings.

A change of dress isn't just for the bride. Ameen's wife and many of the women in attendance soon changed into more liberal attire. Style Number 1: conservative, tone-down, simpler. Style Number 2: colorful, ornate, progressive, and reflective of individual personalities.

He thrives on having opportunities to experience other people and other worlds. He always tries to be respectful of other ways of life, other cultures, and other religions. Nothing is more universal than the joy, laughter, and smiles of a wedding. Unless, of course, it is in reference to his shotgun Mumbai courthouse wedding.

THIRTY-FIVE

QASR-AL-YAHUD (WEST BANK) JULY 25, 2019

It is 3:40 p.m. He is in no hurry since closing is not until five. He has not just physically traveled to the Jordan River, but he has emotionally traveled there because of his decades of brokenness and inner wounds. On his very short must-see list of locations, number one is a visit to Qasr-Al-Yahud, the authentic site of the baptism of Jesus. He was baptized as a child in the Methodist Church in Culpeper, which gave him street credibility to be labeled a CINO. He is free from his psychological chains, living in a new world. It is something he never imagined. His fine-tuned emotion and sensitivity to his intersection with the Jordan River are overwhelming.

Prior to his trip, he had learned of a secondary Jordan River location. It is farther north in Israel, near the mouth of the Sea of Galilee. Qasr-Al-Yahud is in the West Bank, which explains why the busload of pilgrims tends to include the Israeli stop, with far fewer tourists at Qasr. The optics. The politics. The narratives. Since he is not a historian, anthropologist, or archeologist, he googled. He also asked folks who had traveled to the region to ascertain which location was the most authentic.

He is keen to take a dip in the genuine location. He is skilled at logistics, traveling, and moving in and out of countries and cultures. The route to Qasr was to include a stop at the Tomb of Moses and a brief Mud Spa in the Dead Sea. He has checked, rechecked, and triple-checked the closing time. He has emailed for confirmation. The website listed 5 p.m. He had Ameen contact the Qasr-Al-Yahud management multiple times before the trip and on the day of the trip to confirm that it is 5 p.m. in both English and Arabic. When he arrives, he knows he has plenty of time.

Wearing a long white immersion robe that he purchased on site, he steps into the refreshingly chilled water of the sacred river. His Ganges. His Western Wall. His Mecca. Since an eye infection in ninth grade, he has always worn glasses and not contacts. He removes them to be free, to fully immerse himself, but it is a choice that renders him partially blind. The Jordan is not a mighty raging river with river rafting tours navigating the spiritual rapids. It is more like a large creek, about 60 feet across. On the Jordanian side, diagonal to him on a platform, a small group of about a dozen folks are singing hymns. Near him, sitting on a bench, is a small group of about eight. They are glued to their iPads, gadgets, and earbuds.

He is the only person actually in the water. It is quiet. It is serene. The sky is a deep blue. It is very hot outside, but it is refreshing in the water. In his right hand, he holds a small laminated photograph of his mother. His mother was afraid of deep water. Someone had pushed her into a pool as a child, and she nearly drowned. It was a fear that stuck with her. His mother never had the opportunity to visit the Holy Lands, a place her rather conservative self would have deeply appreciated. His mother is with him, in spirit and as a laminated memory. Both he and his mother were going to be going underwater as many times as felt right. In his church, he has no rules or dogma. It is simply what feels right in his heart. He waits for the iPad group to disperse since he is self-conscious and a bit selfish. He wants to be completely alone with God. As he is waiting, a white dove appears from the grass and circles three times. It is highly poetic and so powerful that the appearance of the dove catches the attention of the iPad group. It draws their eyes away from the digital screens.

It is no illusion. His moment has arrived.

The little boy who climbed up through the treehouse door into a world of darkness, and the boy who had run away from everything spiritual his entire life, is now underwater. The boy who never felt truly clean, no matter how long he stood in the shower, is washing away all of those thoughts, washing away all of those negative internal belief systems. The boy, now a man, is cleansing his soul and seeking to align his True Self.

He emerges from the water, takes a few breaths, and goes under again. Each time he holds that laminated photo of his light, the PhD in kindness, his mama, all sense of time stops. A flood of memories race through his mind. Every second. The rustle of the water. The silence around him. Tranquility.

HOLY LAND DRAMA

"Leave now! You must go!" shouts a male voice.

His eyes are closed and his head is tilted back in the water. His Zen-like state of peace is broken.

"Leave now! You must go!" the voice repeats.

He opens his eyes, but he can't see the distance. He just knows he's the only one in the Jordan.

"Leave now!" the voice shouts again.

Eyes squinting in the sunlight, he replies, "Not sure if you're talking to me, but I can't see. I have to get my glasses." Reluctantly, he stops his prayer, climbs out of the water, and fumbles around for his glasses. He looks toward the top of the stairs and sees a Palestinian man and two male Israeli Defense Force soldiers. All three are staring at him.

"Fast! You must leave now! Come on!" The shouting voice is coming from the Palestinian. It is the first time any Palestinian has shouted at him.

He's dumbfounded and perplexed. The IDF soldiers are mute and stand behind the shouting man.

"I don't think it's five yet! Let me check my phone," he replies. He grabs his phone and looks down. 4:18 p.m. Huh? He is totally confused. "No, it's not five yet! I still have lots of time," he replies, getting slightly annoyed with the tone and attitude being projected toward him.

"We are closing! You need to shower and change!"

WTF? He doesn't need forty-two minutes to remove a wet robe, throw his dry shirt on, and head to the parking lot for his ride. He's in the Jordan. He's in prayer. He's not Armenian or Greek Orthodox or Catholic. However, he does have Methodist roots, is a full-blooded CINO, and has a sixth sense for the big picture. Reluctantly, he grabs his daypack and walks to the stairs.

At the top of the stairs, two more Israeli soldiers approach, both female. Now there are four soldiers from the IDF, straight out of Central Casting.

Two handsome males with chiseled faces and physiques and two stunning females with long flowing hair. Crisp military uniforms. Weapons. Gadgets.

He is not a gun expert. He's never shot a gun. The soldiers have heavy weaponry, some kind of long gun, similar to the AR-15 style artillery endorsed and promoted by the Republican Party in his motherland. The kind of guns that shred organs. The kind of guns that promote an image of power. The kind of guns that blow holes in innocence.

He notices two soldiers chewing gum. None of the four soldiers acknowledge him. They don't speak to him, not even a word. His eyes only witness a few smirks. The Palestinian is the Qasr site manager. The manager stands in the middle of all the guns, appearing frustrated at having to shout to the dripping wet, increasingly Agitated American in a Foreign Land. He feels the energy. He senses the attitude.

If it were a courtroom, he continues to argue his case in his mind. *Why was his quiet prayer interrupted? What's the emergency? Is a new section of the Trauma Wall being inaugurated? Is another bulldozer being christened? Perhaps YHWH has called the soldiers for dinner? Maybe there's an audition in Tel Aviv?*

Soon, he receives his answer. The Palestinian has lowered his voice and calmly explains, "They are ready to go home. We have to do whatever they say. We have no choice."

His mind says, *excuse me?*

BIRTH OF A GANGSTA

The small Fiat speeds out of the gates of Qasr-Al-Yahud and across the arid Judean landscape. Ameen is at the wheel as he rides shotgun. His INFJ mind is racing to process the sudden turn of events. It feels very much like an Ice Cube moment. "Why We Thugs?" underscored his mind.

He realizes that he was kicked out of the Jordan River for no reason. There doesn't need to be any reason. He was the only one left at the site and the IDF soldiers decided to go home early. He chose not to engage in an argument with the soldiers out of respect for Jesus and his beloved mother, even though he was madder than a wet hen.

His very first iPhone selfie in the Jordan River was at 3:42 p.m. His very last iPhone selfie was at 4:12 p.m. By 4:53 p.m. he is seated at a hole-in-the-wall eatery in Jericho, having another chicken shawarma. Technically, there are still seven minutes until closing at 5:00 p.m.

For him, it isn't about White Privilege since he had left his card back in America. He isn't trying to be difficult, petty, or rude. Rules mattered until they did not. It is about the principle of the moment, the big picture. It isn't about him; it is about the abuse of power.

What if a family from a remote corner of America or Europe or South America was on their bucket list trip to the Jordan? What if other souls, from obscure places in the world, sought to wash away the hurt, the suffering, the pain, and the broken pieces of their lives? What if there had been a delayed flight, a flat tire, or a bout of morning sickness for an individual who was arriving just as the soldiers were departing? Is it normal practice for soldiers and police to disrupt and shut down intimate prayers in mosques, churches, temples, and synagogues? Or is it Occupation etiquette?

It is about all the little people in this world, the commoners, from every walk of life, who follow the rules, play by the book, and do the best they can in life. It is about the imbalance of power — financially, militarily, and psychologically — across humanity, regardless of nation, gender, religion, ethnicity, or culture.

In the most basic translation, it is about hearts and minds.

THIRTY-SIX

THE BUS

He finds himself on another bus. It's not LA public transit, headed toward Paramount Pictures. It's not a sleeper bus with bunks, honking a loud horn, heading toward Mumbai. It's not America's pride and joy, Greyhound. Rather, it's the Holy Land Express, a short hop from Bethlehem to Jerusalem.

On board, the passengers are mostly Palestinian — men and women, young and old. There are three White faces: a priest, dressed like one, a nondescript male, and Bredbhai. The bus stops at an Israeli checkpoint. A door in the rear opens. All of the Palestinians quietly stand up, exit, and proceed to stand in a single-file queue outside. They appear to be everyday folk, sons and daughters, husbands and wives. He and the two other White people remain seated as a soldier with a machine gun steps onto the bus for a quick passport check. He feels very awkward. Why did all the brown people exit the back of the bus? Why is he also not standing in a line outside? He feels as if he's on a segregated bus, and it is something he has never experienced before. The segregation aspect is more jarring than the weapons.

He observes the queue outside. He watches as a female soldier scans identification. The male soldier from the bus is now back outside. Ever since his train ride in India way back in 1992, attitude was something that has always bothered him. It's not the ID checks that strike him, it's the way in which they seem to be conducted. A jerk of the head. A long stare. A smirk.

He is not a newbie traveler. He's not looking to start something. For decades, across thirty nations and dozens of trips back and forth to India, he has gone through checkpoints and has had regular encounters with security and immigration officials. He has traveled in low season and high season, through crowded airports and train stations and empty ones. In fact, of all his global travels, the biggest attitude he personally ever faced was once on arrival in Dublin and once on arrival at Stansted in London. Both times were White on White interrogations and were anxiety-inducing suspicious interrogations. Even in those instances, immigration officials did not jerk their heads with such an air of attitude. Perhaps it is the American-made Ares Shrike 5.56 machine gun that includes "attitude" in the operational instruction manual.

The scene he is living in makes him feel ill. In his mind, it feels more about dehumanizing than it is about security. His ancestors owned slaves, owned other human beings. He thinks back to his childhood in that North Carolina courthouse, working on that merit badge. His mind races. He was born in 1975. He has not seen separate toilets. He has not seen the separate water fountains. He has not seen the lunch counters. He never sat next to Rosa Parks. He didn't see Union and Confederate Troops *Marching Through Culpeper*. He didn't experience the Civil Rights Movement. He didn't experience the Dandi Salt March.

He grew up in a world in which those events were in the rearview mirror. He grew up in a world where equality existed, at least on paper. He never witnessed the movements, the awakenings, or the breakthroughs in society.

Safety and security are undeniable. Everyone in the world deserves to be and to feel safe. Israelis and Palestinians deserve to live in a world free of violence, strife, and fear. Those are human rights. However, something about the bus and the implementation of the checkpoint didn't vibe well. *This is not normal. This is not humane. This is not a way to live.*

WHICH COLOR ARE YOU?

He is no expert, but he has learned a bit about the Israeli ID system. There are various classifications, including Jewish Israeli Citizens, Palestinian Citizens of Israel, East Jerusalem Palestinians, West Bank Palestinians, and Gaza Strip Palestinians. At the heart of every democracy is, of course, a multi-layered human classification system. Each ID card came with a list of rules and regulations, perks.

To drill it down a bit, Palestinian Citizens of Israel are actually barred from living in 68% of towns in Israel by admissions committees. West Bank Palestinians are barred from living in all but 40% of the West Bank due to Israeli settlers and military presence. Absolutely jaw-dropping, are the large red signs in Hebrew, Arabic, and English that read, "This Road leads to Area 'A' Under the Palestinian Authority. The Entrance for Israeli Citizens is

Forbidden. Dangerous to Your Lives And is Against the Israeli Law." There are literally large red signs everywhere, promoting fear. Road signs of fear. He has never witnessed such signs.

He isn't a highly trained, seasoned diplomat armed with U.S. government-issued talking points about geo-political strategies and forbidden to ask questions or entertain feelings in his heart. He is a tourist from Judean Culpeper. In his quest for a deeper dive, he reads a book by Jewish American Professor Dov Waxman, *The Israeli-Palestinian Conflict: What Everyone Needs to Know*. He appreciates the book a great deal. The book doesn't preach, step on the scale, or subliminally attempt to convert. There is no CliffsNotes version, just a nuts-and-bolts articulation of what led up to the moment he is experiencing as he sits in what feels like a segregated bus. The irony is that his experience in the West Bank has been nothing like the image projected by Western media. It is a recurring theme in his life.

BREDBHAI PHILOSOPHY 101

He arrives at the Damascus Gate of the Old City with the wheels of his mind spinning as fast as a charkha. He imagines that he has retired from the CIA Humanitarian Division, and based on his highly sought-after resume with his film degree, is hired by a lofty Ivy League American College as a Professor of Philosophy. His first class would include a light exercise, apocalyptic America with several key backgrounds.

First, the Supreme Court has abolished the Separation of Church and State, ruling in favor of Biblical Law. Secondly, Congress has abolished the separate but equal branches of government, allowing for any Supreme Court decision to be overturned with a simple majority vote in Congress. Thirdly, all Americans are issued color-coded IDs based on race, class, political party, and NRA membership affiliation.

Scenario #1: Washington D.C. is surrounded by a 35-foot border wall. A bus from nearby Arlington is stopped at the I-66 checkpoint. Cars with D.C. plates are not allowed out of the city, into Virginia or Maryland, as it is against the law and the drivers may not return to D.C. alive if they venture out on the other side of the wall. At the bus stop, the White people remain sitting since they have "Preferred Global Entry Status." Meanwhile, all POCs (Persons of Color) — Black, Latino, Asian, Indian, Native American, and Pro Bono Attorneys — must exit through the rear of the bus and stand in line while D.C. protective services, armed with AR-15s, check IDs and issue long stares. Inside the compound walls of Washington, a narrative has been created about Virginians. The narrative references that the Confederacy is still alive, that General Lee has risen from the dead, and that small-town militias are active. Not only are the citizens of the D.C. unable to vote, but there is a weight of heaviness and fear about people from Virginia.

Scenario #2: New walls have been built — 45-foot walls, 5 feet thick — around the entire state of Vermont and the 14th District of New York. The government has defined Progressive as Socialist and therefore, a threat to Theocracy. Vermont is much smaller than Texas, so the cost of a wall is minimal and Canada has agreed to pay for it. A certain quota, 30% of the Non-Socialists Citizens of Vermont are provided ID cards and are allowed to live in Vermont as permanent residents but have no voting rights. The remaining 70% of the Non-Socialists Citizens of Vermont are provided restricted ID cards and are relocated to a camp in a fully militarized compound deep in the heart of the Adirondacks, away from Amnesty International drones. The

14th District of New York is too urban, too diverse, and too populous; hence, 14th District residents are provided ID cards and barred from entering any square inch of American territory. In response to complaints and hardships, America enforces an out-of-sight, out-of-mind policy.

Scenario #3. White Supremacy is on the rise. Domestic American Terrorism has skyrocketed 750%. There are rural base camps deep within the woods of the Western Territories, specifically Northern California, Eastern Oregon, and Eastern Washington. Weapons and money are smuggled in from rogue nations, nations determined to undermine the United States. Whites, lone wolves with anger management issues and a fear of change have gathered together, radicalized to defend "freedom." Armed militia units, strapped with multiple AR-15s, are operating from jacked-up trucks and have driven into cities and surrounded federal buildings. Denial has finally begun to wane in the Party of the Elephant. The school shootings, church shootings, grocery store shootings, concert shootings, and Wednesday afternoon mass casualty events are also administered by White people who had bad days and did not feel loved. Autocracy, Socialist Right-Wing Politicians, and a near collapse of the Constitution have led to a donkey bonanza. Some Red States have turned Yellow. Some Red States even turned Gay. Congress has authorized an extensive wall from the Canadian border in the State of Washington down to San Diego. California, Oregon, and Washington have a physical barrier, not just mental and spiritual, from the rest of America. The Republican Minority living in these regions are allowed to retain their 2nd Amendment weaponry, all of it, but are issued color-coded IDs in accordance with security clearance. Those Republicans with Green IDs are allowed to enter 70% of San Francisco, 50% of Los Angeles (the 50% without celebrities and cliffside mansions), and 80% of San Diego. Those Republicans holding Red IDs are barred entry into SFO, LA, and San Diego, not even for an augmentation, tummy tuck, Botox injection, or to pick up supplies at the Mall of Cannabis, not even at Christmas.

THIRTY-SEVEN

JERUSALEM

He didn't know much about Judaism. He is a CINO, a late bloomer, and has always considered himself theologically challenged. Of course, he is able to write a very long list of celebrities, journalists, and entrepreneurs who identified as Jewish; however, knowing a person is much deeper than knowing of them.

He didn't grow up in New York or Los Angeles or Chicago. He grew up in small-town America. He grew up with Jesus, public school Bible trailers, and next to "Jack and Diane." He never met Moses or Charlton Heston. While there were Jews in his midst across rural Virginia and Culpeper, no one ever handed him a pocket Torah or invited him over for a bait-and-switch youth party and compelled him that he had a choice to make or be condemned to Hell.

He spent most of his entire professional life in India, a nation of 1.3 billion people and only 5,000 were Jewish. He's never met a Jewish Indian. In fact, he knew more Parsis than Jews in India.

He is a riveting gray zone Gen Xer, living in an era between past social justice movements and present-day pronoun debates. He has seen *Schindler's List* at the Uptown Theater in Washington D.C. While he isn't an actual historian, he certainly is aware of World War II and the travesty of the Holocaust. Based on recent news reports, the burning bush seems to have engulfed the entire region. Climate change has impacted the Santa Ana Winds and blown them clear across the world and into the Holy Lands for decades and centuries.

To him, it seems that most of the world isn't really bothered about the region. From a psychological perspective, silence is a great enabler of trauma cycles. Perhaps he has stepped into the origins of such lofty travel slogans as: "Don't Ask, Don't Tell" or "What Happens in Jerusalem, Stays in Jerusalem."

JEW FOR A DAY

He sits at a long table with a white cloth. He is wearing khaki shorts, a navy-blue shirt with a ring collar, and a bluish Kippah. It's Saturday evening. In accordance with the bylaws of his branch of Christianity and his affiliation with the CliffsNotes Edition of the Bible, he is not forbidden to wear a Kippah or to partake in the weekly tradition of a Shabbat family meal. His unincorporated "Church" has a congregation of one; therefore, he didn't have to endure gossip or eye rolls as he breaks bread, the traditional Challah, and sits with his middle-class Jewish host family smack dab in the heart of Jerusalem. He can allow himself to be fully immersed, free from anxiety, and not be bothered about being excommunicated. Hashtag gangsta.

It's a small flat on the third floor with no lift and perfect GPS coordinates. He is literally having his first Shabbat meal just across the street from the Israeli Prime Minister's residence whose personal invitation he has yet to receive. He is spending a few nights in a room the size of a walk-in closet and that suits him just fine. He is a fifteen-minute walk from the Jaffa Gate Entrance to the Old City.

The extended table takes up the entire living room. He is surrounded by nine others. Samuel, his host, is of Romanian Jewish ancestry and manages a small shop within walking distance. The shop, which has everything from books to home goods to toys, is multi-generational. It is a business established by Yosef, Samuel's 92-year-old father. Yosef lives on the ground floor and makes it up to the third floor for Shabbat dinners every Saturday.

Inside Samuel's office at the shop is a black and white photograph of Golda Meir, the first and only female Prime Minister of Israel. The photograph was taken when Golda, who was affiliated with the Alignment Party, visited the shop with her trademark cigarette.

Samuel's marriage to Rachel is a second. She runs a small daycare at home during the week. Samuel and Rachel have three young children. Samuel's two adult children from his first marriage, Noah and Hannah, are also present. Samuel runs the Airbnb homestay as a side gig on the weekends. It is a creative and authentic way to share a bit of Jewish culture with international travelers and to help with the cost of living in Israel.

He is a total sponge. The food is delicious. Green borscht. Coffee and wine beef stew. Mamaliga. Parve Chocolate Cake. He manages to balance his Kippah while eating. The family is warm and gracious. He is learning that there is an Orthodox Shabbat, Regular Shabbat, and West Coast Liberal

Shabbat. He has asthma and is typically allergic to dogma — of being wrapped in rules and rituals so tightly that he was prevented from being curious or reaching out across town, across the country, or the world. He quickly realizes that his host family is a down-to-earth, chilled-out, and middle-of-the-road Regular Shabbat kind of family. Shabbat lasts from Friday evening until Saturday evening. In Orthodox lanes, there is a total absence of any work on Saturdays. There are apartment building elevators that are programmed to be fully automatic during the Sabbath. The elevator doors would open and close all day long since residents are not allowed to touch the buttons. The non-traumatic capacity of the mind to adhere to a very rigid point of view and set of belief systems is exemplified across the world in every religion as well as the scientific community.

His time with his Jewish host family, his experience, and his observations are exactly the kind that he sought. He always prefers a deeper meaning — beyond the superficial, beneath-the-surface pleasantries.

As the evening begins to linger, a bit of heaviness seems to fill the room. As with any dinner party or family event with lots of conversation, there is a vibe and lots of topics covered. He is just a middle-class bloke from Virginia, but intuitively, he absorbs the energy and emotions of those around him. The heaviness isn't his or his past trauma. It is more of a sense of burden, an unconscious stress to be Jewish.

Judaism, comprising 0.2% of the world's population, is nearly 16 million — of which over 82% reside in two countries, Israel and America. The rest of the world is home to small populations, including those 5,000 in India whose forefathers sought to escape Greek persecution.

Samuel shares with him that the family has traveled twice to Europe, once to Romania and once to France. Samuel's face lights up thinking about those trips to Europe. Ironically, Samuel felt much freer in Europe. The idea that one could feel safer outside of their home country, their native place, is profound to digest. To have love for a country, a culture, and faith in the heart is one thing; however, to have a mind weighed down with stress, anxiousness, and a level of fear is indeed heavy to absorb.

Behind the smiles, the flags, and the national pride is a traumatic bond of running for thousands of years. First, he isn't in Kansas anymore and the separation of church and state does not apply to a theocratic democracy. As with Christians, not everyone is an Evangelical. To be a non-practicing Jew or an independent thinker and live under the strict interpretation of the Torah can be a heavy proposition. Secondly, living in a militarized zone and the shadow of a projected narrative is stressful. The big red road signs warn of potential death. The walls. The machine guns. The wars. The bombs. The rockets. The stones. The ego-driven reckless rhetoric from narcissistic dictators in surrounding lands.

He understands from his life that smiles are often deceiving as smiles hide pain.

EGGSHELLS

He sits at the dinner table. He is at a crossroads in his life. He was released from ADX Willow Tree, but he has not fully healed. He had been silenced for decades, but he is now feeling more free and more willing to express himself, his voice, and his perspective.

His natural instinct is to want to share stories of his adventures in the West Bank. He quickly learns that sharing upbeat stories about Palestine isn't received well and does not seem to match the national narrative. To him, wanting to share out of innocence of the moment is exciting; however, it could be a potentially triggering event in the minds of his host family. He quickly reads the room, feels the energy shift, and recalibrates himself. Immediately, he shuts the door on any further sharing of his experience with Palestinians and this saddens him a great deal. The last thing that he wants is for his words to hurt another. It is notable to him that even though the door to his birdcage is open, he could not fly.

In Israel, he is sensitive and a bit reserved to ask questions, much less a political one. He feels the walls of stress everywhere and opts to observe, absorb, and feel the experience. He doesn't want to be labeled antisemitic for sharing the concerns of his heart nor does he want to judge or offend anyone unintentionally. Hashtag Bredbhai Wallenda.

"They teach all the kids in school. They have it in the books. They teach them how to kill a Jew!" shares a very spry 92-year- old Yosef.

He sits in silence, listening. While he understands that evil existed, he has just spent half his Holy Land trip in Palestine, interacted with dozens of Arabs, and never heard any snide or derogatory comment uttered against Jewish people. Manger Square. The gas station. The wedding. His Bethlehem flat. School kids. Nobody. He hasn't felt that kind of low vibrational energy toward Jews.

On the contrary, he felt free in Palestine. He felt open, as if he were traversing India. The people he has witnessed in the West Bank are human souls living out their lives with decency and humility, just as Samuel's family is doing in Israel. The only thing between them is a 35-foot wall and a projection. He respects Yosef and understands that Yosef had a front-row seat to the Holocaust. Yosef has been on the receiving end of hate. The cycle of trauma and triggers runs deep and would always exist until there is healing.

"My suggestion to you is not to mention anything about the West Bank," Noah casually advises him after dinner.

Do what?

"It will be easier for you at immigration if you just don't mention anything about the West Bank," Noah continues.

He is beginning to feel as if he has done something wrong. He learns that "Don't Ask, Don't Tell" really does exist. He learns that "What Happens in the West Bank, Stays in the West Bank!" really does exist.

Noah is being honest, heartfelt, and authentic with him, the American guest. Noah is trying to protect him from the powerful police and security services. His mind and heart races. That anxiousness from his first cab ride in Jerusalem begins to filter back into his being.

Certainly, the Mossad would have tracked every inch of his global footprint, his arrival in the backdoor from Dubai to Amman to Tel Aviv. Certainly, the Mossad knows that he is in the CIA-Humanities Division. He assumes that Israel, perhaps in coordination with America, has a spy satellite hovering over Ramban Street just waiting for him to exit the three-story flat and head to the Western Wall to pray. He has washed away his sins in the Jordan River even though the IDF kicked him out. He is an Eagle Scout. He is an honorary Gandhian. He has no plans to lie to Israeli immigration officials when he departs. He isn't the American President. Tweet. Tweet. Hashtag 45.

WAR SUCKS, BRUH

Had he been twenty years younger, his foreign policy bandwidth might have been summed up to: "War Sucks Bruh! Like really Bruh, it sucks! Bruh!" End of thought. Period. Bruh. However, his INFJ head needs just a little more substance beyond the cranium void and weed smoke.

As he walks down Gershon Agron Street, heading toward the wall — not the trauma wall, the Western one, the sacred one — he passes by a tiny United States diplomatic office, the U.S. Office of Palestinian Affairs. The stars and stripes of his muthaland fly overhead. He has a lot to digest, a few ideas of his own, and thinks perhaps he might jot them down and slip a note under the doorway at the little office on his way back.

PALESTINE PENNY DIPLOMACY

The concept is very straightforward. For each 100 million dollars of American military funding sent to Israel, one penny would be issued to the West Bank and Gaza. However, these would not be ordinary pennies with scuff marks, faded bronze, and tire tread. These would be handcrafted freshly minted pennies with shiny images of Abraham Lincoln. A high-level State Department delegation would travel on board a private jet. The pennies would be in specially crafted boxes. There would be elaborate ceremonies with large American flags, newly built stages, and a C-Span television crew. Jericho. Hebron. Bethlehem. Jenin. A team of well-diggers would be brought in to dig Wishing Wells. There would be all the pomp and ceremony of a State Dinner with the theme "Make a Wish." The only condition required to receive the penny is that the wish must be non-violent in mind, body, and soul.

IT'S A JOINT FAMILY BRUH DIPLOMACY

India is the land of the joint family. It is a nation of over a billion with dozens of political parties, cultures, languages, and religions. India possesses the diversity of Europe and could have easily broken into a series of fragmented nations as opposed to one single democracy.

Joint families are loud and boisterous. Joint families don't always see eye to eye. Joint families argue, love, and forgive. Joint families often pool resources to provide opportunities, such as study abroad, for nieces and nephews of more humble means. The heart of the "It's A Joint Family Bruh Diplomacy" would center around the birth of a new narrative, a human one, a narrative in which Jews, Christians, and Muslims view one another as "bhai" and "ben" as opposed to "Other."

CHILDHOOD TRAUMA COALITION

A final foreign policy outline would deal with the mental health and emotional well-being of children. Unfortunately, social workers and child therapists from the United States would not be available as they are on call for school massacres. However, child specialists from across the world would be brought in. Large "innocence" bubbles would be created, stress-free zones for Jewish kids and Palestinian kids. Entry would be forbidden to politicians, narcissists, and clergy.

THE WALL

The Western Wall is like Fashion Week in Milan. The hats. The hats. The hats. He knows the British wear large hats, but the British have nothing on these Shtreimel fur hats. The style. He felt like a judge on *America's Next Top Model*. He observes the intensity of the faces. Some men walk faster than a bullet train in China. He knows the Western Wall isn't going anywhere since it has been there since 19 BC. He knows that New Yorkers could cover 21 blocks a minute, but the Shabbat folks are setting Olympic records.

In the distance emerges The Big Daddy, The Grand Poobah. The "Don" of Jerusalem. He sees a large-framed and stout older man with a long gray beard and a fur hat that could have been a cover shot for *L'Officiel Hommes*. The man walks with style and grace as if a holy man, a wealthy man, a prophetic man, or possibly, a mob boss like his mother.

He visits the Western Wall twice. It is on his second visit that he writes a little note for world peace and sticks it inside a crevice. He places his hand on the wall and prays. He has prayed at a Buddhist temple in Thailand, a Hindu temple in India, and the Mosque of Omar in Bethlehem. Prayer is universal.

OUT OF DARKNESS

The Mediterranean summer sun is intense. Beads of sweat drip from every pore of his body. He is parched, and his water bottle is empty. He is alone but determined to walk the entire campus and visit each memorial.

He is at the Yad Vashem, the Holocaust Remembrance Center in Jerusalem, a 45-acre site. He has allotted five hours in his schedule, but he is approaching the eight-hour mark. He tends to get overwhelmed in museums with the crowds, the noise, and the distraction. Outside, he is able to think, feel, and absorb in silence. He walks through a maze of natural bedrock. The sandy-colored rock has been carved and stands a good three stories high. This one memorial covers 2.5 acres. Etched in the stone, in various sizes, are the names of Jewish communities around the world. In some places, only the name remains. It is written in Hebrew and Latin. 107 Walls. Valley of the Communities. He sees names he recognizes. Krakow. Berlin. Kiev. He sees places he hasn't heard of. He sits. He stands. He walks. He watches the sharp contrast of light and shadow. The Valley is peaceful. He finds it ironic that there are 5,000 city and town names etched in the stone, and there are only 5,000 Jews in India.

His intention this morning is to better understand the root of such evil. Where does that level of hatred begin? How is it possible to harbor such hatred in the heart for a fellow man? He remembers the images he saw moments earlier in the museum. Cartoons. Slogans. Caricatures. Words. Words used to malign. Words used to divide. Words used to degrade. Long before the first train to Dachau, the dehumanization had begun.

He thinks about misinformation and fake news. He thinks about the demonization of Americans in this day, of immigrants, of small-town folks, of big-city folks, and of politicians with differing views. Narcissism hammers away a fixed viewpoint, a fixed narrative to manipulate others. Drip by drip by drip by drip. A mind subjected to a lie, an untruth, and a conspiracy theory is primed for radicalization. Silence enables a puppet master (charismatic leader) to skillfully tug at the fears, insecurities, and vulnerabilities of a wider community.

He continues to sweat profusely as he takes a seat in the Valley of the Shadow of Death. How does the human mind become so desensitized?

The desensitization to slavery. How does one sit in a home with human beings out back that were bought and sold?

The desensitization of the caste system. How is it possible to drive past a slum and not feel anything?

The desensitization of gun violence in America. How is it possible to accept cameras, armed police, armed teachers, active shooter training, and dead children as normal?

The desensitization of Others. How is it possible, in the 21st century, to ride on a segregated bus?

MOUNT OF OLIVES

He sits on a stone wall beneath an acacia tree watching the sun begin to set over the heart of Jerusalem's Old City. The Dome of the Rock. Church of the Holy Sepulchre. The sound of distant car and bus engines reverberates off the ancient walls. Below him is a field of tombs, each piled high with stones. He wonders what it was like when Jesus entered the city on a donkey. He wonders if Jesus would have been live streaming on Facebook or sending out tweets along the way. He wonders if the Disciples would have been busy making TikTok videos. He wonders how many online trolls would be posting hate messages in pajamas while sitting in their basements. He wonders if God's Law took into consideration global population growth and the fact that the Earth was the same size, less the volcanic expansion and tectonic shifts.

When Moses led the Israelites in 1500 BC, the world's population was 50 million. In 30 AD, when Jesus rode into town for the last time, the world's population was 300 million. In the 21st century, that figure is close to 8 billion. The same earth. The same land. The same human ego.

It is easy to get lost in the current moment, the present life, and the narratives woven. In many lifetimes over thousands of years, Jerusalem was ruled and conquered 17 times. Nearly half of the world's eight billion inhabitants have a basic ideological, spiritual, and heart-based connection to the city. Jews. Christians. Muslims. He wonders about the intersection between God's Law, Civil Law, and International Law.

He has always understood the fight centered around two paths, a two-state solution (Israel and Palestine) or a single state (Israel). In his mind, at the heart of each path are human rights, human dignity, and equal representation. While he isn't a geo-political expert, his short but transformative experience has opened his eyes to an imbalance in human rights. To his surprise, he stumbles across a contextual nugget of information that, in many ways, makes some sense to him. Corpus Separatum. A Latin term for "separated body," Corpus Separatum was a key part of the United Nations Partition Plan for Palestine in 1947. Resolution 181. Due to the number of holy places, the sensitivities, and international significance, an area including Jerusalem and Bethlehem was to become a separate body administered by the United Nations or International Council. No fighting. No power grabs. No bias. No destruction of property. No bombs and no guns.

At the same time in the world, India gained independence on August 15, 1947. The wheels begin to turn inside his mind. Which nation was tied to India and also tied to the Palestine Mandate? England. The British Monarchy had their hands in both cookie jars. What if? Hmmm... What if Resolution 181 was resurrected and India became an exporter of non-violent diplomacy? What if the 21st Century transformation of the British Monarchy, in collaboration with India and the United States, leveraged peace-building and soft diplomacy to establish a Corpus Separatum for the human race, a true light with global ramifications?

Footnote, his mama was also born in 1947. Corpus Separatum, Bruh.

FAITH

He closes his eyes. He sits in the same spot. Day has turned into night and the lights of Jerusalem twinkle. The hum of traffic is just a trickle. Faith has brought him to the Mount of Olives. Faith is his inheritance, a gift from his mama. Faith had allowed him to break free from ADX Willow Tree. Faith was with him in court as he fought against domestic violence. Faith is with him in the mirror. Faith has carried him through the pain of losing his children. Faith has led him to the mountaintop in search of the message he has always carried within his being but could never decode. Faith is beginning to twist and turn his Rubik's Cube in order to align his Mind, Body, and Soul.

THIRTY-EIGHT

INTO THE WILDERNESS

It is love at first sight. There is an instant connection, an immediate attraction. I feel giddy. There is just something about those headlights and that busted tail light. She is one of a kind, unfiltered, authentic, and original with all her dings and dents. She looks like a rugged and rough hot mess, the way I used to feel inside. She doesn't have a fresh paint job. In fact, the actual letters of the word "Mitsubishi" seem to dribble down the back tailgate. Her tires are the off-road kind and she is a 4-wheel drive, the regular kind, not the jacked-up American-style kind with airplane exhaust systems often seen in the hinterlands. The only things missing from this old beat-up Mitsubishi are a large flag mounted in the back that reads "Freedom" and a bunch of gaudy bumper stickers with slogans that read: No Weapon Formed Against

Me, Social Media Sucks Bruh, Peace, Love, & Bhindi Masala, Revelation:1947, and "Gangsta Rap Made Me Do It."

It's mid-morning as I stand at the edge of the Judean Desert, several miles south of Bethlehem, looking out across the vast barren rocky and dusty terrain. No, I am not being held hostage. It is quite the contrary. I am surrounded by Ameen, a couple of Ameen's friends, and a local Bedouin. The Bedouin is a legit hardcore Bedouin, a camel herder that is seeking to branch out into adventure tourism and has spent $500 to acquire the old truck with green Palestinian plates. I don't know why but the Bedouin, with his tall wiry frame, non-stop talking, and high-pitched voice reminds me of J.J. Evans from *Good Times*.

I am the Guinea pig, a test market. We are gathered at the edge of the desert with plans to journey out to a small cliffside cave overlooking the Dead Sea. The plan is to have a cookout with kebabs, hummus, salad, and soda. No weed. No meth. No booze. No Xanax. Just a real-life off-the-beaten-path adventure.

The plan is to chill, eat some good grub, and watch the sunset over the Dead Sea before returning to civilization under the starlight. Ameen has packed everything. We have grills, charcoal, mattresses, and blankets. Once, in Ahmedabad, I had moved from one apartment to another by camel, all my worldly possessions strapped onto a cart. When the camel arrived at my new place, it took a ginormous dump. The things we do for love, for passion, for vision, for purpose. The Mitsubishi is an upgrade. I'm in absolutely no hurry to return to a cookie-cutter life in America, swallowed up by the black hole of Rinvoq, Skyrizi, and Ozempic ads. Ugh!

I am at the end of my two-month journey, and my cash flow is a little tight. My bank accounts have never been all that boujee to begin with. Never in a million years did I expect to be in the Holy Lands. I am super focused on balancing the experience of cultural immersion with Jews and Palestinians while trying to be a "faithful" Christian lad by checking off a few historic sites.

My original plan was to travel from Bethlehem up to the Sea of Galilee and essentially be a tourist. I wanted to see some Biblical places, places where busloads of pilgrims travel. The Sea of Galilee is in Israel which means that I need a taxi/driver with blue tags, Israeli plates. However, the blue tags meant triple the price! Having lived so long in India, my mind is habitual with always converting prices into Indian rupees and U.S. dollars. I tend to be thrifty, not frugal. I like to maximize the ROI for every dollar spent anywhere in the world. Going to the Sea of Galilee would be a 16-hour day trip and would cost a fortune, but the CINO in me said *just do it, just charge it.*

And then I remembered something Ameen said days earlier... I quizzed Ameen on arrival about any sort of activities or things he could recommend, and Ameen vaguely referenced a cookout over the Dead Sea. While I believe that Jesus is worth the money, I consider myself to be somewhat of a Progressive Christian so the desert cook-out makes more sense to me. It has a larger-than-life feeling. It is a feeling of charting a new direction forward into the desert, into the unknown. There are no roadmaps.

Some folks explore space while others explore the bottom of the ocean. I tend to poke and prod humanity. A symphony of timeless biblical hymns fills my mind as I hold onto the rollbar while standing in the back of the truck as we traverse down gullies, over boulders, and across the barren desert wilderness.

Check out my Mitsubishi. Hashtag Lauryn Hill. "Fu-Gee-La." Rakim. "When I B On Tha Mic." Gang Starr. "Mass Appeal." DMX. "Lord Give Me

A Sign." Emerson, yo. Transcendentalism, yo. Thoreau, yo. Sinclair, word up. Muckrakers, word up. Smashing Pumpkins. "Disarm." Tiesto. Armin. Sama Abdulhadi. Nora En Pure. And rounding out the playlist, Bette Midler's "Wind Beneath My Wings," a favorite of Mom.

EVERYTHING LINES UP

Alignment isn't finally learning how to master a Rubik's Cube. It is not that final twist where everything falls into place, and you can finally put it away on the shelf only to discover it again decades later while you are cleaning out the basement.

Alignment is as organic and ever-changing as the cells and microbiology that make up the human body. Alignment is not an item to schedule on your Google calendar or an hour of goat yoga. Alignment is not an alert from your watch, or phone, or a welcome message when you arrive home.

Alignment requires constant tuning and refining. The heart, the mind, and the soul are like an instrument, a work of art, a masterpiece. There is no one-size-fits-all approach. Alignment is as unique to each soul as DNA. Alignment isn't leaving the 80-hour workweeks, frozen microwave meals, and keeping up with the Joneses to travel to Cambodia for a one-hour Karma Session to find instant inner transformation.

The journey through life is like floating in a dinghy across the ocean of time. The forces of nature, the ebb and flow of life, the peaks and valleys of life, the wrong turns, the pain and trauma, the sense of self... all of it is constantly weathering the human body. The visual of my Mitsubishi truck seems to be reflective of our collective human journey.

At times, we do get it right. The moment one steps through a moment of alignment is a feeling like no other. The right place. The right time. The right decision. An inner knowing. A feeling. A sense, a sixth sense. A momentary glimpse of revelation that you are indeed in the exact place you are meant to be.

Standing at the rear of the old truck in the hot West Bank sun was one of those moments for me. I had no idea what to expect or what the road ahead in life would mean. All I knew is that I have faith in God and faith in me that somehow, someway, I'd make it. If I had realized that a random picture taken in the back of the truck was going to end up on a book cover about my life and take three years to manifest, I would have most likely overthought, ended up posing for dozens of pics, and missed the Dead Sea altogether.

I'm not really sure if we had a Plan B. I am riding in the back of the truck and am holding on to the roll bar as my fearless guide, the Bedouin J.J. Evans, navigates more and more ruts, boulders, and a few spin-outs. I'm not exactly sure if we have the Palestinian version of AAA or how long it would have taken to get a tow. I haven't really considered a flat tire, or a "puncture" as they say in India, or what if I might have needed to go take a dump without any privacy. All I know is that we are the only ones in the desert that day, and it feels as if we are driving into something extraordinary.

Quiz me on the Bible and I'd fail. The land we are about to trek across, I'm sure, has not changed much in 2,000 years. It is the same land in all those stories and with all those eccentric Biblical characters, and yet here we are, crisscrossing in the footsteps of history. The emptiness. The vastness. The freedom. The imagination. The dreams. The contemplation. Whatever we are doing, or are about to do, is some dope shit! I have this feeling of anxiousness, this anticipation of having a face-to-face, a heart-to-heart, a sit down with God. It has that epic vibe. As much as I get annoyed with human beings, especially myself, I really do love people. However, I crave moments of solitude, complete solitude, where I am disconnected and off-grid. Guru Bredbhai.

FAIRY TALES

Solitude blending with captivating landscapes equals perfection. I am sitting in the middle of a calendar shot for July 2019. The entire Dead Sea stretches out before my eyes. Our little Mesa-Verde-like cliff dwelling is nearly 3,000 feet above. A hawk flies and circles below. The silence and serenity are occasionally broken by the sound of a 55-seater tour bus traveling on the road below. The sound echoes up the plateau wall. The spiritual pilgrims on that bus have no idea that I am sitting 3,000 feet above, feasting on savory grilled kabobs, hummus, pita bread, and salad. I never want to change the channel. The 85-inch Neo QLED 8K Smart TV cannot compete with what I am witnessing. I have Dolby surround sound as well in the form of an Arab J.J. Evans who is talking nonstop in Arabic.

I wonder what it will be like when I arrive back in America. Fairy tales and happy endings are great, but real life tends to be a bit more complicated. For a moment, I allow the world of fantasy and make-believe to permeate my mind. If I, alone, were able to write the arrival scene at Washington Dulles Airport, I would be inclined to give it a bit of a Bollywood flare. I imagine walking through the doors at baggage claim and locking eyes with Isabella. This reunion would be followed by a slow-motion run and romantic embrace.

I imagine being reunited with my kids. Their happy faces, smiling faces. Cody would be eager to show me a brand-new polished gemstone that he has recently discovered, and he would share with me the first chapter of a superhero animated story recently written in one of the writing notebooks I had given him.

I imagine my sweet Little Ana, with the same missing front tooth and messy hair, galloping into baggage claim riding the horse from *Spirit: Stallion of the Cimarron.*

Maybe there would be fake snow falling outside the airport, in July, like a Hallmark year-round Christmas movie with cameras on dolly tracks and cameras on cranes. Outside of Dulles Airport, all of us would pile into the Jeep Liberty complete with a horse trailer. After that, maybe we'd just drive all night back to North Carolina, to the beach, to make another drip sand castle.

Writing the fairy tale ending is easy, but living the fairy tale is not in my hands. Only God can write my arrival scene and all the chapters that will ultimately follow. Learning to let go of expectations, dreams, and timelines often seems to conflict with my inner lighthouse of hope. The perpetual crossroads of knowing when to hold on and when to let go isn't part of my formal education at super boujee USC.

A MOMENT WITH GOD

As much as I am enjoying the peacefulness, the aromas, the company, and the visuals while laying back on a mattress in that little cliff cave, something within me begins to stir. I need to step away for a bit. It is time to have that word with God to further process the algorithms within me from my Holy Land junket.

The wind. The wind. The wind. As soon as I step out of the cave and onto the barren moonscape, the wind hits me. It is a warm desert wind that is constant, always blowing from the West to the East out toward the Dead Sea. As I begin to search for the perfect perch, the perfect place to park myself, I begin to feel as if, after 43 years, I am walking across the stage to receive a PhD in Life Experience.

It has been decades since I walked across the stage at the Shrine Auditorium, literally underscored by the soundtrack of *Star Wars*, to receive that highly sought-after scrap of paper. I remember driving aimlessly across the freeways of Greater Los Angeles, feeling as though I had a message to share with the world. I was frustrated and did not understand why I had jumped off a cliff and into the world of entertainment. I had been searching outside of myself, not realizing that the story I had to tell was within me.

I remember my life in India and the constant gnawing within my soul telling me that I needed to connect the dots, that somehow all the slingshots would line up. My life often feels like a pinball machine, so I am enjoying the stillness of the moment. Perched on a rock high above the Dead Sea, the fog in my mind begins to lift a bit as I begin to receive my internal download from Spirit and present my dissertation to God in the form of questions of course. I shake hands with the wind. In my head, I switch on Neil Young's "Throw Your Hatred Down" with an extended guitar solo.

TOP SECRET

CONTAINS SENSITIVE COMPARTMENTED INFORMATION

ALL INDIVIDUALS HANDLING THIS INFORMATION ARE REQUIRED TO PROTECT IT FROM UNAUTHORIZED DISCLOSURE IN THE INTEREST OF THE NATIONAL SECURITY OF THE UNITED STATES. UNAUTHORIZED DISCLOSURE SUBJECT TO CRIMINAL SANCTIONS.

ISSUED BY

EMBASSY UNITED STATES OF AMERICA

INDEPENDENT CITY OF JERUSALEM

WORLD HERITAGE CITY FOR ALL NATIONS AND ALL FAITHS

CABLE SENT TO:

VATICAN CITY

SINGAPORE

MONACO

MAILROOM, KINGDOM OF HEAVEN

DECLASSIFICATION FORBIDDEN

BY THOUGHT

BY TWEET

How is it possible, O Lord? For You to anoint Thou,

A perfect man. A man who has never made a mistake, has never told an untruth.

A man who lives, breathes, and works tirelessly for humanity such as You.

How is it possible, O Lord?

A perfect man who respects all women, minorities, men, and especially immigrants.

A perfect man that makes perfect calls, a man who does nothing wrong, perfectly.

A saint, O Lord. Tweet Tweet Hashtag 45.

"Bredbhai," utters the baritone voice of God.

I look up in disbelief. God really does have an accent.

"Ignore Thou man with a golden toilet. Ignore Thou man with a tiny vocabulary. Ignore Thou man who holds an upside-down Bible."

How can they, O Lord? How is it possible that clergy and rabbis and members of the flock worship Thou as an idol, before You, O Lord? Thou that seek to only worship Thy Self.

"Fear not, Bredbhai. Remember, I can see what you cannot. Stay on your path. Have faith in humanity. Sometimes tests are needed for growth. Tweet Tweet, as you say, is a test."

It takes me a minute to process such a profound revelation. Afterward, as a gust of warm arid wind blows, my mortal human mind is filled with both gratitude and more questions.

Dearest God,

I am grateful for the time spent with my Divine Children, Little Ana and Wild Cody. Thank you for gifting me the opportunity to redo my childhood, to be silly and goofy and innocent and free. Thank you for letting me experience the joy of fatherhood. My mom never got the chance to have the title, Grandma. I know that my second father and even my father would love the chance to be a grandpa. Just a little hint.

God, I am grateful for my haters. I've been in some very low, low, *low* vibrations. I've faced the wrath of the Warden Shilpa and Lucifer Jenkins.

Through the darkness, there is light. I accept that You are in control of my slingshot machine. Had you not taken Cody and Little Ana away from me, had my heart not been broken, had my vessel not been shattered, I would not be here at this very moment in time.

Why is there a wall around Bethlehem?

I am genuinely shocked. Not only is it a physical barrier and an eye sore, but to me, it's a psychological barrier. Bethlehem is a place of peace, a little Manger scene that kids and families put up each year, all over the world, at Christmas. I guess they should sell Manger scenes nowadays with an optional wall. A two-foot barrier wall to keep the Manger scene separated from the rest of the house. All the live nativity scenes at churches and in towns could feature a replica of the giant Wall of Bethlehem behind the Manger and the Wise Men. While we are at it, maybe the Manger could be updated to a Cave-like structure.

Where is the flock?

2.4 billion people. One-third of the world's population. 157+ countries. All the yard signs. All the bumper stickers. Jesus. Jesus. Jesus. All the flags. All the images. And somehow, I feel like the only one having a cappuccino in Manger Square, hanging out on the West Bank. Speechless is an understatement.

I mean, God, you know me, I was late to the party. I felt like I had to check and recheck my GPS to make sure I was in the right spot. Yes, there are a few tour buses here and there and a few Orthodox Clergy lurking around. I know people come for Christmas once a year, but I am flabbergasted to feel as though Bethlehem is very much the same sleepy town that has existed for thousands of years. A footnote.

Did you ever consider writing a passage for Bethlehem to be a "mandatory" pilgrimage?

I know the Bible has a lot in it. It is a bit of a heavy read, that's why I use the CliffsNotes version. When I say pilgrimage, I'm talking about a once-in-a-lifetime kind of goal. A rite of passage in a sense.

In Islam, there are lifetime trips to Mecca and Medina. In India, there are sacred temples high up in the Himalayas that tens of millions of Hindus make an effort to reach at some point in their lives. And here, in Jerusalem, it seems like just about every Jew is at the Western Wall. To me, that demonstrates the depth of a belief system and the importance of a place, irrespective of whether or not a follower is orthodox or progressive. Perhaps, if there is ever a rewrite of "The Newer/Newest Testament," then maybe there could be a line or two added about a once-in-a-lifetime pilgrimage to Bethlehem.

Is there a Plat?

God, you know the Bible is a little vague in terms of specifics. It's a bit like how folks speak in rural Virginia, "Over Yonder. Down the holler." I'm not a historian, but it seems to me like Your Law and Civil/International Law are out of alignment. The real estate sign that hangs in the region says "Always and Forever in Dispute." But, at my house, I have a plat that lists everything. The plat specifically lists the square footage, the right of ways, the easements, the utility lines, and every other little detail. Without a plat, it's messy. It's like if an American owned seven acres for generations, all legally stolen from the Native Americans of course, only to wake up one day to the sound of nail guns and construction crews building a house in the middle of the seven acres. When confronted, the new settlers simply reply, "God says it's mine!"

Can you imagine the reaction in America? You know America thinks it's a non-violent nation, with 500 million guns. So, God, like a plat could really help. Perhaps there is something buried in Uzbekistan or Liechtenstein or Benin or somewhere in Azerbaijan. Something with an official Seal of God that the archeologists and cultural anthropologists can authenticate. Then, me and You could take it to two courts, pro bono of course. First, we could file a motion with the United Nations. Secondly, we could file a motion within the court of public opinion.

Is tolerance good enough, or is it a low bar?

Tolerance is one of those lofty English words to include in the name of a museum or an international conference of world leaders. However, is the idea of tolerance truly aspirational enough? It's kind of like, "Hmmm. Yeah, I guess I'll deal with you. Just don't mix with me. You stay in your box, and

I will stay in my box." It just seems like an odd juxtaposition. We seek to colonize Mars but tolerate humans. To me, aspirational ideas are larger than Self. It is a mix of idealism and pragmatism, the slug that's always moving and always in search of the light. What do you think, God? Has social media derailed the train and exacerbated the lowest vibration of the human ego? An idea that seemed like a promise, but has become a plague.

Where is the boundary between defense and dehumanization?

God, this is by far my heaviest question today. It is emotionally heavy, gray, layered, and nuanced. Every human being in the world most certainly has the right to exist. Each person should have the right to defend against harm, both physical and psychological. But what I have witnessed on this trip, on both sides of the wall, is heartbreaking. My entire life, I was overly guarded against men. Never again. Never again was I going to be taken advantage of, traumatized. Never again was I going to feel helpless and trapped. In response, I built high walls and higher belief systems but backed myself into a trap. Dehumanization starts small. It starts with a thought, a belief system, a taunt, an eye-roll, a head jerk, and a seesaw that is unbalanced. Unhealed trauma enables a person to dissociate.

What if Judaism and Jews are the keys to world peace?

I say this to you, God, as a Christian. Follow me on this line of thought. The world's population is 8 billion. Jews represent 15 million or 0.18%. So why the hate? Why the antisemitism? There are 26 million Sikhs and 4 million Jains in the world, and yet those religious lanes are not demonized and persecuted. In fact, for thousands of years, antisemitism has never been an issue in the land that is India. Is it a Jesus thing? Because Jesus wasn't exactly an advocate of violence.

Let me sharpen up my math skills a bit — 8 billion people minus 2.4 billion Christians equals 5.6 billion people in the world who don't follow Jesus. Nobody trolls the Buddhists. When exactly did Jewish people plot to take over the world? Sounds like fake news, a projection, a lie instigated by a manipulating, self-absorbed, and twisted narcissist.

Let's establish an Intrinsic Case Study in which we define Hitler as not a man, but as a demon, a manifestation of a Satanic entity. The good versus evil battle for the soul of humanity. What if the world had a second chance, a redo? What if Hitler had succeeded, in totality, in the perpetration of Evil so that any chance of aligning the Rubik's Cube of world cultures, religious, and non-religious lanes would have ended in the gas chambers? What if this 0.18% of the world is actually the final piece required to complete the puzzle of humanity, creating an image of hope, possibility, and transformation? Maybe it's time to bring in the Hindus for India to export non-violent soft diplomacy. That's another billion people right there. Add in the Secular folks and the Buddhists for another 1.5 billion. That's approaching 6.5 billion people. The heart of the Intrinsic Case Study revolves around the idea that all the lanes in the world lead to Jerusalem. It has nothing to do with religion or dogma or the building in which one prays. It has nothing to do with conversion or confusion or lane jumping. It has everything to do with creating a buffer, a protective zone around that 0.18% of the world, Judaism, both physical and psychological. Perhaps it is a test for the world, to utilize human capital and nonviolence to twist the Rubik's Cube into alignment.

Which is more important, real estate or humanity?

James Madison proposed the 2nd Amendment in the American Constitution. Was Mr. Madison's intention to promote the killing of school children? Theodor Herzl, in the late 1800s, articulated and promoted his vision for a Jewish State. One man. One man's lifelong pursuit. At what cost to humanity?

God, I have a different perspective, one that is not bound by the topography of rocks, stones, and deserts but by the topography of the heart. In my humble view, I submit to you that the greatest threat to Jewish people is a lack of awareness and understanding by the rest of the world. I grew up in the most powerful nation on Earth, yet I know very little. I think about the hundreds of tiny villages I've visited across India and in other parts of the world, places in which there would be zero knowledge of Judaism, Jewish people, or Jewish history. There is great irony in the fact that an ancient Hindu symbol for prosperity and good luck was hijacked by Evil. The ancient Indian swastika symbol is seen all across India, in towns, cities, and villages. It is a symbol painted on door frames, walls, and temples. It is a part of the innocence of life.

On the other side of the wall, the Nazi Swastika was responsible for the killing of six million Jews in a single war. I think about the school children all across the world in which there is no historical reference to Hitler, no awareness of the Holocaust.

I think about all those times in India when everyone called me Catholic because that was the perception. I never bothered to explain what a CINO really is. I think about those school children whose first introduction to Judaism is a tank, a bulldozer, a bomb, or a derogatory chant against Arabs.

Is Occupation the best strategy to win the hearts and minds of billions around the world? Or was the answer revealed in 1947?

What about the British Monarchy?

Who can carry the ball, light the torch, and thread the needle? Governments can't since there is always an election, a point to be scored, a voting block to pander to, or a war to start. Politicians can't since they are mostly attorneys and that presents its own set of ethics issues. Religious leaders tend to get bogged down in the nitty-gritty of strict interpretation and dogma. My first suggestion is the United States, my homeland; however, I'm not sure if America has the appetite or bandwidth. America is already spread thin. It's focused on banning books, setting up weed dispensaries next to every blue mailbox, laminating copies of the second amendment, debating pronouns, considering a rewrite of the Constitution, and preparing to add indictment as a prerequisite for holding the highest office. It's a heavy lift.

What about the British Monarchy? You know, my lineage is British even though my bloodline is more *Oliver Twist* than Royal and any hint of a bloody accent has long since vanished. England was tangled up with America, India, and the Palestine Mandate. Throughout the thousands and thousands of years of history, the Brits were the last ones to call the shots, to cut and run. At that time, the plan was two states and a corpus separatum. Perhaps an evolving 21st-century Royal Monarchy could establish a forward-thinking moonshot, the Bethlehem Peace Project, a non-political, non-partisan, secular initiative. A new King Charles could bring back the old gang, Washington, and New Delhi to flesh out the details.

MIRACLE REQUEST

I know this is the land of miracles. I'm familiar with the fish, the wine, the fig tree, the Raising of Lazarus, the Lepers, the Blind, and that little Water Walk. Don't get me wrong, those are fine miracles, just fine they are. But I am thinking of an update. After 2,000 years, maybe it is time to add a new Miracle to the list? I have a suggestion, but it's just a rough sketch at the moment. I have a name for it. It's called the "MATCHING GRANT MIRACLE." That's right. A bit of NGO lingo. Again, God, this is a rough outline, not a formal presentation. My muthaland, America, according to Mr. Google, spends $3.8 billion of taxpayer funds each year for weapons systems, domes, and militarization of the Holy Land. Bombs and weapons are just a language that my country understands very well. It is part of the DNA.

The idea, God, is that You tap into the hearts and minds of Christians around the world. Perhaps a whisper. Perhaps a revelation. Perhaps a dream. Perhaps a calling. I tend to think it is not the kind of request for a rigid evangelical hardliner, but You might surprise me. So, let's say 10%; 10% of 2.4 billion people works out to 240 million. That's a lot of people. The matching grant would be for those 10% of "selected" Christians to invest 16 hours annually toward the Palestinians in the Occupied Territories. 16 hours times 240 million works out to a "human capital" investment of 3.8 billion hours, one hour for every US dollar spent on weapons. The numbers are flexible, but You have a master list, a soul list, so You know whom to inspire.

The core principle behind the MATCHING GRANT MIRACLE is to realign Christians with Muslims to build bridges, de-escalate, foster trust, and ensure the protection of our Jewish brothers and sisters. There would be some ground rules. A moratorium on conversions. There would be absolutely no Bible-Koran-Torah exchanges. No conditional-based love. Everybody remains on their respective team. The beauty of this Miracle Request is that it's inclusive, weapon free, and eco-friendly. The 240 million individuals that You call will have their own brilliance, their own light, their own experiences, their own skill sets, and their own passions to bring to the table. That, in itself, is dope. It's an outline, not a pipe dream.

Remember, I'm a weed-free non-violent hawk. The tools of soft diplomacy can be used such as Sister City Engagements, student exchange programs, inbound tourism to Bethlehem and the West Bank, artistic collaborations (music, art, film, dance, etc.), volunteer service programs, economic and trade links with Palestine, inter-faith conferences, Boy Scout/Girl Scout programs, Sports programs, links with Refugee camps, counselors and trauma specialists, and maybe a Christian/Arab cornhole tournament. The MATCHING GRANT MIRACLE is of Biblical proportions. A Biblical flood of humanity. For that reason, I am throwing out the Bat-Signal from the top of this cliff, across the Dead Sea. It's also a Mayday signal since we humans clearly could use a bit of assistance on Earth.

In the Name of the Father, the Son, and the Holy Spirit...

Amen.

EPILOGUE

The front passenger side tire is flatter than a blueberry pancake. The rear left tire also has a puncture but with a slower leak. He sees the word Michelin on the tire but doesn't know if perhaps they are the black market imitations of Michelin's that are not rated for Judean desert travel. There is just one spare. He stands around the old busted-up Mitsubishi along with Ameen and Ameen's friend. Everyone looks to Bedouin J.J. Evans for guidance. The expansive Dead Sea glistens in the late evening sunlight three thousand feet below. Next to them, is a large red road sign with a flashing light on top that reads: "Warning. You are entering the world of FICTION. Travel may be treacherous. Kindly hold on to hope."

He really enjoyed the kababs but wished he hadn't eaten so much. Between the food and the lengthy prayer session with God, he had planned to ride in the back seat of the truck back to Bethlehem rather than walk. He is last, of course. The asthmatic athlete of the year, bringing up the rear... Bedouin J.J. is a mile ahead, but the desert wind carries the soundwaves of J.J.'s voice back to the rear. Suddenly, the barren rocky ground begins to shake a little. Everyone instantly stops in their tracks. Racing toward them at a high speed is not a tow driver with Palestinian AAA Roadside Assistance, but a jacked-up old Ford F-150. It has tinted windows and is dark red, Hell's favorite color. Two large flags blow in the wind. A Confederate flag and a Nazi flag. He, Ameen, the friend, and J.J. are strung out across the desert, speechless and frozen. His heart starts to beat fast. A bead of sweat forms on his forehead. His core body temperature begins to heat up. A glimmer of PTSD and anxiety begin to overwhelm him. Trauma triggers. The big red truck looks awfully familiar, and it's got Virginia tags.

Lucifer's truck begins to pick up speed, as a plume of dust trails! The ground continues to rumble. From the back bed of the truck, two fire-breathing demonic half-man, half-serpent figures sway back and forth. He closes his eyes. He focuses his mind. Inside his head, he says in a low whisper, "Devil, I rebuke you."

He opens his right eye. The truck is closer and closing in on Bedouin J.J. He closes his right eye. He tries to focus. His mind is more forceful the second time. "Devil, I rebuke you!" Within milliseconds, to everyone's surprise, the demon truck suddenly veers off course, flies past everyone, and barrels at 105 miles an hour off a cliff. Four stunned faces peer over the side of the Judean Cliff. Huh? There is confusion. There is no sign of the truck. No wreckage. No damage. No ball of flames. It just vanished. Poof.

Ameen turns to him and asks, "Did you see that?"

He nervously shakes his head back and forth. "Yeah. It was real."

An illusion. A mirage. A projection. Everyone takes deep breaths of validation.

Two hours later, the sun is beginning to set. The group walks much closer together. In front, there is only desert as far as the eye can see. To the north, south, east, and west of them, it is all desert. As the group nears a large boulder, heads abruptly jerk left.

"My baby's name is Beebe!" says the boulder. The boulder speaks in a familiar voice to him. The boulder speaks in the voice of Little Ana. "My baby's name is Beebe! Beebe!"

J.J., Ameen, and Ameen's friend all turn to look at him, the foreigner. A large monarch butterfly appears out of nowhere and begins to fly around the group. A bright red handsome cardinal flies in. A couple of deer appear near the boulder. In unison, the animals and the rock continuously repeat, "Beebe! My baby's name is Beebe!"

J.J. rubs his eyes to make sure it's not a hallucination. Ameen turns to him again. "Who is Beebe?"

He is very relaxed and at ease. "Little Beebe Lissette. A French name, with Hebrew roots. Means God's Promise." He interrupts himself, "Long story. Maybe one day I'll share."

Darkness has come to the desert. The group marches on as a brilliant display of stars shine overhead. Far off in the distance are enormous shafts of light. It's not the North Star. These are beams of light coming from the ground up into the sky. He and the others march through the night, heading toward the light. He appears hot, dusty, parched, and a few pounds lighter in the morning sun. The hum and buzz of civilization are around him. Camels. Herders. A few cars. He hands Ameen his camera and poses for a quick picture next to a sign that reads: "Bethlehem. One of the World's Top 10

Small Towns." He hugs Ameen and gives a respectful Namaste-style greeting to J.J. and Ameen's friend. "We made it! You guys are awesome. Go on, I think I'm gonna explore a bit."

He quickly realizes that Bethlehem is not the same place he left 24 hours before. He sees a line of tourists waiting to board a tram. It's a rather unique-looking tram. It is as if the Universal Studios tram hooked up with the Warner Brothers VIP tour cart and gave birth to the Holy Lands Tram. Shiny chrome wheels. Massive hydraulics. European EDM/House Spiritual.

He overhears the bubbly female tram driver who religiously goes over her memorized shtick. "Hands and legs inside the tram at all times. As a reminder, our CEO, Mr. God, would like to remind everyone that this is a non-segregated ride. You may be seated next to persons from across the globe of all faiths and backgrounds. And for those Americans on the tour today, you may even be seated next to individuals that voted for Tweet. Tweet. Hashtag 45. Our CEO, Mr. God, reminds us to practice the art of forgiveness. We all make mistakes!"

His eyes are wider than they've ever been. The loud megaphone is still on blast as the tram begins to depart.

"Ladies and Gentlemen, it's not uncommon on the tour that you may experience supernatural events. The list of medical conditions is mentioned for a reason. I've been working here five years and have encountered sudden snowstorms, seismic events, lightning bolts, and once the entire tram was elevated and suspended in mid-air to allow a herd of camels to pass."

The outskirts of Bethlehem appear much more robust and busier. There are tons of foreigners, many wearing T-shirts that read: "I survived the West Bank." Ahead of him, he sees a large and architecturally dramatic building.

It's a museum. Outside the museum, children are crying and being consoled by their parents. A man standing near the entrance appears to be in a total trance. He looks up and sees the name of the museum. THE EGO OF MAN: THE INSTITUTE OF TRAUMA. His face cringes in a WTF? moment.

The tranced-out man jarringly grabs his arm and looks him in the eye. The man says, "Don't go in there! Whatever you do, don't go!"

His eyes are curious as he peers into the museum. He sees a kaleidoscope of images. Projections. Sculptures. The sounds of war. The images are haunting. A young mother ties her daughter's shoelace as boarding begins for American Airlines Flight 11 on September 11th. Headline news scrolls of global massacres. Sinjar. Bor. Hama. Battle of Jolo. Guangxi. Indonesia 1965. Bodo League. Rwanda. Bleiburg. Wola Poland. Balkans. Merindol Massacre 1545. Punic Wars. Three Kingdoms War. Baga Massacre. Crusades. Hundred Years' War. Huguenot Wars. World War I. Partition of India. Godhra. Vietnam. Korea. Auschwitz. Esterwegen. Mauthausen. Ukraine.

He sits on a bench in the shade, drinking a large masala chai with ginger. His face appears shell-shocked and weathered. He reaches into his daypack and takes out a tiny bottle of Old Monk Rum and pours a little into his chai. His face is caked with desert dust. His hair is messy. He wears his trademark attire: olive shorts, black Henley with dried body salt sweat rings, sturdy shoes, and high-powered prescription goggles. An older South Korean woman in her early 60s sits next to him. He gives a double glance and stares at his chai. The woman is dressed in a period costume from 5BC.

"Are you okay?" the woman inquires.

"I'm good. Just recovering from the museum. I didn't even go inside. Drained the life right out of me," he answered.

"Healing becomes difficult when we sit in our trauma."

He's impressed with the woman's intuitive perceptions of life, but he is perplexed by her wardrobe. "What's your story?"

"I'm an extra!"

His face perks up. "An extra?"

The woman's eyes widen. "You don't know? It's the biggest film production in the history of cinema. 555,000 extras!"

He takes another sip of his spiked chai. "Mam, I've been in the desert. I think it was a day, but I'm not really sure."

The woman leans in and is eager to share more. "It's Hollywood. The legendary Cecil B DeMille has risen to make one last film. It's called *The Essence of Man*. That's all I know. The story and script are under lock and key in a gold box carried around by huge bodyguards. I'm just an extra!"

He walks slowly up a very steep and winding narrow lane much closer to the old town, the heart of Bethlehem. He sees a cluster of massive searchlights on the side of the road. A closer look reveals an engraving that reads: "Property of Paramount Pictures." He realizes that these are the lights he had seen while traversing the desert overnight.

The crowds around him are much thicker now. It is a mix of locals, shopkeepers, costume-wearing extras from across the world, transport vehicles, equipment, bounce boards, and curious religious pilgrims. As he gets closer to Manger Square, he sees a very different kind of security detection machine managed by officers wearing white uniforms and having no visible weapons. To his right, down a hill, he sees a large holding area with what appears to be a crowd of primarily older White men dressed in high-dollar suits. In front of him, another man in a flamboyant suit triggers the security detector and is turned away. A sign next to the scanners reads: "Truth & Ethics Detectors." Suddenly, one of the uniformed guards shouts out, "If you are a lawyer or a politician, entrance may be a challenge. Please meet with your group at the bottom of the hill."

He, like all the regular unanointed folks, easily makes it through the Truth & Ethics Detectors. Out of the crowd, emerges a face he recognizes. A woman in her mid-40s, friendly glow, and wearing a lanyard. They both stop in their tracks.

"No way. Kate?"

"Brad?"

"Yeah, Paramount Class of '97." Kate smiles as she reflects.

With a bit of humorous sarcasm, he says, "Yeah. I was the "Man Without a Face"! Xerox Boy. I am real and do have an actual face."

By this point, Kate is laughing. "They called me 'Non-College Educated Farmer Kate.' She's from Manhattan. Dramatic pause. Kansas. Followed by laughs and taunts!"

He smiles and shakes his head. He then notices Kate's lanyard. His eyes widen. "A.D.?"

Kate appears to be a bit humbled. "Yep. Assistant Director. Under Mr. DeMille. I have no idea how I landed this gig!"

He looks at Kate and is serious. "Ah, maybe talent. Congrats Kate! I'm really happy for you."

"What about you?" she asks.

He looks around and looks down for a second. He has no lanyard but is confident. "I transitioned a bit, into lighting. Grip. Gaffer. Electric. A bit of an awakening. Realized I like to light shit up."

Manger Square and Bethlehem in general have been turned upside down by all the comings and goings related to the epic film shoot. He finds himself walking along the 40-foot border wall, and he hears lots of loud shouting. "Traitor! Traitor! Traitor!"

He looks up and sees a man in his early 20s rappelling down the side of the wall. He looks around for any film cameras but doesn't see any. The man wears a long beard and has long flowing hair. The man, in a rush, bumps into him. "Where's the audition?"

"For what?"

The man looks at him like he's crazy. "For Jesus."

"Look, I don't know anything about this movie, but I'm sure casting was already done." He notices the man wearing a Star of David necklace and is perplexed. The man sees and senses his confusion and asserts, "I'm Religiously Neutral."

He looks at the man, blankly.

"I'm Jewish Orthodox. I'm Messianic. I'm Christian. I'm Nonbinary. I'm spiritually fluid, Bruh!"

He looks at the man with confusion and a loss for words.

"You won't understand. You're too old. Probably 40!" says the aspiring actor before rushing off.

His mind drifts in and out of a dreamlike state as he walks into the middle of a "Jesus" audition. He sees a military platoon-style formation. He overhears a casting director arguing and seems to be at his wits' end. The casting director looks at a single sheet of paper. "Carpenter. Mid-30s. That's it! No other details?"

He walks through the rows of aspiring "Jesus" supporting characters. Scruffy beards and long hair are a common theme. Black Jesus. Asian

Jesus. Latino Jesus. Indian Jesus. Middle-Eastern Jesus. Gender Fluid Jesus. Biracial Jesus. Gen Z Jesus. Millennial Jesus. Tall Jesus. Short Jesus. Thin Jesus. Rambo Jesus. White Jesus. And Santa Claus. Huh?

Yep, Santa Claus. Father Christmas. Saint Nicholas. Saint Nick. Kris Kringle. He approaches Santa Claus and isn't sure if it's the Old Monk chai impacting his senses or if it really is a youthful Jack Nicholson. It certainly looks and sounds like Mr. Nicholson.

Distinctive tone. Powerful delivery. "They can't cancel me! They can't cancel Santa Claus."

He glances up at the sky and then to Santa asking, "Let's go in the shade and have some Masala Chai?"

Santa continues to rant, "Boycott everything. Cinemas. Streaming. Gadgets. This is a global travesty. They are trying to steal my day! It's my day! I give out toys to all kids. Kids that are loved and kids that are unloved. Toys. Jewish kids. Muslim kids. Hindu kids. Buddhist kids. Doesn't matter. Everybody likes a toy! What do these guys do, huh? Give out Bibles. This is my square. Gotta stand my ground! Can't cancel me!"

He looks Santa in the eye, gives a head bobble, and utters a few words of broken Gujarati. "Arre, Santabhai! Shanti. Arama Karo."

He walks past more film gear, large cranes, and equipment. He passes through an area that is surprisingly quiet, a rare place where he finds himself alone. He isn't alone for long, since an oversized hologram soon emerges in front of him. It's the late one-of-a-kind agent Martin Baum, sitting behind a large desk at an office in Beverly Hills.

"I'm not just gonna send Dickie your script! Who do you think I am? I'm not just gonna send Dickie your script! Who do you think I am? I'm not just gonna send Dickie..." Marty rants angrily.

He stops walking and looks at Marty. "Relax, Marty. Just relax. I moved on."

He hasn't realized how incredibly famished he is and luckily enough, he wanders into a mythical-sized craft services area. It's a global cuisine fest with dietary sensitivities of course. There are so many lanes. Kosher. Halal. Vegan. Pure Vegetarian. Gluten-Free. Nutri-system frozen meals. Sweet Tooth delights. He loiters around the Fast-Food Lane, eating an imported five-pound patty melt from Whataburger with spicy ketchup and a Coke Zero. Next to him, is the A-Lister food cart. Norwegian Fish Diet. Sirtfood. Baby Food Jars. Large heavy-duty white plates with a single grape and a single walnut topped off with a microscopic spec of non-fat Greek yogurt.

His personal satellite dish, his head, his INFJ wiring, overhears a far-off heated conversation between movie producers and bigwigs back on Melrose. One producer holds the phone out at arm's length.

The mob boss, studio boss on the other end shouts, "Who the hell names a film *The Essence of Man*? Nobody gets it. Nobody! It doesn't test well. Attention spans are short. Marketing has no idea how to sell this concept in a millisecond."

The producers look at each other, happy to be far from Los Angeles.

"Who gives a fucking blank check? No budget. No timeline! No release dates! Who the fuck greenlight this?"

As the shortest producer, with LA hair and LA shades, sheepishly says, "You did, sir?"

He watches in awe as Cecil DeMille frames a shot. There's a dolly track and camera. It is an intimate scene in the heart of Manger Square. There are two boys around ten years old. The first appears to be an Orthodox Jewish boy with payot sidelocks and conservative threads. The second appears to be a traditionally dressed Orthodox Muslim boy. Both kids appear to be waiting.

"Where is he?" inquires the Jewish boy.

"Where do you think? Eating!" replies the Muslim boy.

A third boy, having a round face, freckles, and a BMI of 43, sprints across Manager Square. The Catholic boy is dressed in a crisp Sunday suit with two of the white shirt buttons popped open. By now, Mr. DeMille is seated on the dolly with the DP. The young Catholic stands in between the other two boys.

The Jewish kid looks at the Catholic and says, "You've got ketchup."

"What?" exclaims the Catholic, as he huffs and puffs from the run.

"Ketchup. On your cheek! The other side too. They have napkins," the young Muslim boy proclaims with an eye roll as Mr. DeMille shouts, "Action!"

He finds himself a couple of stories up on the top of a concrete building. He stands next to the Unit Photographer, a very artistic woman with long gray hair, pointy thick specs, and a wrist full of beads and threads. The photographer is also part philosopher and stands next to a heavy-duty tripod and a camera with a dope lens. "Leica Elcan 90mm. Only ten ever produced. Picked it up at an Air Force rummage sale."

He is a bit startled. "The Air Force has rummage sales?"

"This little gem was created for aerial night vision. I tinkered with it a bit for tonight. Gonna be brilliant."

"Tonight, what?"

The woman leans in. "The sky will be filled with illuminated kites. Like Uttarayan in India. Going to be breathtaking. Bredbhai, with this lens, we can change the way we view the world. This lens is pure. This lens has its own sixth sense. It's not only the air we breathe, Bredbhai, it's about human existence. We are at a crossroads. Do we live in an A.I. world or a real world with a beauty inside each of us?"

He finds himself deep underground in an ancient sandstone room. He stands near a light box. This isn't an ordinary light box. It is nothing like the circuit breaker box found in middle-class suburban garages. This is the kind of lightbox that existed before Edison. Suddenly, he hears a loud noise, the whirling buzz of a helicopter! Perhaps a Boeing AH-64 Apache. In the blink of an eye, *BAM, BAM, BAM.* He screams, "Jesus Christ!" as four members of the Israeli Defense Forces bust down the door and surround him with weapons pointed. He is different this time. Calm, cool, collected, and confident inside and out.

"I forgot this is a No-Knock country, but really guys? A little over the top!"

"Who are you?" shouts a soldier. "Show us your identification?"

"Who am I? Can I open my backpack? I have in my possession the most powerful book in the history of mankind." He glances into the eyes of each soldier as he slowly reaches into his bag.

"Y'all look familiar." He stands and prepares for the reveal. "It's not what you think. Not the Bible. Not the Torah. Not the Koran. It's the Blue Book! Passport. United States of America. Valid everywhere except North Korea, Iran, and apparently the Jordan River!"

The IDF soldiers stare at the American.

With a hint of White privilege, a dash of American self- righteousness, and a glimmer of Churchy judgment, he opines, "Let's lower the guns. Did I pay for those? I pay taxes, you know, when I have any income!"

A tremor begins to shake the room. Everyone looks around. They are startled and unsure of what is happening. Sudden darkness. Blackout. Sudden light. Surreal. The light flickered only for a second, but everything has changed. The soldiers, the same two men and two women from the Jordan River, are no longer wearing military gear. Nope. They appear to be ramp models. Louis Vuitton. Armani. Dior. Gucci. Prada. The soldiers are understandably bewildered.

He is dressed the same in a black shirt with crusty salty dried sweat marks. Wait. What? Huh? He is wearing a lanyard. The lanyard has his photo on it. It reads: "Bredbhai. Gaffer — Trainee. *The Essence of Man*. Director — Cecil B. DeMille." He proudly holds up his lanyard. "My secondary ID."

"Come here, let me show you something." He dusts off the ancient circuit breaker. "You see all these circuits? Horizontal. Not Vertical. No hierarchy. Everybody has a circuit. Christian. Jew. See right here. Judaism. Written in Hebrew and translated into 25 languages. Muslim. Hindu. Buddhist. Miscellaneous. Agnostics. Scientists. Every lane has a switch."

The young soldiers are distracted from his lecture as they feel much lighter in boujee designer threads.

"These are not normal circuits. Not made in China. In the garage, you can just flip, flip. Done. These here, they require lots of torque. Super heavy." He notices something hanging on the dress pants of one of the female soldiers. "You forgot to cut the tag off."

He looks back at the massive circuit breaker box. He raises his hands but is careful not to touch it. "Before you interrupted me, I was reading the instruction manual. This box is connected to humanity. The switches can't be flipped individually. All of them have to be flipped at exactly the same time. A reset. A reset of the hearts and minds. Don't you see, this is the power grid to peace? But I ain't gonna touch it!"

"No. Let me try..." replies a buff male soldier.

He raises both hands to block the soldier. "No. No. No. It's not that simple. There are 888 pages of warning instructions, and I'm just a trainee. If our timing is off, if we mess up, it's game over. I can change a lightbulb and that's about it." He picks up his daypack and begins to exit. "Now, if you'll excuse me, soldiers, I believe Mr. DeMille is expecting me on set. To move some wires. Have fun in Milan. Peace Out, Bruh!"

He emerges from the underground room feeling captivated. Darkness has settled onto Bethlehem, and the sky is filled with thousands of illuminated kites. There is pin-drop silence. An overwhelming flood of emotions well up inside him. His heart rate increases. He feels that click again, the click of momentary alignment. He looks up toward the sky.

"I'm home, Mama. I made it."

A few teardrops of rain fall from the sky and onto his hand. He glances at his hand before looking back up to the sky.

"I know, Mama. Me too. I'm gonna keep fighting."

NOTE TO THE READERS

Dear Distinguished Reader,

Thank you for your curiosity and for taking a moment out of your life path to read a few words that I have jotted down. I am honored and humbled to enter your mind. I wanted to take a moment to share a bit of insight into the creative decision to write *Alignment* outside the literary box by using a third-person narrative.

Firstly, the idea of sitting down to tell my story, to essentially write about myself and have to use the word "I" page after page, was a tremendous barrier. Frankly, it was a non-starter. For many decades, I have lived in or adjacent to the worlds of narcissism and the idea of *me, me, me, me, me*. I had writer's block before I had written the first word.

How could I best deliver my story to your mind? How could I thread the needle between a story about me that is really not about me? I charted a course in third person and put my faith in your sophistication and understanding that the dude you see in the truck on the cover... Well, this is "his" story.

Secondly, my job as a writer is to take you on a journey. As for an autobiography, I wanted to bring you inside my mind as it intersected with life. On any film set, you will find a dolly track — a train track with a rolling platform and a mounted camera to follow the action. The image for *Alignment* was for you to be seated on a 43-year-long dolly track and be as close as possible to the action, drama, tragedy, and humor, without any barrier. The third-person narrative made that possible.

Finally, the narrative and creative style of storytelling lends itself to serve as an extension of authenticity for my story and my voice. The transition to first person "I" in Chapter 38 is intentional. It is symbolic of finding one's voice, life path alignment, and self-worth. It is symbolic of stepping into a new world, a new version of Self, for the first time. The idea is that you and I get to step into that new world together.

In Love and Light,
Bredbhai.

OPEN LETTER TO THE PRIME MINISTER OF INDIA

Honorable Shri Narendra Modi,

Myself Bredbhai. My native place is Amerika. My village name is
Culpeper. You may not remember, but twenty years ago we met once on a
stage in Ahmedabad. You were Chief Minister of Gujarat at the time, and I
had just produced *EKTA*, the Gandhi-King play in collaboration with Manav
Sadhna and Darpana Academy of Performing Arts. You presented me with a
shawl. It is memorialized in a photo. We shook hands. You may not recall,
but you said to me, "Today's your lucky day."

I wasn't able to respond to you at that time since I tend to get lost in
my thoughts, and I was a little nervous around world leaders and famous
personalities. However, I now have an idea for your consideration. I was living
in Ahmedabad during the tragedy of the riots and the earthquake. My heart

hurt in those days. I consider Gujarat to be my second home. Gujarat has provided me with a wealth of experience, personal inspiration, much laughter, delicious home-cooked food, lots of masala chai, and a 24-hour electric grid!

My idea is for India to step away from the sidelines of world affairs and to engage as an exporter of peace and nonviolence. India, as you know, is the largest democracy in the world, a stable and secular one. India has a unique opportunity in this 21st century to engage in proactive soft diplomacy. Both of our nation's histories are intertwined with that of England and the British Monarchy. What if India collaborated with the United States and the United Kingdom, in partnership with King Charles and The Prince of Wales, to seek and bring greater peace and stability to the world through resolving the conflict between Israel and Palestine? India has a lot to offer the world. It has the right temperament and a proven track record, vis-à-vis August 15, 1947.

Your consideration on the matter is greatly appreciated.

Jai Shri Krishna!

Respectfully,

Bredbhai.

POST EPILOGUE NOTE

As of the publication of *Alignment*,

I never saw my kids again,

Not since the tornado ripped through on Valentine's Day

Cody and Little Ana

Will forever remain in my heart.

God had a slingshot for me,

An abrupt reroute into INFJ hibernation.

A global pandemic settled across the land,

My world travel ceased,

My small business imploded,

My immune system battled long haul,

And all manna ceased.

Yes,

God had a different plan for me.

A whisper

A tug at the soul

It's time

To find the right words

To share a message with humanity.

Tweet

THE PRINCESS BED

During the production phase of *Alignment*, I came across an old iPad. It was one I hadn't turned on in a long time. The iPad had been a birthday gift from Isabella. On that particular birthday weekend, all of us stayed in a little cabin in the mountains. Cody baked me birthday brownies, and Ana woke up filled with excitement and eager to watch me open my gift.

A few months later, I was attacked.

I hadn't turned on the iPad in several years and when I did, it was like opening a time capsule. I had only used the device a few weeks and the last image saved in the library was a picture of a princess bed, a child's bed. I had recently asked Isabella what she thought about her and the kids moving in with me. My home office was going to be Cody's room. A smaller bedroom was picked out for Little Ana. The fairy tale princess bed was an indication of where my mind was as I was planning to set up the kid's rooms. A joint family, Bruh.

Life changes in an instant. One storm has the potential to reshape your life.

On July 17, 2021, soon after the first draft of *Alignment* was completed, I converted the empty room that was to be Little Ana's into my very own church, my church of one. In India, all of my friends have some version of a temple inside their homes so it just made sense to me.

Of course, it's not an ordinary church by any means. In addition to a little Christian artwork and oversized brass candles, I have a comfy orange Buddhist prayer cushion, a Chakra poster, a jar of mustard seeds, a 200-year-old family Bible, and an array of Libra crystals. Oh, and a beautiful weathered chalice picked up at an antique store for a few dollars. Totally Boujee!

STORM CLOUDS

The idea that I could just saddle up and ride off into the sunset as an INFJ cowboy filled with inner peace, happiness, and respect as a human being might be possible in a movie, but it is not quite in real life... You see, narcissists are not happy campers when a "target" escapes prison. The idea of empowerment, growth, and living a life free from puppet strings is a reality that a narcissist has a challenge reconciling with.

Lucifer Jenkins and Warden Shilpa have been the gifts that continue to give over the years. One would think that I was in possession of actual highly classified documents based on the ongoing efforts to gather intelligence with regard to my comings and goings. I've had scruffy White men in trucks parked outside, watching my home. I once caught Lucifer himself parked a few houses down in the opposite direction. He was stalking me. At the time,

Mr. Jenkins was under a two-year No Contact court order. However, narcs tend to violate boundaries, it is part of the whole entitlement schtick.

I decided to drive down the street to document the location of the vehicle with my iPhone. My mind wasn't sure if it was Lucifer but my intuition and vibe felt that it was. As I neared the truck, Lucifer exploded. Lucifer began throwing violent punches inside the truck, and he sped out of the neighborhood at a dangerous speed. Rather than pursue more justice, I decided to establish my home church and seek to pursue Divine justice instead.

Warden Shilpa periodically violates the Freedom from Interference boundary by seeking to exploit any potential vulnerability in my No Contact wall — the wall established in Ocean Springs, Mississippi on my 48-day road trip. Over the years, I've received a series of harassment calls from across the United States from a strange male Indian voice. Efforts have been made to sabotage much of my youth education work in India. Security cameras have picked up a few drive-bys. Occasionally, I would receive outreach from distant folks regarding unsolicited advice for healing my "depression." I'm not depressed. I'm free.

Alignment has been written from inside the storm clouds.

THE SHORT CUT

In honor of the short cutters and line breakers, I've composed a brief summation as it relates to the thematic content behind *Alignment* — AKA the CliffsNotes version. In light of the AI revolution, I'd prefer not to have technology interpret my thoughts and feelings. I'd prefer to share those myself.

ENGAGE WITH THE WORLD, DON'T JUST TROLL IT

TRAVEL OUTSIDE YOUR BOX

LIFE IS SO MUCH MORE THAN A TWEET

NEVER HARM A CHILD. EVER

NEVER CLOSE THE DOOR ON HOPE. EVER

GANGSTAS COME IN ALL SHAPES, SIZES, ZIP CODES AND FLOWS

LET THE AIR OUT OF THE HATE BALLOON. REFOCUS THAT ENERGY

WORDS DO MATTER. THEY OFTEN LINGER FOR A LIFETIME

PTSD'S A REAL BITCH

FOLLOW YOUR HEART, EVEN OFF A CLIFF (METAPHORICALLY)

OUTER SPACE IS COOL AND ALL, BUT HUMANITY IS DOPE

LEAVE THE WORLD BETTER THAN YOU FOUND IT (LOW BAR)

FIND YOUR PATH AND YOUR PURPOSE, AND NEVER LOOK BACK

WALLS GO UP AND WALLS COME DOWN

EDUCATION DOESN'T END WITH A SCRAP OF PAPER

RED FLAG WARNING: PERFECT POLITICIANS

ACKNOWLEDGMENTS

My Dearest Family, Friends, and Special Loved Ones

Elaine

Every Teacher & Professor in my life.
You all inspired me!

Pilots and Flight Crews across dozens
of airlines over decades. The magic of flight.

My Doctors and Nurses in India who healed me
numerous times during my Indian odyssey.

Everyone at Manav Sadhna.
You will forever be in my heart.

The Citizens of Gujarat State, India

Qatar Airways (IAD-DIA-AMD)
My Flagship Carrier for Many Years!

IHG Hotel Group (Worldwide, Bruh!)

The Late Dr. George L. Maison,
Inventor of the Asthma Inhaler (circa 1956)

Dunkin' Donuts
(Mocha Lattes & Low Carb Boston Cremes)

Small Business Administration (SBA)

The U.S. Department of State;
For Building Walls Around Me & Telling Me No

AVES

Writing *Alignment* would not have been possible without the inspiration, the antics, and the sheer chaos of my backyard crew, my feathered friends. Your individual personalities, sounds, quirks, sheer appetite, and mating rituals allowed my mind to unwind each day of this journey.

Shout out to a few standouts:

Big Red. My cardinal-in residence and backyard property manager who keeps tabs on everything.

Big Red's Girlfriend. I'm not sure if you both are married or just nesting, but y'all look good together.

Mr. Fee Bee. My powerful little chickadee that always seemed to show up at just the right time to bring inspiration, joy, and that nudge to hang in there and keep moving forward.

Mourning Doves. Y'all remind me of my old self — anxious, jumpy, and always looking over your wings. The blessings and spiritual overtones of your visits were always on my mind.

Little Wren. I'm so in awe of you that I never gave you a nickname. Celtic culture associates wrens with creatives. Poets, artists, musicians, and writers. That alone speaks volumes.

Tiny. My bilingual Ruby-throated hummingbird with annual trips from a cliffside estate in Honduras to an American small-town backyard. It should be noted that Tiny has been fully vaccinated, has an up-to-date Covid booster, and has a valid visa granted by the U.S. Embassy in Tegucigalpa – Avian Division. Tiny travels to America as part of the "SBP" Summer Breeding Program which promotes cross-cultural ties between nations.

ONE MORE THING...

In compliance with eco-friendly
literary publishing standards and practices,
Project 10-15 is fully

Tweetless

Subscriberless

Social Media Allergic

Algorithm Free

www.project10-15.org

Printed in the USA
CPSIA information can be obtained
at www.ICGtesting.com
LVHW092321271223
767606LV00021B/156/J